MAKING A LIVING

Chad Montrie

The University of North Carolina Press ∗ *Chapel Hill*

Making a Living

WORK AND ENVIRONMENT IN THE UNITED STATES

Portions of this book are based on previously
published articles: "Continuity in the Midst
of Change: Work and Environment for
West Virginia Mountaineers," West
Virginia History *1 (Spring 2007): 1–22;*
"'Men Alone Cannot Settle a Country':
Domesticating Nature in the Kansas-
Nebraska Grassland," Great Plains
Quarterly *25 (Fall 2005): 245–58; "'I Think*
Less of the Factory Than of My Native
Dell': Labor, Nature, and the Lowell 'Mill
Girls,'" Environmental History *9 (April*
2004): 275–95. Used by permission of the
publishers.

Library of Congress Cataloging-in-
Publication Data
Montrie, Chad.
Making a living : work and environment in
the United States / by Chad Montrie.
p. cm.
Includes bibliographical references and
index.
ISBN 978-0-8078-3197-7 (cloth: alk. paper)
ISBN 978-0-8078-5878-3 (pbk.: alk. paper)
1. Labor — United States — History.
2. Environmentalism — United States —
History. I. Title.
HD8072.5.M66 2008
331.0973 — dc22
2007044718

12 11 10 09 08   5 4 3 2 1

Title page illustration: J. W. Barber,
"East View of Lowell." Courtesy of the
Center for Lowell History, University of
Massachusetts Lowell.

For Bob Foreman

Contents

Acknowledgments

As is always the case with a book, I could not have written this one but for the support, assistance, patience, and good humor of many different people. I now have been privileged to work with Sian Hunter at the University of North Carolina Press on two separate projects. This time around, like before, she helped me broaden the scope of my research and deepen my interpretation. Anonymous readers also provided several sets of reviews that challenged me to make critical, necessary changes. And other staff at UNC Press, including Nathan McCamic, Paul Betz, Ellen Bush, and Liz Gray, were models of professional competence when it came to an appraisal, copy editing, and all the additional, important steps along the road to publication.

The archival research for this book was generously funded by the History Department, Division of Social Sciences and Humanities, and Provost's Office at the University of Massachusetts Lowell. I received one of the university's Healey Grants, as well, and an Office of Research Administration/ Scholarly Research Forum Grant, which allowed me to make one last trip to Detroit. Archivists at the Center for Lowell History, National Archives, Kansas State Historical Society, West Virginia University, and Walter Reuther Library at Wayne State University were kind and knowledgeable, especially Martha Mayo, a walking trove of Lowell history. For articles, books, and various primary sources acquired through interlibrary loan and virtual catalogue, I relied on the diligent labors of Rose Paton and Debbie Friedman.

My dual interest in labor and environmental history was first nurtured at the University of Louisville, where I had the good fortune as an undergraduate to be mentored by John Cumbler. Taking his courses and engaging him in many conversations outside of class convinced me that the two fields could and should be brought together. I also received early encouragement for the endeavor from the late Hal Rothman. In his last year as editor at *Environmen-*

tal History, he published an essay I wrote on mineworkers and opposition to strip mining, even though (in my mind) it still bore marks of unseasoned scholarship. That article helped me get a book contract as well as a job, and it opened the way to this second book, too, so it was no small thing what he did.

Finally, I stand on the shoulders of my family, past and present generations included, whose dutiful work carried me to graduate school and an academic career. My Grandpa Leo, for one, was on the night shift at Dana Auto Parts in Toledo, Ohio, and, by rights, a member of UAW Local 12, which meant my father as well as some of my uncles and aunts attended the union's summer camp at Sand Lake, mentioned in chapter 5. My stepfather, Bob, for another, has made a living, with a good amount of satisfaction I think, landscaping yards and remodeling homes. I learned a lot from him over the years, and that is why his name is on the dedication page. My teaching, research, and writing are also sustained by the concern and care of my mother, my sisters, my daughter, Phoebe, and my partner in thoughtful conversation, Susan Loucks. Each of them deserves all the gratitude I can muster.

MAKING A LIVING

Introduction

"When one speaks of increasing power, machinery, and industry," Henry Ford wrote in 1922, "there comes up a picture of a cold, metallic sort of world in which great factories will drive away the trees, the flowers, the birds, and the green fields." This was how he began an early memoir, on the defensive, and the rest of the book was an answer to both skeptics and critics. The bleak and foreboding imagery, Ford contended, was not right. It was a mischaracterization of what would happen with the advent of new technology and the spread of factory production. Machines, he insisted, were but a means to an end, tools for doing labor more efficiently and with less drudgery, which was how they "set us free to live." Through industrial innovation and its proper application people did not have to give up "living" because they were too busy "providing the means of living." Labor-saving technology could liberate humankind for "the pleasant things" of life. "Unless we know more about machines and their use," Ford argued, "we cannot have the time to enjoy the trees, and the birds, and the flowers, and the green fields."[1] This answered the problem by turning it on its head.

Like most of his contemporaries, Henry Ford believed that labor and leisure were two separate things, an idea based on a real division of time that had evolved with industrial capitalism. According to this view, it made perfect sense to pursue any innovations that lessened the amount of work people had to do to satisfy their needs, whether they were making cars or growing wheat. Even on his farm in Dearborn, where Ford had spent his youth and cultivated an interest in steam engines, he returned with a plan for doing everything by machinery and studied economy. "We are not farmers," he explained, but "industrialists on the farm." Yet in defending the machine age, Ford overlooked what was at the heart of many people's wariness about industry. He dismissed the criticism that his methods of car manufacturing—

not merely the tools used—actually made the work more rather than less onerous, by deskilling and regimenting labor and turning it into a repetitive operation. He had heard from "parlour experts" that repetitive labor was "soul- as well as body-destroying," but his own investigations, "the most thorough research," had not found a single case "of a man's mind being twisted or deadened by the work." Anyway, the average worker wanted a job "where the creative instinct need not be expressed," Ford maintained, one "in which he does not have to think."[2]

Contemporary autoworkers, apparently, did not share all of these assumptions. They accepted the division of time into work and leisure, the former belonging to their employer and the latter belonging to themselves, and they organized a union at least partly to increase their time off, by cutting hours and expanding vacation benefits. They wanted to be away from factories, however, because work there had become such an intensely disagreeable and alienating experience. The changed circumstances of their labor, transformed into toil, made improving the quantity and quality of their leisure even more imperative. "The worker in this assembly-line age needs recreation," explained the United Auto Workers Recreation Department director. It was important to relax after a hard day's work, she said, and "physical activities" were critical for maintaining good health. But there was the matter of certain "mental and spiritual cravings," or "hungers," as well, particularly the need to create something, if only "a vegetable garden, out in the back yard." On the auto plant assembly lines there was "nothing creative, or combative, competitive, adventurous, or social," and that left workers feeling a lack, which necessitated concerted efforts to fill the void.[3]

By the 1930s, in fact, many autoworkers had already begun to deal with the objections of their work lives by developing an avid interest in sport hunting and fishing. "Farming was better than working in the factory," historian Lisa Fines explains, quoting two former employees of Reo Motors, and "hunting was better than farming."[4] This statement, set against Henry Ford's industrial vision of farming as well as his apology for factory production, suggests the ways changes in people's work were entangled with changes in people's relationship to the natural world, as well as the implications this had for leisure. "Hunting and fishing must be thought of as recreation out of doors," declared a journal for one of the largely working-class sportsmen's clubs in Michigan. Just as important as "downing game," it said, was "the God-given opportunity to get away from teeming cities and the rush of everyday living and plant your feet on the good soil of a quiet backwoods trail."[5] Following this line of thinking, factory men (and some women) went hunting and fishing not only to find a quality of life that had become more elusive with the onset and spread of industrial capitalism, but also to experience a more direct if idealized connection to the land.

On its own, technology was not the primary factor degrading labor and undermining the "unity of living and active human beings with the natural, inorganic conditions of their metabolism with nature," as Karl Marx wrote.[6] Technology certainly played a role in this process, yet putting it exclusively front and center misinterprets the past. Besides the fact that such an interpretation rests on an overly sentimental understanding of premodern work, it misses other important aspects of the way labor establishes people's relationship with nature. How work was done, why it was done, and to what end mattered a great deal as well. When twentieth-century Detroit autoworkers developed a romantic sensibility about outdoor recreation or, for that matter, when antebellum Lowell "mill girls" looked back longingly to their old rural homestead, they did so for many reasons. Assembly lines in auto plants, or rows of looms in the first brick factories, were more than just machines to them. They were part of a whole system or mode of production.

Making sense of all this, a complicated story of work and environment, is now possible in part because environmental history has begun to mature as a field, with a few notable scholars even taking tentative steps toward integrating the concerns of labor history. First, these scholars have begun to establish the contours of organized labor's participation in public health, resource conservation, wilderness protection, and modern environmental campaigns, writing unions and labor coalitions into the narratives of those movements. Second, they have started to interpret the history of human beings' relationship to nature with class as a category of analysis, while also attending to the ways cultural constructs such as race, ethnicity, and gender have conditioned that same relationship. Third, several historians have opened up a theoretical discussion about the connections between labor and nature, suggesting that we cannot understand changes or continuities of one without considering changes and continuities in the other.

Although there is some overlap between the articles and books that initiate a "contributory" environmental history project (writing organized labor into the narrative) and those that take up class as a category of analysis, most early studies are largely of the former variety. This includes Robert Gottlieb's *Forcing the Spring* (1993), Jim Schwab's *Deeper Shades of Green* (1994), Rosemary Feurer's chapter on unions and the Missouri Valley Authority in *Common Fields* (1997), and Robert Gordon's separate accounts of the United Farm Workers' and the Oil, Chemical, and Atomic Workers' environmental activism, the one published in *Pacific Historical Review* (1999) and the other in *Environmental History* (1998). It includes as well Scott Dewey's survey of organized labor's critical involvement in the origins and evolution of modern environmental consciousness and activism. In a 1998 *Environmental History* article with broad scope, Dewey went so far as to label some American unions "proto-environmentalist" for their prescience and timely concern, and he uncovered many cases in which workers parted with their employers on various environmental issues, rightly giving particular attention to the United Auto Workers' participation in campaigns against air and water pollution.[7]

The truly groundbreaking book, however, one that brought unions into the account of environmentalism in a sustained local study *and* introduced class as a category of analysis, was Andrew Hurley's history of Gary, Indiana, *Environmental Inequalities* (1995). "My aim," Hurley wrote, "is to approach the process of environmental change as the product of competing environmental agendas forwarded by specific social groups," which in the case of post–World War II Gary included industrial laborers in the United Steel Workers Union, African Americans, and middle-class whites.[8] Similarly, in *Environmentalism and Economic Justice* (1996), Laura Pulido examined Mexican and Mexican American farmworkers' campaign to organize the United Farm Workers and address their exposure to toxic pesticides, as well as a grazing conflict that pitted Hispano sheep ranchers against mainstream environmentalists. In both cases, she proceeded using the dual lens of class and ethnicity, drawing on theory about "subaltern" groups. And, published somewhat later, my own book, *To Save the Land and People* (2003), discussed the way Appalachian farmers as well as miners, who were members of the United Mine Workers, aligned with and parted from national environmental groups in the battle to reign in strip mining, often along the lines of class.[9]

Less concerned with unions but ardent to reveal class as a factor conditioning people's experience with nature, Richard Judd's *Common Lands, Common People* (1997) and Karl Jacoby's *Crimes Against Nature* (2001) also helped immensely in moving us toward a hyrbid environmental history. Judd's book displaced elites such as George Perkins Marsh from the pantheon of authors of conservation to discover the motives and methods for improving soil fertility, maintaining woodlots, and conserving fish and game in the communitarian ethics of New England's small farmers.[10] Likewise, Jacoby studied conservation from the bottom up and found common people practicing what he termed a "moral ecology," paraphrasing E. P. Thompson, one that "evolved in counterpoint to the elite discourse about conservation, a folk tradition that often critiqued official conservation policies, occasionally borrowing from them, and at other times even influenced them."[11]

Yet perhaps one of the most important essays for bridging environmental and labor history, Richard White's "'Are You an Environmentalist or Do You

Work for a Living?'" (1996), is notable in part for its neglect. In his piece, White insisted that work was and is a primary means for human beings to gain experience and knowledge of the environment. "Coming to terms with modern work and machines," he wrote, "involves both more complicated histories and an examination of how all work, and not just the work of loggers, farmers, fishers, and ranchers, intersects with nature." This set new parameters for future study and seemed to enable and encourage collaboration between scholars laboring in different fields, but environmental historians have largely declined to use it as a starting point or guide for investigation.[12]

One exception to this is Kathryn Morse's *The Nature of Gold* (2003). Also heavily influenced by William Cronon's *Nature's Metropolis*, Morse examined the Klondike gold rush with a focus on work, nature's commodification, and markets. In miners' journeys north, in the hunting, fishing, and store purchases they relied on to feed themselves, and certainly in their search for gold, she explained, they were, more or less, connected to the natural world. "As workers and travelers in a distant corner of the North American continent, always in need of food, supplies, shelter, and transportation," Morse wrote, "the miners criss-crossed the border between a local subsistence economy and the decidedly nonlocal mining economy that brought them to the Yukon." In that way they experienced both a preindustrial immersion in and an industrial capitalist alienation from nature. They changed the local landscape too, and participated in the ongoing transformation of the expansive North American environment beyond.[13]

Other studies, by labor historians, have investigated mining in the West with an eye toward nature as well. Laurie Mercier's *Anaconda* (2001), for example, included consideration of the way workplace hazards in a smelter town stimulated labor militancy and led some workers to develop a growing concern about air pollution.[14] More recently, Thomas Andrews revisited the mining history of Ludlow, Colorado, in a dissertation, "The Road to Ludlow" (2003), with brief attention to coal mines, homeplaces, and hinterlands as part of a larger "workscape" for industrial labor. Andrews also demonstrated an awareness of the links between labor and nature in a journal article, "'Made by Toile?'" (2005), explaining how work and workers disappeared from tourists' views of the Colorado landscape.[15] And, even before this literature on the West started to appear, historians began to consider coal mines in the East as work environments. In particular, Alan Derickson's *Black Lung* (1998) and Barbara Smith's *Digging Our Own Graves* (1987) both told the story of the struggle to deal with coal miners' pneumoconiosis.[16]

Still, the labor historiography attentive to the environment is much smaller than the environmental historiography attentive to labor and class. There is more that could be done by labor historians to integrate work and environment in their interpretations of the past, and this is not simply a benign suggestion for bringing new topics into the field. Labor historians *need* to do this. Labor history is incomplete without environmental history, just as it would be greatly lacking without social history, women's history, the history of race and ethnicity, immigration history, and the history of technology. Paying attention to workers' relationship with the natural world through their work can and will alter the way we think about their experiences during industrialization, their changing identities, their varied and evolving culture and values, their efforts to create and maintain unions and other social organizations, as well as their role in politics.

Making a Living is meant to be a step in this direction, by examining aspects of the historical relationship between labor and nature during the rise and advance of industrial capitalism in the United States. It builds on the relevant literature in environmental history, the more limited scholarship in labor history, as well as many traditional primary sources, including diaries, correspondence, memoirs, company store records, oral history interviews, union journals, newspapers, drawings and photographs, government reports, and others. Using these materials, often in new ways, it looks at how the evolving means, circumstances, and ends of work were inextricably linked to the changing ways people used and thought about the physical and organic environment.

Taking this tack, the book necessarily draws on the theoretical insights of Karl Marx, for his explanation of historical materialism (which starts with the premise that people have history because they must produce their life as social beings) and more specifically for his exposition of alienation (which is, in his view, inherent to historical change). Marx's general philosophy of history and its various aspects both incorporate the natural world, since humankind is itself part of nature, and because people must transform their environment not only to live but also to realize their distinct "species powers," namely the capacity for self-conscious creative activity. So these ideas allow us to see the connections between labor and nature as well as people's estrangement from one and the other, two parts of a single (though complicated) process.

According to Marx, writing with Friedrich Engels, the "first premise of all human history is, of course, the existence of living human individuals," and "the first fact to be established is the physical organization of these individuals and their consequent relation to the rest of nature." As people act to satisfy their needs, their capacity for this activity evolves, their social organization changes, and they acquire new needs. With historical development of their productive powers and social relations they change their relationship to the natural world as well.[17] People are a part of nature, but nature is outside of humankind, too; and it is the object transformed to meet our most basic needs and accomplish all manner of other ends. "In creating a nature which is adequate, in producing food which he can eat, clothes he can wear and house he can live in," philosopher Bertell Ollman clarified, "man is forever remolding nature, and with each alteration enabling his powers to achieve new kinds and degrees of fulfillment."[18]

At another level, nature is also the instrument by which humankind experiences self-realization; consequently, when society evolves to various levels of production in which workers are alienated from their labor and its products, they are estranged from the natural world. Under capitalism, the power of living beings for creative productive activity is largely reduced to a mere means to satisfy animal needs, when they are forced to sell their labor power for a wage and give up claim to the products of their labor. This severs most of their remaining organic connections to nature and thereby compounds an actual and sensed estrangement from self, although it is not complete. Workers are not entirely bereft of ways to respond and resist, and they certainly do so, a fact that *Making a Living* attempts to reveal and explain.

Yet it is important to acknowledge at the outset that other environmental and labor history grounded in Marx's understanding of how change happens in a capitalist society has not drawn on his ideas in quite the same way, particularly in terms of understanding alienation. In *The Five Dollar Day* (1981), for example, Stephen Meyer chronicled and interpreted the decline of skilled, autonomous craft production with the advent of scientific management and introduction of new technology, leading to considerably altered (degraded) relationships between workers and the labor process, their products, and one another, as well as the managers and owners of the companies that employed them. "Workers cease to be human beings," Meyer quoted one Ford worker as saying, "as soon as they enter the gates of the shop." Likewise, in *The Fall of the House of Labor* (1987), David Montgomery charted the erosion of skill, as well as the assaults on mutualistic values that accompanied such work, during the late nineteenth and early twentieth centuries. He portrayed these changes as part of an effort to reconfigure work to meet the needs of an evolving capitalism and connected it to developments in labor organizing and political affiliation, toward a radical militancy grounded in opposition to employers' drive for "rationalization."[19]

While labor historians have focused exclusively on alienation as a matter of labor and social relations transformed, however, environmental historians have tended to see people's estrangement from nature as part of economic change, but without much attention to work. In *Dust Bowl* (1979), for instance, Donald Worster pointed to cultural values, such as narrowly viewing nature as a source of profit and assuming the right to dominate and exploit the land for material gain, as part of an explanation for why western farmers overworked the land and created the conditions for devastating dust storms. "There was nothing in the plains society to check the progress of commercial farming," he wrote, and that "is how and why the Dust Bowl came about." Similarly, in *Nature Incorporated* (1991), Theodore Steinberg investigated industrial capitalism in New England as "a profound restructuring of the environment" that had at its core the commodification and mastery of nature.[20]

Making a Living ventures to bridge these different approaches, drawing on unrecognized common theory and shared subject matter, to tell a story that should resonate with scholars working in both environmental and labor history. From the early nineteenth century to the close of the twentieth century, the book argues, the exploitation of American workers intensified while their sense of separation from the natural world became more acute — but they did not simply allow this to happen unchallenged. As many accounts have pointed out, they practiced all kinds of informal individual and group protest in fields, mines, and factories, and they frequently organized themselves into unions and political parties to assert their collective power more purposefully and effectively. Workers also relied on a myriad mix of responses to their estrangement from nature, particularly new interests in literary romanticism as well as old and new interests in hunting and fishing. These responses were not unrelated to their various forms of resistance to economic exploitation, and in doing what they did workers provided the foundation for modern environmental and environmental justice movements.

Still, the narrative of workers' evolving relationship with nature is not a linear one. It is complicated by time and place as well as gender and race, and *Making a Living* is organized with that in mind. It consists of six chronologically arranged case studies — young, female textile workers in antebellum New England, black male plantation slaves and newly freed African American sharecroppers in the Mississippi Delta, homesteading women in Kansas and Nebraska, native-born coal miners and their families in southern Appalachia, male and female autoworkers in Michigan, and Mexican and Mexican American farmworkers in southern California. Each of the cases deals with workers who confronted an industrial transition, people facing significant changes in the conditions, methods, and purpose of their labor, but each also reveals particular and even unique experiences.

In this book, "industrial" change is not exclusively something that happened only to men working with heavy machinery in dark mills, although that is the typical understanding. It is, rather, a process of change that affected many different kinds of workers during the nineteenth and twentieth centuries. It introduced a set of innovations for doing labor, or getting labor done, that affected even people who worked independent of an employer or capitalist and that did not necessarily involve the introduction of new technology. Likewise, "work" is a category broadly defined, encompassing a wide range of activity, sometimes done for a wage or piece rate and sometimes done without pay. In this and other respects, the selected case studies are about people with much in common. But they represent a diverse perspective, too, exploring the lives of different groups of workers in a variety of occupations, at distinct moments in the American economy's development, and in a number of different environments.

Looking at environmental and labor history this way moves materialism beyond a "stages of history" approach, with social relations, productive forces, and a "superstructure" of politics, law, and culture advancing according to a strict, predetermined model. It also allows for a more complicated examination of how people experienced many facets of alienation. Threaded throughout the story are changes in work with the introduction of industrial production methods, transformation of labor as a consequence of technological developments, loss of control over land and tools and the concentration of wealth, and an important rural-to-urban shift, all of which contribute to variants of estrangement from labor and nature. Yet the differences revealed by the six case studies allow for a more sophisticated analysis of change over time, giving cultural variables equal attention with economic factors and leaving room for historical agency, demonstrating that it mattered who and where you were and suggesting that there were no set outcomes.

Chapter 1 follows young women from New England farms to the new textile mills of Lowell, Massachusetts, where they exchanged their place in a family production unit primarily concerned with subsistence for industrial wage labor oriented toward an expanding national market. This migration and the accompanying change in work brought about a change in their relationship with nature, all of which was permeated by gender conventions. The labor young women did in hill and valley homesteads as well as the spinning and weaving they did in new brick mills abided by a generally shared understanding of what it meant to be female, although that definition was in flux. In resisting exploitation "mill girls" claimed the Lockean rhetoric of the Revolution as their female inheritance, calling themselves "daughters of freemen," disinclined to abide wage slavery and willing to organize, write, speak in public, and initiate strikes in order to be taken into account. They also came up with their own working-class version of literary romanticism, using it to indict industrial capitalism for separating them from an eminently preferable rural, agrarian life, the virtues of which they lauded using more traditionally feminine sentimental language and style.

In Chapter 2, the book turns to Mississippi Delta male slaves and share-croppers, who cultivated and harvested some of the cotton used in New England textile mills, and it highlights the importance of race and gender as well as class. In the antebellum and postbellum South, race was at the center of a set of evolving social relations that determined to a great extent, or at least heavily influenced, how blacks as well as whites thought about and used the natural world around them. Gender, which was conjoined with race, did this too, demarcating the landscape and giving meaning to the labor people did there. It suffused the act of making a living from the land with notions about manhood and womanhood, but even more so it cast and conditioned black men's resistance to economic exploitation. That resistance included various forms of independent production, particularly hunting and fishing and gardening, which partly repaired a rift between themselves and nature. After the Civil War, as wage laborers and sharecroppers, black men continued to engage in this independent production for many of the same reasons they had done it during slavery, and with similar results.

Shifting the focus to the West, and a bit forward in time, Chapter 3 examines the lives of women settlers on the Kansas and Nebraska plains, from their initial encounters with an open and seemingly wild land to the years after their families had achieved more control over nature and established modern homes. Although these women were one step removed from industrial capitalism and wage labor, the work they did and the relationship with the environment that entailed was affected by larger trends of economic change as well as movements for "scientific farming" and "domestic economy." How they understood gender changed as well, as comparatively fluid roles and expectations during the early years focused on survival were replaced by more rigid, traditional conventions as time passed and life became more predictable. In the process, the antagonistic attitude many women had toward the grasslands at the start evolved into the kind of romantic thoughts and feelings Lowell mill girls had embraced decades before.

Returning to the themes of persistent hunting, fishing, and gardening, Chapter 4 traces the ways mostly white, male native-born residents of southern West Virginia dealt with a multifaceted transition from farming to coal mining to factory work. Still practicing largely subsistence-oriented agriculture into the late nineteenth century, these men first did wage work in mines and woods on a temporary and seasonal basis, to earn money that allowed them to continue farming. By the beginning of the twentieth century, many had moved their families into company-run camps to dig coal for a living, although initially they had considerable freedom to work when and how they pleased. They also held onto parts of preindustrial life by cultivating large gardens, hunting game in nearby woods, and fishing in local streams along with their wives, sons, and daughters, depending on the task. Over the course of the next few decades, however, coal operators standardized production and introduced new technology while conditions in the company towns deteriorated. Miners responded by organizing unions, often relying on the local landscape for subsistence to tide them over during long and hard-fought battles. When the coal industry started to atrophy in the late 1920s, and especially after the onset of World War II in the 1940s, mountain dwellers took their families north, to work at Akron rubber plants, Detroit car shops, Chicago packinghouses, and other urban-industrial workplaces, where they were witness to another degree of dual alienation from their labor and nature both.

Chapter 5 picks up the story there, investigating the lives of Michigan autoworkers, many of whom had come from the rural South or Midwest. In Detroit, Flint, Lansing, and other towns and cities the migrants confronted repetitive, dulling work on assembly lines, in gargantuan plants that polluted the air and water of local and distant communities. To deal with a profound sense of estrangement from the natural world and with the other stresses that came with factory labor, in the 1930s and 1940s an increasing number of these men (as well as some women) took up or renewed their interest in hunting and fishing. And they established or joined existing sportsmen's clubs, at first with an exclusive focus on conserving fish and game but eventually broadening their scope to include advocacy for environmental protection in general. At the same time, autoworkers organized a union, the United Auto Workers (UAW), which responded to its members' sporting interests and environmental concerns by promoting recreational committees, running a summer camp, lobbying for pollution control laws, and encouraging grass-roots campaigns to clean up neighborhoods. By the 1960s, in fact, the UAW had begun to take a leading role in building a modern environmental movement.

Although organized labor's participation in environmental advocacy tended toward passing stronger regulatory legislation, sustaining what might be called "mainstream" environmentalism, some efforts aided the rise and spread of "environmental justice" activism, too. Chapter 6 examines this contribution through the United Farm Workers (UFW) campaign to organize mostly Mexican and Mexican American migrant labor in southern California vineyards, orchards, and lettuce fields. Although initially focused on improving wages and basic working conditions, the UFW quickly turned its attention to the issue of pesticides, which, like growers' voracious need for cheap, migrant labor, seemed to be a an essential component of profitable, industrial agriculture. The land and its fruits in southern California were commodities, as was the farm workers' labor power, and exploitation of both nature and workers simply followed, on a grand scale. To empower migrant field hands and protect them from agricultural chemicals, the union started by César Chávez organized a militant, confrontational social movement along ethnic lines. In this way, Chávez established or at least demonstrated an organizing model that poor and minority activists dealing with toxins and other environmental hazards could and did use in the future.

Taken together, the six chapters suggest there is a link, although not a straight or uninterrupted line, between antebellum mill girls' protests against urban-industrial life and mid-twentieth-century farmworkers' efforts to reign in a deadly industrial agriculture. There were, as noted, many differences between workers, depending on their time, place, gender, race, and other factors, but they had much in common as well. With the onset and spread of industrial capitalism they faced many changes in the way they had to make a living, often including new material circumstances as well as alteration of their relationship to the natural world, changes that were inextricably bound. In response to these shifts, workers called on ideas and practices that were both old and new, not only to understand what was happening to them but also, at least sometimes, to have a hand in shaping the content and destiny of their lives.

1

I Think Less of the Factory
Than of My Native Dell

Labor, Nature, and the Lowell Mill Girls

In 1840, as part of a defense of factory life in Lowell, Massachusetts, textile operative Sarah Bagley pointed out that "mill girls" were not really "so far from God and nature, as many persons might suppose." They managed to maintain their relationship with nature, and nature's God, by cultivating roses, lilies, geraniums, and other plants in pots on the mill's window sills, giving their work rooms "more the appearance of a flower garden than a workshop." The perfume of the flowers supposedly pervaded the air, inspiring the operatives to praise God for such rich blessings and filling them with happiness.[1] Decades later, in a memoir, Lucy Larcom recalled how she and other mill girls would take their only summer holiday, the Fourth of July, rising early to walk down some unfamiliar road and collect wild roses. "No matter if we must get up at five the next morning and go back to our humdrum toil," she wrote, "we should have the roses to take with us for company, and the sweet air of the woodland which lingered about them would scent our thoughts all day, and make us forget the oily smell of the machinery."[2]

Although written for different reasons, and with distinct audiences in mind, the explanations each of the operatives offered for mill hands' attachment to the flowers in their workrooms suggest the challenge capitalist industrialization posed to traditional relationships with the natural world. For workers and many other antebellum New Englanders, the new brick factories threatened to displace other, more direct and satisfying experiences with nature. Even in coming to their defense Bagley revealed the new distance mills created between workers and God's creation, while Larcom penned a more critical recollection about how flowers served as fresh balm and escape from daily toil among stinking machines. In the writings of both women, the influence of the romantic poetry and literature of the day is clearly evident, but it is equally apparent that the factories where they labored provided actual points of comparison to memories of former lives, real and imagined. A significant change was taking place across the region, and Bagley and Larcom were marking its occurrence and beginning to interpret its meaning in a variety of ways.[3]

Before migrating from family farms scattered about northern New England, women operatives viewed nature largely in utilitarian terms, a perspective grounded in daily, direct use of the environment for the subsistence and comfort of themselves and other family members. Recognition of nature's beauty and a sense that it was a manifestation of God were sentiments not entirely absent from their consciousness, but ones not prominent or pervasive either. After their migration to work in the mills, the operatives were less able to see how their labor was any sort of productive exchange with the environment, and they felt increasingly estranged from the natural world. For many of the mill hands, nature was no longer a place where work was done but rather a thing apart from labor, something exclusively "out there" to be brought into the mills in rarefied form if it was to be present at all, and the aesthetic and spiritual dimensions of the environment assumed a new importance. More often, nature was a place for casual leisure, meditation and academic study, and, particularly when there was a chance to return home, temporary or permanent escape. In fact, this evolving view of the natural world became an important but sometimes understated part of the operatives' resistance to mill labor. The grumbling, "turnouts," and turnover that began so soon after the women's arrival in Lowell were not only about wage cuts, boardinghouse rates, and the mill girls' refusal to be "slaves" to industrial tyrants. They were also about the operatives' separation from a factual as well as fictional rural landscape, one they believed was more healthy, beautiful, spiritually meaningful, and conducive to the development of good morals.

DOMESTIC PRODUCTION

The majority of women who worked in the Lowell mills of the antebellum period hailed from parts of New England first settled by whites in the decades leading up to the Revolution. This included southern Maine, southeastern New Hampshire, the hill country between the Merrimack and Connecticut river valleys, and southeastern Vermont. Between 1790 and 1830, white settlers also moved beyond alluvial bottomlands as well as farther north into the mountains. Maine's population increased threefold and Vermont's more than twofold, while the number of residents in New Hampshire nearly doubled. By the first decade of the nineteenth century, however, the earlier-settled sections of these states were already starting to see a noticeable population decline, as young men and women left for land out West or took jobs in cities of the East.[4] As out-migration increased, soil fertility declined, and markets encroached, subsistence-oriented agriculture gave way to raising sheep for woolen mills, which reached its height in the 1840s but thereafter could not compete with the wool-growing farther west. By the 1850s, most of the descendants of the original white inhabitants who remained had turned to making a living as dairy farmers.[5]

Prior to the economic and demographic transformation of New England, girls and women on the region's farms did a variety of tasks essential to the family economy, with a few opportunities for local trade. There was, of course, a gendered division of labor, but well into the first half of the nineteenth century the "women's sphere" encompassed quite a large number of productive activities. These included feeding poultry, milking cows, making butter and cheese, tending the garden, gathering berries and other wild edibles, preserving and pickling, shucking corn, paring apples, making cider and applesauce, cooking, washing, tidying the house, making soap and candles, preparing flax and cleaning fleece, spinning, knitting, weaving, and dyeing cloth, as well as bearing and caring for children. Female household members worked both outdoors and indoors through the various seasons of the year, and they did it alone, in pairs, and as part of larger groups.

Some girls and women saw parts or even all of their work as onerous, drudgery that brought little satisfaction. Tasks such as cooking and spinning, which had to be done every day or constantly through the week, could be tedious. Heavy labor, such as doing the wash, brought complaints too. Writing to a cousin from Bristol, New Hampshire, in 1845, Malenda Edwards bemoaned the toil that delayed her from attending to her correspondence sooner. Both of her parents were in bad health and neither had their usual hired help, which put additional burdens on her. "I have got the most of my wool spun and two webs wove," Edwards wrote, "and at the mil land have been out and raked hay almost every afternoon whilst they were haying." One morning she had fainted "and had to lay on the shed flour [*sic*] fifteen or twenty minutes for any comfort before I could get to bed." This rest cost her, though, because the next day she had to "wash churn, bake and make chese and go over to Daniels blackbering." She accomplished each of the tasks but the berry picking, as it had become "so tremendous hot I dare not venture out so far."[6]

Yet a greater number of women on New England farms did not see their work, or most of it in any case, as either dull or unbearably difficult. In this preindustrial age there was not always a clear line between work and leisure, and numerous tasks were welcome occasions for enjoyment and fulfilling demonstration of skill. Young girls and older women usually could set their own pace, rarely had to deal with arbitrary or demeaning oversight, and routinely had the chance to socialize with both men and other women as part of their work. Typically they were among those who used or otherwise relied on the products and services of their labor, of which they were rightly proud. Just as important, their work and leisure provided a direct relationship with the natural world, one that sustained a utilitarian view of the environment but did not exclude observations of beauty and spiritual meaning.

Making soap and doing the wash, however much disliked by women, both required some knowledge of how nature could be put to use. Soft soap, for laundry, was the end product of leaching wood-ashes in a barrel to make lye and boiling this in a great pot outdoors. A harder soap, for toilet use, could be made from bayberry tallow.[7] Making the soft soap as well as actually doing the wash required a plentiful supply of water with the right pH balance, which could be corrected by adding soda or lye. When young Tryphena Ely White first moved out to central New York in 1805, she recorded in her diary that their kettle of boiling soap "does not seem to do well," because "we were obliged to make it of river water," which was too soft. Later that month, she "washed some muslins and fine cloaths which had lain a good while dirty, waiting for rain water." To whiten clothes or remove stains, White also would have had to wait for a good spell of sunny days in order to lay the garments out under the sun, taking them in at nights to prevent mildewing.[8]

Similarly, women transformed parts of nature into a useful product when they made candles from bees' wax, deer suet, moose fat, bear's grease, and mutton tallow. Naturalist Peter Kalm noted the use of the waxy berries of the bayberry bush in candle making as well, explaining that Swedes called the plant tallow-shrub and the English sometimes called it "candle-berry tree." To start making candles women saved their cooking grease, robbed their bee hives of some wax, or collected berries in the autumn and set aside a day or more to produce the family's yearly stock. Nicer candles, as Catherine Beecher explained, were made by pouring a mixture of melted tallow around wicks set out in molds. Dip candles, made by repeatedly dipping wicks in a kettle of tallow, were easier and cheaper to manufacture. A variation on this process substituted common rushes with parts of their outer bark stripped away for wicks that were then dipped in tallow or grease and allowed to harden.[9]

The production of textiles, which changed so dramatically later in the nineteenth century with the advent of fully integrated, water-powered mills, required intimate knowledge and direct use of nature too. Farm families usually planted a field of flax for linen cloth in May, which was weeded by young women or children in bare feet, to prevent them from crushing the tender stalks. Later, in June or July, boys and older men pulled the plants, removed the seeds, and dried and broke the stalks. After a few other steps, women put the flax fibers on the spinning wheel, bleached the thread with water and ashes, wove it on a loom, and bleached the linen again in the sun. As for wool yarn, that usually came from the family's own sheep. After women picked over the raw fleece, it was carded, combed, and greased, spun into skeins on a wheel, either knitted (after a good washing) or used for weaving on a loom, and then sent to the local fulling mill. To color the wool women used a variety of natural dyes derived from the bark of oak, hickory, sassafras, and birch trees as well as boiled pokeberry, onion skins, pressed goldenrods, and black walnut hulls.[10]

Among the other more common daily experiences that rural girls and women had with domestic animal products were milking and turning milk into cheese and butter. "In those summer days," recalled Sarah Emery of her early life in Newbury, Massachusetts, "mother and Aunt Sarah rose in the early dawn, and, taking the well-scoured wooden pails from the bench by the back door, repaired to the cow yard behind the barn." The women milked the ten cows owned between them, and Sarah's mother made this into cheese four days of the week, leaving the task to the aunt the other days.[11] More frequently, milk was turned into butter by churning the skimmed cream. In 1839, after moving out to Franklin, New Hampshire, "to live in the woods among the stumps and owls," Olive Sawyer "made eleven hundred weight of new milk Cheese [and] 4 hundred of butter cheese beside considerable skim milk cheese."[12] This sort of work required that women pay some attention to what their cows were eating and the quality of the water they were drinking, the characteristic habits and behavior of the individual milk cows, and the passing of the seasons that brought warmer or cooler temperatures requiring different milking methods.

Likewise, women took responsibility for their family's poultry. They raised geese for feathers and food, according to Alice Morse Earle, letting them roam "the streets all summer, eating grass by the highways and wallowing in the puddles." Three or four times a year, pickers plucked the geese, securing the birds' heads in stockings or a "goose basket" to prevent biting. The down made bed ticking, and the quills, pulled only one from each goose, were used for pens.[13] The women raised chickens and turkeys as well. Between working about the house, making a cape bonnet, and noting the apple tree blossoms on walks through the orchard at her family's New Hampshire homestead, a young Sally Brown rounded out one day in March 1832 by making a turkey cage. But while women sometimes marketed surplus eggs their hens produced, it was up to the men to sell the chickens and turkeys. Later in the year, Brown's father went to Ludlow with "his poultry" and "sold turkeys for seven and chickens for six cents a pound and my stocking yarn for five shillings a pound."[14]

On what were likely rare occasions, young women challenged conventional gender roles and hunted small game or fished in the local brooks or ponds. In her diary entry for 4 June 1832, Sally Brown noted catching two partridges, probably using snares. Similarly, Tryphena White recorded one late June day that after chores that included housework and weeding in the garden, "towards night I went down to the river with my hook and line to catch some trout but had no success."[15] More in line with traditional expectations, however, women usually took other opportunities for relatively passive experiences with wildlife. Susan Emery remembered long afternoons sitting upon the sill of the open door as her "fingers kept time to the murmur of the brook or the song of the birds in the willows bordering the silvery stream just beyond the gravel path, edged by flowers, the perfume of which, mingling with that of the lilacs and sweet briar, filled the air with grateful odor."[16] But moments of distanced observation could be permeated by fear as well. White's journal includes numerous entries about rattlesnakes, which struck terror in women and men both. A couple of days before she went fishing for trout, when she was out picking greens with her sister Polly, they encountered a rattler, and a crowd of hesitant men and women soon gathered. That particular snake escaped before they could kill it, yet many others did not.[17]

The female members of farming households also gained firsthand experience with the many faces of nature, and some of the intricacies of ecological relationships, by cultivating vegetables, herbs, and flowers. Anna Howell kept a record of her gardening interleaved in agricultural almanacs and regularly mentioned the many hazards she encountered. Unrelenting storms through the month of May in 1819 and 1820, for example, destroyed the sprouts of her nutmeg melons and watermelons the first year and her cucumbers and watermelons the next, forcing her to replant.[18] Late frosts in the spring and periods of drought in summer killed plants too, a problem Howell sometimes remedied by replanting. Other times she simply accepted lower yields or none at all. May entries for 1821 suggest that was a bad year for "worms," which "destroyed all my early corn and the greater part of cucumbers." Days later Howell was busy "replanting cucumbers and Nutmeg melons the 3d and 4th time [and] Replanting water melons." This was not her first damaging visit from insect pests, but the infestation started Howell thinking, and the next month she recorded a way to prevent "the yellow winged bug" from destroying cucumber plants by planting an onion in each hill and between peas.[19]

Women did not always view gardening as a battle against fickle weather or ravenous bugs, though. Sarah Emery fondly recollected the great variety of medicinal and sweet herbs as well as the flowers her grandmother cultivated. Some criticized her for such "fiddle-de-dees," and pronounced the plantings "vanity," because they did not seem as useful as turnips, leeks, carrots, or other vegetables. Emery reasoned, however, that God had decked the whole universe with beauty and that "pretty surroundings" made people "happier and better." "Grandmam'" considered it part of women's duty to make their homes agreeable in this way, and Emery "was sure her good sisters-in-law and other croakers enjoyed a bunch of pinks or a rose as much as any one, and her mints and sweet herbs were in great demand, especially lavender, to strew in drawers among linen."[20] Tryphena White was more inclined to complain about the heat of the day, which forced her to get up before sunrise to weed the family's garden, but an entry recording her visit to a neighbor indicates that women could take great pride in the patch of ground they transformed. Mrs. Hopkins took White "all over her garden [to] see everything she had in it" and delayed her return home, but with "a posy of pinks and a handful of young onions for salad, and one cucumber, which was the only one she had big enough to pick."[21]

Finally, the girls and women of New England farms witnessed the bounty and beauty of fields and forests on frequent trips to gather wild herbs, pick berries and flowers, and sometimes just take a stroll. One day in mid-September 1832, for example, Sally Brown finished her chores "and went to the mountain to get some Pyrola [wintergreen] to send Mrs. Webber." This plant, according to Lydia Maria Child, was "considered good for all humors, particularly scrofula," and some called it "rheumatism-weed" because a wintergreen tea supposedly soothed that disorder, which might have been Mrs. Webber's particular affliction. In any case, throughout the summer months, Sally had also made other trips with her friends, Susan and Marcia, to pick strawberries, currants, raspberries, blueberries, and blackberries. These were for eating fresh and as preserves, of course, but like wild herbs the berries and parts of berry bushes had medicinal uses too. Child noted that blackberries were "useful in cases of dysentery" and recommended a tea made of the roots and leaves as well as a syrup.[22] And, not incidentally, there was the pleasure and healthful benefit of walking to get them.

. Later, after they had migrated to Lowell and other textile towns to work in the mills, young women like Sally would look back longingly on the days they spent roaming hillsides and walking along brooks, gathering in the woods and meadows. Then, however, it was not so much the herbs and berries they missed but real and imagined opportunities for reverie and delight in nature, wandering that was as much leisurely or spiritual excursion as purposeful labor. This sentiment developed in tandem with profound economic and social change, when industrial capitalism intervened to upset the women's world, compelled them to indict the cities and factories they encountered, and led them to invoke both old and new ideals in praise of agrarian life and rural landscapes.

MILL LABOR

The city of Lowell, Massachusetts, was carved out of land on the banks of the Concord and Merrimack rivers, once the site of two important Native American villages at the Pawtucket and Wamesit Falls. In the middle of the seventeenth century, the missionary-minded John Eliot successfully petitioned the Massachusetts General Court to establish 2,500 acres there as a praying town, straddling the mouth of the Concord River, with exclusive rights of use for the local indigenous population, which had been decimated by disease epidemics and numbered only in the hundreds.[23] By the early eighteenth century, however, following King Philip's war and continued hostilities with white settlers who coveted the area's fertile lands, most of the Indians left for the Connecticut River or points north, and their land claims went extinct.[24]

Throughout the rest of the eighteenth century, and past the turn of the next, the people of what was then East Chelmsford were engaged primarily in farming and fishing for subsistence as well as market trade. Taking advantage of the falls on the Concord River and River Meadow Brook, local residents also built various kinds of mills along the waterways, including grist mills, fulling mills, iron mills, and eventually spinning mills. Decades before the Boston Associates harnessed the Merrimack River for manufacturing, in fact, there was already some industry in the area. To the west of the Concord, however, the land was a mix of woodlots, fields, orchards, houses, and a couple of dirt roads. Several systems of locks and canals were completed there by 1814, linking up Concord, New Hampshire, and Boston, but new settlement and commerce did not significantly transform the environs until the mid-1820s, when the Boston Associates moved in and built many more textile mills on the Merrimack.

By the late 1830s, Lowell was a bustling place with twenty-eight mills employing 8,000 workers, the great majority of whom were women from the New England countryside. They worked at the many machines powered by turning waterwheels in basements below, producing sheetings, calicoes, broadcloths, carpets, and rugs for a growing market, an experience quite different from what the operatives had been used to at home. Now they were

wage laborers, working under central supervision, making products for un-
known consumers, and usually living in one of the many boardinghouses
scattered about what was quickly becoming the second-largest city in the
state.[25]

The new factory labor also severed the direct relationship women migrants
once had with nature through work. They were confined to the "built environment" of noisy workrooms in sprawling mills for hours on end, employed at tasks that seemed distanced from anything like transforming parts
of the natural world into useful products. To be sure, Lowell's perimeters
were at least semirural, the mills there were crafted edifices of brick and wood
often edged by flower gardens, and it was raw cotton and wool that the
workers manufactured into finished goods. But the experience simply did not
compare to living and working on the women's native homesteads. This
seems to have become more evident as the years passed, and it played an
important part in the women's growing disenchantment with mill labor. The
otherwise tame writing in literary experiments such as the *Lowell Offering*
included numerous expressions of disillusionment with factory life and pin-
ing for home. These often centered on differences in landscape and were
coupled with romantic musing about the beauty and spiritual fullness of
nature. Such sentiments also factored into the militant resistance mill hands
began to organize in the 1830s as well, finding their way into columns of the
radical *Voice of Industry*.

There were some operatives who felt fortunate to leave off having to "pick
rocks, and weed the garden, and drop corn, and rake hay."[26] Sally Rice left her
parents and siblings in Somerset, Vermont, in the 1830s, first to work on a
farm in New York and then to labor in a Connecticut mill, but she never
wished to return to her old home. "I can never be happy there in among so
many mountains," Rice wrote after a brief visit back to Somerset, and she
pledged not to settle on the family's rocky farm "in that wilderness."[27] Others,
such as Harriet Farley, emphasized the pastoral quality of the mill village as
one of the attractions of the factory system. Home manufacture in old England, she argued, was an ugly life of poverty and discomfort. Textile manufacturing in places such as Amesbury, Massachusetts, however, was different. The town was situated, "as is almost every factory village, in the midst
of most attractive natural scenery." At any rate, Farley maintained, mill girls
were not permanent wage laborers and frequently returned home for a few
weeks or months, where a "change of air and diet are conducive to health."[28]

Yet many of the female operatives in Lowell who put pen to paper, in
correspondence, diaries, literary journals, and operatives' newspapers, were
less than enthusiastic about work in the mills there. Among the more com-

mon objections was the routine confinement among clattering machinery and noxious lamp smoke. After working in a weaving room for only sixteen weeks, Susan Brown complained of being "immured within the massey brick walls of a hateful factory" and declared her intention to return to her family's home in Epsom, New Hampshire.[29] Likewise, while she sometimes found the work agreeable, Lucy Larcom had her moments when "the confinement of the mill became very wearisome to me." One June day, when the weather was fair, she leaned far out of the window, trying to escape the "clash of sound" inside and, looking at the distant hills, cried out "Oh that I had wings!"[30] Although writing under a pseudonym, Harriet Farley also described feeling cooped up in the mill where she worked. Looking out of the window at "the bright loveliness of nature," she felt "like a prisoned bird, with its painful longings for an unchecked flight amidst the beautiful creation around me."[31]

The desire for release from the mills was prompted both by what operatives could see and sometimes hear outside their workrooms as well as by the conditions within them, a contrast often employed by factory critics. "The graceful form, the bright and sparkling eye, the blushing cheek and the elastic motions of 'Industry's Angel daughters,'" did not belong "to Lowell Cotton Mills, but to New England's country Homes," where "the fair cheek, kissed by the sunlight and the breeze, grew fresh and healthful."[32] In fact, operatives frequently fell ill from their work and left their positions for days, weeks, and even months to recuperate. Permielia Dame made her way from Rochester, New Hampshire, to the Lowell mills in the mid-1830s, but soon after wrote her brother about becoming sick and taking an absence. She had intended to answer his last letter earlier, Dame explained, but "my health being very bad and my eyes very weak that I was obliged to leave the Factory for a short time." She made a short trip to Boston, but this did not help, and so she took more time off and "went to New Hampshire and there visited all our friends and connections."[33]

The conditions operatives experienced in the red brick mills depended to some extent on their particular job and where they worked in the multistoried factories. Each stage of the production process had its own floor, with machinery powered by a waterwheel in the basement. At ground level was the carding room, where operatives worked loose cotton into roving, continuous strands that drawing frames stretched and recombined before it was wound on bobbins. Spinning frames on the next floor then twisted the coarse roving into yarn of variable thickness. Filling yarn made this way went directly to the weaving room, but workers running the warping and dressing machines above turned roving into warp yarn too. Power loom tenders on the next floor used both types of yarn to produce a finished cloth. Lastly, in a cloth room, workers "measured, folded and batched the fabric for subsequent bleaching, dying, or printing and eventual shipment to selling agencies in Boston." Throughout the whole process women predominated, although men held all the supervisory positions and operative jobs in the carding room. Women held the rest of the machine-tending jobs, running drawing frames, double speeders, and spinning throstles — the lowest-paid positions — as well as looms, and winding, warping, and dressing machines — the more skilled and better-paid jobs.[34]

Upon first arrival, however, regardless of where they worked, most hands were surprised by the general noise level from clattering machinery and the suffocating smoke from the many oil lamps. Factory windows were numerous and tall, set in repetitious rows from one end of a building to the other, to make better use of natural light. But they were kept closed even on the hottest summer days, and steam was sometimes sprayed in the air inside, both practices necessary for maintaining the proper humidity that kept threads moist. Working from five in the morning to seven in the evening, with a half hour each for breakfast and dinner, the operatives also inhaled dangerous amounts of cotton fibers. When they started becoming more militant and creating lists of their grievances, many of the women cited workroom conditions as detrimental to their health. "We are perfectly certain, from personal observation," wrote one trade unionist, "that these long hours of labor in confined rooms, are very injurious to health, and we doubt whether it would be using too harsh terms to say, that the whole system is one of slow and legal assassination."[35]

The world outside the factory was clearly viewed by most mill hands and other observers as preferable to that inside the mills. This explains, in part, the popularity of outdoor leisure activities, which assumed a new importance in the urban-industrial context. Operatives frequently used the time they were not expected to be at work for walks around Lowell as well as more ambitious excursions elsewhere. Lucy Larcom recalled making herself familiar with the "rocky nooks along Pawtucket Falls, shaded with hemlocks and white birches" and dotted with "strange new wild flowers." She and her companions also occupied their free time with walks to where the Concord met the Merrimack, around the old canal path, and up Dracut Heights "to look away to the dim blue mountains." But the women did not have to go far to see nature, she claimed, because it came up close to the mill gates. "There was green grass all around them; violets and wild geraniums grew by the canals," Larcom remembered, "and long stretches of open land between the corporation buildings and the street made the town seem country-like."[36]

From the beginning, mill owners had made some effort to beautify Lowell as part of their paternalist scheme. They instructed managers to maintain flower gardens just outside the factories and, because the original mill acreage was mostly cleared farmland, they oversaw tree planting. Kirk Boott gave particular attention to establishing lines of elms along Dutton Street and the Merrimack Canal, which others continued after his death. Starting in the late 1820s, workers used the strip of land between the street and canal as an unofficial promenade, which operative Maria Currier called a "delightful retreat." And opportunities for pleasant strolls within Lowell increased in the 1840s, when the city purchased land for the North and South Commons, a total of thirty acres, also accessible by tree-lined paths. Not long after this, a group of prominent citizens founded the Lowell Cemetery on forty-five acres along the banks of the Concord River. Its design included winding paths that followed the hilly contour of the area as well as a lake.[37] In a poem about the place, operative Lydia Sarah Hall described it as "that forest wild . . . like a spot enchanted," where the "tearful eye of nature glistened" to look on the dead gathered in the ground.[38]

Despite the various local sites for taking leisurely walks, however, some mill hands felt compelled to wander a greater distance, seeking out more of an escape. Like the short jaunts closer to "home," these explorations occasionally served as inspiration to wax lyrical. This is evident in an article entitled "A Morning Walk," signed by "V. C. N.":

> I had wandered forth ere yet the sun had commenced his course in the heavens, and directed my steps to the banks of the Merrimack that so carelessly was rolling its tranquil waters to mingle with the great deep . . . and resumed my walk to gaze upon the glories and beauties of the waters, the woods, the fields, and the sweet, blue heavens that with tinseled clouds and gorgeous drapery, enclosed the scene: and while beholding all that was around me, and calling before the mind, as far as memory and imagination would enable me, the events of the past and future, I was led to think upon the Creator of them all. . . . I sat musing thus till roused by the peeling tones of the bell which told me that I was wanted, when I arose and walked into the city where, as usual, all was noise and bustle, but my mind had enjoyed a calmness and serenity not easily effaced, and I felt that I was much profited by my morning walk.[39]

Women operatives commonly expressed such reverie in their writing, both private and published. What they meant to convey, apparently, was the rapture to be found in getting closer to a natural world denied them in the factories and sometimes the city itself.

To get even farther away from Lowell and intensify their rapture, workers also took trips that required travel by stagecoach or train, trips that they could make in part because they were wage earners. One woman made a July 1842 excursion to Lebanon Springs, on the other side of Worcester, and wrote a brief account. "Those who have for any length of time been pent up in a cotton mill and factory boarding-house," she explained, "can appreciate the pleasures of a journey through the country, when the earth is dressed in her richest roves of green, bedecked with flowers, and all smiling with sunlight." What she saw and thoroughly enjoyed was not wilderness, but "farmhouses, gardens and orchards, barns, grass-lands, fields of corn and grain, potatoe plants, wood-lots, pasture-lands, with herds of neat cattle, flocks of sheep, &c., all beautifully interspersed." The trip confirmed for her the notion "that man had made the town, but God made the country."[40] Others deliberately sought out the wild, and they found God there too. Writing from the Mount Washington House in New Hampshire, Sarah Bagley wished her friends were there "to enjoy with us the wild, romantic, mountain scenery around." The view, she said, was "grand and sublime . . . beyond the power of words to describe," and it prompted a soul "to sit still and commune with its Maker."[41]

As should be obvious, the rhetoric mill operatives used to describe various natural scenes, and the emotions their descriptions betray, were at least partly derived from the romantic literary influences of the day. This poetry and literature encouraged a view of nature full of beauty, harmony, and moral symbolism, all of which was evidence of divine creation and design. It was not a way of observing the natural world unfamiliar to the women migrants, some of whom would have read Mrs. Sigourney, John Greenleaf Whittier, William Cullen Bryant, and others before coming to Lowell. Even the *New England Farmer* frequently printed original and previously published items about the sublimity of mountains and valleys and the like, meant for both male and female readers. One column of advice, run after the mills had begun to so dramatically impact rural villages, suggested that farmers' daughters might be enticed to stay at home with a good selection of books and periodicals, a tasteful garden with flowers, shrubs, and winding paths "where she can luxuriate on Nature's charms," as well as a shady bower inviting her to " 'Converse with Nature, and commune with Nature's God.' "[42] But, perhaps ironically, romantic literature was much more available to operatives once they were in the "City of Spindles," and it was urban-industrial life that most encouraged them to embrace its sentimental precepts.

In her memoir of factory life, Harriet Robinson claimed that some women came to Lowell primarily for its circulating libraries, because they "lived in secluded parts of New England, where books were scarce, and there was no cultivated society." While this is something of an overstatement, it is probably

not entirely untrue. Many boardinghouses offered a wide range of periodicals, from *Ladies' Book* to the *Dial*. Spinners and weavers used to read and
write at their machines as well. They brought "their favorite 'pieces' of poetry,
hymns, and extracts, and pasted them up over their looms or frames," thus
skirting the rule against openly reading books in the mill. The more literary-
minded operatives secretly captured their thoughts, according to Robinson,
in notebooks and "on scraps of paper which we hid 'between whiles' in the
waste-boxes upon which we sat while waiting for the looms or frames to need
attention." Some of these workers were among the groups that started the
city's famous literary journals.[43]

Many of the women operatives were not only engrossed in literature and
poetry but also deeply involved in religious worship. In fact, according to
Hannah Josephson, the idea of producing literary journals was first discussed
during "self-improvement" meetings in the vestries of the Second Universal-
ist and First Congregational Churches. Starting in 1840, each "improvement
circle" produced its own publication, the *Lowell Offering* and *Operatives' Magazine*, which were combined in August 1842 as the *Lowell Offering*, under the
editorship of Harriet Farley and Harriet Curtis.[44] In 1845, just two months
before that endeavor folded, the first issue of the *Voice of Industry* appeared,
providing an appealing alternative for the increasingly militant labor force in
Lowell and other parts of Massachusetts. The paper included on its editorial
board the radicalized Lowell operative Sarah Bagley, who had recently engaged Farley in a public debate about whether or not the literary journals
were tools of the mill corporations. Still, like the early magazines and the *New
England Offering* Farley edited later between 1848 and 1850, even the *Voice of
Industry* was filled with countless examples of sentimental stories and poetry
about nature.

Contributors to the literary journals often pondered the seasons, and
spring was a particular favorite, a welcome explosion of color and new life to
transform a comparably colorless and dead winter landscape. In a poem entitled "The Scenes of Nature," a writer named Francine described the April
pleasures of wandering in the woods, when the month's "warmth has waked
the flowers," and listening to the brook, "with sweetest music in its songs."
These scenes that in the "wilds nature has spread," she wrote, caused her to
reflect on the "wondrous lesson" of God's love.[45] But authors had something
to say for the other three seasons too, including winter, coming on "with his
icy train in noble majesty, greeting all that impedes his way with chilling frost
and bright mantles of pure white snow; and in his course imparting many
pleasures in defiance of his dreary aspect."[46] Just as often, they discussed the

changing of the seasons, and plumbed this aspect of passing time for metaphysical significance. "Transient is all earthly pleasure," wrote one operative:

> Joys and grief alternate rise;
> Here we've no abiding treasure,
> Yet it waits for us in the skies.[47]

It was rare that a story or poem that dealt with some aspect of the natural world did not draw a connection to the divine. "It is not possible to hear the sweet music of the birds, warbling forth their notes from every bough," explained an *Operatives' Magazine* author, "without feeling the mind impressed with a sense of the wisdom of our Creator, and conceiving pleasures and delights unlike and far purer than can be gained or conceived of in the crowd and noise of the city."[48] Every part of nature, so full of beauty, harmony, and power, it seemed, was evidence of God's existence and will. The creation was "a stupendous display of power, intelligence, wisdom, and benevolence" marked by "beauty, harmony, and magnificence, in all her wise arrangements." The music of the birds, grandeur of the forest, and beauty of the floweret, wrote one operative, as well as the purling streamlet, majestic river, vine-clad hills, and towering mountains, all betokened "a wonderful exhibition of wisdom and goodness."[49] God's power and worthiness of praise were evidenced in the wild and destructive as well. "In the roar of mighty waters, in the deaf[e]ning combat of the elements above, and in the wild tornado's startling fury and dread effects," maintained Huldah Stone, "we recognize the voice and presence of the Great Omnipotent. Listen we, one moment to the great orchestra of Nature's Temple! O, what strains of harmony swell through its glittering vaults!"[50]

In various other pieces, mill hands held up observations of nature as evidence that they should put time to wise use. "That the earth is a place for improvement is almost too plain to need the illustration," declared one operative, "for wherever we turn we meet with something, which, if remembered and brought into practice, will tend to our advancement." She pointed to the bee and the ant as examples of both industry and economy.[51] But authors also employed the natural world as a foil to critique industry and sometimes the material world in general. In "Alone with Nature," the pseudonymous Adelaide (probably Lydia Sarah Hall) wrote of retreat to "some sylvan spot / Where art, the spoiler, ventures not," and counseled leaving "the haunts of selfish men" to "learn thy Maker's ways to scan" in this "purest of society / With brook and bird, and flowers and tree."[52] Standing to gaze from the "prison walls" of the mill, another poet, Mary, wondered if the river's waters spring "from the hand of its Almighty Giver . . . to add to the miser's gold." No, she concluded, their purpose was to cheer and bless the human race, but they had been turned from that aim "to sap the life-blood from young veins, / And fill the Funeral Urn!"[53]

LONGING FOR HOME

Among the stories, poems, letters, and memoirs written by Lowell operatives in the antebellum period were countless recollections of home. This writing, perhaps more than any other they did at the time and later, best expressed the women's belief in the virtues of rural landscapes and country life. The selective way they dealt with the theme, placing emphasis on certain aspects of their previous experience and excluding discussion of others, also demonstrates how the workers' thinking about the natural world had changed since they came to work in the mills. Other accounts of growing up on New England farms, and the domestic production that was so central to the lives of rural girls and women, were generally matter-of-fact, suggesting that nature's utility was significantly more important than its beauty or divine qualities. This was true of diaries and correspondence written by rural-dwelling women who never went to the mills as well as documents written by operatives before they migrated. Once they had spent some time in the Lowell factories, however, many of the women gave far more attention to aesthetic and spiritual aspects of nature.

Operatives' writings about home make clear that they were using romanticism to develop a critique and even rejection of industrial capitalism. They had come to Lowell for the economic opportunity offered by the mills, and the various attractions of urban life, but their new work and even the city itself was not comparable to domestic production at their home place. Back in the hills and vales, many girls and women had read romantic poems and stories, and this did apparently shape the ways they mused about the natural world around them even then. Yet leaving the farm for the City of Spindles brought them in contact with many other women like themselves, gave them much easier access to the literary creations of romantics, and, most importantly, immersed them in an urban-industrial environment that made that literature more meaningful. Their real, present lives became a point of comparison to the lost rural landscape of their former lives, which they took poetic license to embellish and use as a foil.

Elizabeth Emerson Turner grew up in Vermont, "in one of the pleasant towns of the banks of the Connecticut [River]," a place she later described for the *Lowell Offering* as "diversified scenery of field and forest, hill and plain."

Her native home, or "the old farm" as family members called it, had been settled originally by a grandfather when the "country was still wilderness." In the intervening sixty years since that time, the homestead had become a site for a variety of pastoral delights:

> The sunny hill side, with its beautiful grove of tall maple trees, bringing the merry times of sugar-making to remembrance: the orchard with its excellent fruit — and many a happy hour have I there spent, in rambling from tree to tree, and selecting the choicest and most beautiful apples for my young friends: the old cottage farm-house, with the two majestic elms that overshadowed it, waving and sighing in the summer breeze, or sturdily braving the rude autumnal blast: the garden, its green alleys bordered with flowers of every hue: its cherry trees and currant bushes. Well do I remember the accustomed place of each plant and flower — the lilac and rose-bush, the peony strawberry plant — and in particular a large asparagus bed, which I used to admire in spring for its delicate, pale green leaves and branches, and in autumn for its bright crimson berries.[54]

Having worked in a Lowell mill, Turner developed a great fondness for her former way of life, which might have partly resembled her description but surely was not so free and easy. Interestingly, her estrangement from nature as an urban factory operative seems to have encouraged a more distant relationship with a rural environment as well. In her account, Turner was more a passive observer than a producer laboring to transform nature into something useful.

Betsey Chamberlain, who was born in the New Hampshire town of Wolfeboro and moved to Brookfield after marriage, had similar memories of her homeplace. She described the landscape and life there as distinct from what was to be found in the New Market, New Hampshire, and Lowell mills where she later worked. During childhood Chamberlain "waded the pond for lilies, and the brooks for minnows; I roamed the fields for berries, and the meadows for flowers; I wandered the woods for ivy-plums, and picked ising-glass from the rocks; I watched the robins that built for many years their nest in the chestnut tree; and nursed, with truly motherly care, the early lambs and chickens." There certainly was evidence of work done in these memories, but survival and comfort seemed almost gratuitous, and nature afforded as much enjoyment as it did utility.[55] Likewise, "V." recalled "the many delightful scenes of my native place, including the noisy cascade "whose spattering foam was wont to spread a continual dew upon the flowers I carefully cultivated upon its banks." There was the arbor too, "inviting the wanderer to its cool and shady retreat" and filled with "the melody of happy songsters as they played from bough to bough."[56]

Other operatives made a more explicit contrast between their home and the mills. One mill hand claimed, in "Cure for Discontent," that traveling to her native village in her imagination, while "doing her duty" in the mill, was what made the factory tolerable.[57] But what is interesting is the particular type of mental retreat workers made. In a short piece titled "Thoughts on Home," E. D. returned to "the green hills of my childhood" in her mind, picturing her home amid vines and flowers, with the garden blooming, "the orchard laden with its golden fruit," and a silver stream meandering through the field. This "waking dream" was rudely interrupted, however, by the factory bell, telling her that she was "still a wanderer, far from home and those I love, dwelling where all are strangers, and few are kind."[58] In "Factory Girl's Reverie," another operative lamented being so far from home, to "toil day after day in the noisy mill." She wished to be a child again, to "wander in my little flower garden, and cull its choicest blossoms, and while away the hours in that bower, with cousin Rachel."[59]

Quite often, being homesick and wishing to escape the confines of Lowell inspired the workers to poetry. "I've a pleasant mountain home, / And in summer love to roam," wrote Caroline Whitney, "By the sparkling rill, / That comes dancing down the hill." She loved the "aspect wild" of the mountain walls that hid the family's cottage from the world and longed again for "a rural life / Free from every heated strife."[60] A poem signed "S. A. M." also described the beauty of her family's homeplace as well as the pleasures of fishing in the streams there. She recalled:

Thy fields, thy woodlands, and thy flow'ry meads, .
List'ning to the warblers chanting there
Their joyful notes, [I] have whiled the hours away.
I've heard the murmurs of thy rivulets;
And, seated on their mossy banks, have caught
The silvery trout. . . .[61]

Still others were prompted to make song. In "The Lowell Factory Girl," the singer lamented leaving her "native country" to be "summon'd by the bell" and, declaring the sentiments of so many other operatives, explained, "I think less of the factory / Than of my native dell."[62]

The *Voice of Industry*, it seems, was more inclined to print correspondence from operatives who had left the mills for a spell and wished to remark on their contentment at home. Writing in October 1846, J. R. assured her friends, "think not while surrounded by the green fields, feasting my mind with their beauties, that I do not cast a sympathizing thought to the many shut up in the mills, constantly toiling, without time to look abroad upon the face of nature and 'view the glorious handiworks of their Creator.'" Being home gave her a chance to wander the banks of the river, waters that fed the Merrimack and eventually turned the belts of the Lowell mills. There she listened to bird song but also pondered "the evils growing up in the present state of society, which must undermine all glorious scenes with 'her thousand votaries of art.'"[63] In a letter from her mountain home in Cabot, Huldah Stone addressed the operatives' struggle as well, mixing this with thoughts on the local landscape. Rather than be fooled by "infallible clergy," she wrote, the laboring classes would be better off "studying the beautiful — the sublime, volume of Nature, if we would learn of God aright." In His works, she maintained, there were harmony and grandeur, and by studying the laws that governed this world "science and true Christianity may walk among us hand in hand, causing the waste places around us to become gardens of truth's own planting, in which shall flourish the unfading flowers of virtuous friendships and human sympathies."[64]

The landscapes operatives remembered, however, were not always hills and mountain valleys. In her memoir, *A New England Girlhood*, first published in 1889, Lucy Larcom wrote about growing up in Beverly, a seaside town in Massachusetts. As a child, she roamed freely on ledges overlooking the ocean, studied the wildflowers of meadow fields, walked along the river banks, and explored the treasures of the beaches. "The tide was the greatest marvel," she recalled, "slipping away so noiselessly and creeping back so softly over the flats . . . dashing against the rocks, it drove me back to where the sea-lovage and purple beach-peas had dared to root themselves." Sometimes her brother John would take her with him when he went huckleberrying in the woods, which she liked even better than the sea. He usually left her sitting on a rock where she gazed at the "tall pine-trees whispering to each other across the sky-openings above me." The tress and "the graceful ferns, the velvet mosses dotted with scarlet fairy-cups, as if the elves had just spread their table for tea, the unspeakable charm of the spice-breathing air, all wove a web of enchantment about me, from which I had no wish to disentangle myself."[65]

Later, when Larcom's sea-captain father had made her mother a widow, the family moved to Lowell, and Lucy went to work in the mills. Having been hooked on poetry by Coleridge's "Mont Blanc Before Sunrise," she was fascinated by the other operatives' talk of real mountains and life there. But when she was sixteen years old and her older sisters married and had babies, Larcom eagerly returned to Beverly to help out with the housework. "One of them sent for me just when the close air and long days' work were beginning to tell upon my health," she explained, "and it was decided that I had better go. The salt wind soon restored my strength, and those months of quiet family life were very good for me." When Larcom returned to "daily toil among workmates from the hill-country, the scenery to which they belonged became also a part of my life." Perhaps she meant by this that, having known a sense of escape from the mills on the coast, she could better appreciate what the distant summits offered in the way of retreat. "Every blossom and every dewdrop at our feet was touched with some tint of that far-off splendor," she wrote, "and every pebble by the wayside was a messenger from the peak that our feet would stand upon by and by."[66]

Operatives like Larcom and her workmates had their lives dramatically transformed by the urban-industrial development Lowell mills represented, and their way of thinking about the world around them evolved accordingly. Coming from New England farms, they were familiar with fairly satisfying labor that usually entailed a direct relationship with nature. But work in the textile factories was not like this. Instead, mill hands toiled among noisy machines for a wage, through a regimented workday, with comparably little variety and even much less skill in the work. When operatives responded to these new conditions, as other historians have explained, they employed the Revolutionary rhetoric inherited from Yankee relations, refusing to be made slaves to man or machine. Many of them, both those professing at times to be content with factory work as well as militant union organizers, also embraced a romantic version of nature, which they identified with the homes and landscapes they had lost. In a sense, they cultivated a mental separation to match a real, actual breach from the natural world.

CLASS, GENDER, AND ROMANTICISM

Although antebellum operatives used awareness of natural beauty, harmony, and divinity to *protest* their treatment as workers, others more sympathetic to mill owners' interests employed similar observations to *defend* factory production and urban living. Not surprisingly, these apologists tended to be of a different class than the mill hands. Their competing version of romantic naturalism was influenced by the same sources that inspired the workers, but they turned the rhetoric, insights, and assumptions of writers from Coleridge to Whittier into an argument for economic and cultural progress through industrialization and urbanization. On the one hand, apologists saw the poems and stories in literary journals such as the *Lowell Offering* as evidence of mill work and city life improving the minds of deprived country girls. On the other hand, they pointed to efforts mill managers made to beautify the urban landscape as consistent with ordering and using the natural world for profit.

As they launched America into the industrial age, owners and managers of the Lowell factories insisted that they would operate their mills according to a benevolent plan. They hired young women who had a family farm to return to when production was slack and housed them under a protective regimen when they came to the city to work. "It was a common assumption that girls and young women who were not incessantly occupied," explains historian Hannah Josephson, "were subject to temptation and vicious habits, as well as being a financial drain on their parents and a burden to society." Migration to Lowell to labor for wages and reside in boardinghouses seemed to solve several problems at once, while at the same time providing a "docile and tractable" labor force.[67] When the female operatives began to produce respectable literary journals, as part of church-based self-improvement circles, managers and other observers pointed to them as evidence of the beneficent influence of the mills as well. They missed the criticism of industrialization and urban life threaded throughout submissions to the *Lowell Offering* and *Operatives' Magazine* and regarded the poems and stories as demonstrations of the sort of ornamental education girls and young women would otherwise have access to only through finishing schools. At the very least, the romantic poems, sentimental stories, and literary longing for home stood as proof that mill work did not degrade the minds of operatives in the way of Britain's dark Satanic mills.

Apologists for the new mills also used romantic rhetoric of their own to characterize and reconcile various aspects of the ongoing industrial conquest of nature. In a letter to the editors of a local newspaper, for example, a writer signing himself "Middlesex" took note of the onset of spring and "nature's revival from her long winter's lethargy and sleep." With the change of seasons he proposed more attention be given to planting trees in the city. This was something all "true lovers of nature" would support, but it also fit with utilitarian values, providing residents with the means to cleanse the air. "Much towards the attainment of this end and of the many delightful associations, and the great and unalloyed good attending it," Middlesex wrote, "has been done by the superintendent of the Merrimack corporation the past year."[68] As already noted, Merrimack's Kirk Boott as well as superintendents and staff at other mills gave considerable attention to planting grass, flowers, and trees around their buildings as well as along thoroughfares to make "greenways." Likewise, they developed their horticultural and botanical interests through associations with greenhouses and gardens, through memberships in natural history societies, and by tending elaborate gardens on their estates.[69]

Beyond Lowell, on the family farms that had bequeathed Yankee daughters to mill work, fathers and brothers made little effort to defend the new brick factories and bustling cities, and they displayed only minimal interest in a romantic view of the natural world. Agricultural journals published in the region ran poems such as Whittier's "New England," which spoke of a "land of forest and rock / Of dark blue lake and mighty river. . . ."

> The nursery of giant men,
> Whose deeds have linked with every glen,
> And every hill and every stream,
> The romance of some warrior dream![70]

But women penned most of the original poetry, and scattered observations and stories by both women and men tended to equate romantic interests with femininity. Additionally, while criticism was not consistent, there were some attempts to characterize sentimental pursuits as wasteful dallying. In one fictional tale, written by "Letitia," a young woman is enticed by friends to leave her milking to take a leisurely walk. When she hesitates, they talk about her father as "one of those old-fashioned sort of men that think we ought to do as our grandmothers before us did." Their conversation wrestles with redefinition of gender roles, tending toward limiting "out-door" work by girls and women. Still, at the end, the journal's male editors point to the critical comments of an older aunt in the story as more wise, insisting that "expensive and effeminating pride in the daughters of the farmer deserve a sneer."[71]

Evidently, both middle-class, male urban dwellers and the men of farm families had ideas about nature that often diverged from the those of female operatives. When Lowell mill girls marshaled romantic rhetoric to express their estrangement from the natural world and criticize the factories and city they held responsible for this loss, their thinking was very much shaped by particular class interests as well as time-bound definitions of gender. It mattered where they stood in relationship to the means of production as well as what it meant to be a woman in the early nineteenth century. This is not to suggest, however, that men were spared an experience of separation from the physical and organic environment. The lives of men who worked the land or performed some manner of industrial labor, in particular, were transformed by many of the same changes that first affected female mill operatives. As subsequent chapters demonstrate, the alienation of these men from nature was acute and real, and they too struggled to make some sense of the rift.

2

Living by Themselves

Slaves' and Freedmen's Hunting, Fishing, and Gardening in the Mississippi Delta

The story of Yankee mill girls' venture from New England farms to urban factories demonstrates the importance of both place and work in shaping people's relationship with the natural world. Yet theirs is not the only story. Examining other regions and sectors of the American economy in the same period or at different times complicates the historical narrative. Former slaves in the Mississippi Delta, for example, who cultivated the cotton used in textile mills, stayed much closer to home, near the rural plantations where they were born and raised and worked for much of their lives, yet they also witnessed a significant transformation in their labor and social relations. Capitalism came to the countryside as well as the cities, and the economic and social change it wrought was not entirely a process of linear declension.

In the Delta, the focus of this chapter, slaves obviously benefited from emancipation, but their experience is, of course, more complicated than that. In bondage and in freedom, black men and women resisted exploitation by a myriad of means, and that resistance impeded somewhat not only their abuse as laborers but also estrangement from their work and environment. When field hands and sharecroppers engaged in various forms of independent production, namely a combination of hunting, fishing, and gardening that was relatively outside the control of a master or landowner, they avoided to a limited extent the dual alienation that Karl Marx was just then beginning to understand and explain.

It was not always clear to outside observers, however, what exactly was happening. In 1867, reporting from his subdistrict headquarters in the Gulf Coast town of Pascagoula, Mississippi, Freedmen's Bureau officer George Corliss bemoaned the local freedpeople's seemingly underdeveloped work ethic. Many of them "are industrious and frugal," he explained, "while others are inexcusably idle and slothful, some of the latter manage to exist by fishing, hunting, &c." Corliss claimed, for the most part wrongly, that the men and women just released from bondage were "usually satisfactorily paid" by their employers, often their former masters, and he believed that grievances about wages were rarely an excuse for a lack of work discipline and respect for labor contracts. In his general frustration, blinded by a belief in "free labor" and hindered by racism, he misunderstood the situation. Some freedpeople did fail to follow through on their new commitments to work white planters' fields, but it was typically not because they were lazy or slothful.[1]

One of the things the Pascagoula case demonstrates is the way prevailing social relations conditioned blacks' interaction with the environment. This had been true when they cultivated cotton, sugarcane, rice, and indigo as chattel, and it remained so when they worked those crops for a wage or share after the Civil War.[2] But viewing independent production as a form of re-sistance to exploitation—a way of contesting slavery, wage labor, and white supremacy—also reveals links between labor and race relations and African Americans' relationship to nature. Through hunting, fishing, and gardening, black men, in particular, often sought and found supplements to family sub-sistence, freedom from oversight and physical abuse, as well as opportunities for asserting their masculinity. They bargained for access or stealthily escaped to a different part of the natural landscape, to use it in ways at odds with how they labored in fields for slave-owning planters or profit-minded, postbellum landowners.[3]

SLAVERY

By necessity this chapter casts a wide net for sources that speak to slaves' and freedpeople's experience with the natural world, the varying ways in which they used it as well as their thoughts about it. But the primary geographical focus is on the Mississippi Delta. Over the course of the nineteenth century this area, land that originally sustained the Choctaw, was transformed from a "wilderness" into a critical part of the Cotton Kingdom. When white mi-grants and black slaves first moved into the Delta in the 1820s pressure in-creased for Indian removal, and the federal government made several treaties with native residents toward that end. By 1832 aspiring planters had acquired unhindered access to territory along the Mississippi River, stretching from Hinds County in the south to Tunica County in the north. During the ante-bellum period most plantations were confined to this strip along the water-way, silt-laden land that was more easily cleared than what could be found in the interior. After the Civil War, however, cotton cultivation spread through-out the rest of the Delta. Between 1870 and 1900, as railroad lines expanded in tandem with clear-cutting timber operations, cotton acreage doubled and land prices soared.[4]

In the first years of plantation settlement, thick canebrakes and deep woods of oak, elm, and sweetgum covered the flatlands, while massive cypress and cottonwood trees dominated the swamps. Wild animals, including deer, bears, panthers, turkeys, geese, ducks, possums, rabbits, squirrels, as well as a variety of birds populated the land in abundance, and fish ran heavy in creeks and streams. On his Bolivar County plantation, former slave Louis Hughes recalled regular nightly visits from hog-stealing bears and numerous occasions listening to howling wolves. Issaquena County planter J. F. Griffin wrote about "catching 500 pounds of fish per day, when high waters brought 15 to 30 pound buffalo fish up into the ditches on the plantation."[5] Even after the war, in fact, most of the Delta remained uncultivated, either plagued by periodic flooding or lacking transportation, and much of what had been tamed by human hands began to grow wild again. When Hughes returned to Mississippi in the mid-1870s he saw many dilapidated houses and overgrown fields. "The entire country [we] passed through," he insisted, "looked like a wilderness."[6]

Clearing the Delta land and planting it to cotton was grueling work, made more taxing and oppressive by having to do it as chattel for someone else's gain. Typically, seaboard slaveowners planning to move to the area sent a group of young bondsmen, under supervision of a white kinsman or overseer, to ready a new estate for planting. Alternatively, they hired available slaves already carried to the Delta by other planters. Girdling and felling trees was men's work and they predominated among the frontier labor force, but more often than was the case back east women and even children sometimes joined them rolling logs, grubbing roots, digging stumps, and burning canebrakes. When they set the cane on fire, Louis Hughes recalled, "the cracking that would ensue was like the continuous explosion of small fire crackers."[7] The rough clearings this labor made were usually planted to corn first, and only after the fields were fully improved did they grow a staple crop.

The cotton cultivation that followed was a year-round ordeal. At the beginning of spring slaves deeply plowed a selected field, worked the soil into ridges, and planted seed. Soon after, they scraped the fields of weeds with hoes and turned the loose soil around developing cotton plants with bulltongue plows. This work was repeated every twenty days or so until late July, when the crop was briefly left untended and hands were set to clearing or other tasks. In mid-August the first bolls opened and picking began, work that did not end until December or later, with masters expecting 250 pounds or more cotton a day from each able-bodied slave. And in the few weeks

before the crop cycle started again, there was time for more clearing, drain-
ing, and various preparations.[8]

Not surprisingly, most if not all slaves objected to the arduous and often
tedious labor on cotton plantations. When Maryland slave Charles Ball was
sent to a South Carolina cotton plantation he quickly developed a hatred for
the picking season, outdoor work that would have ended by November on
his former Chesapeake tobacco estate, leaving only processing that was "comparatively a work of leisure and ease."[9] On the frontier, George Skipwith, sent
by his Virginia master John Cocke with other slaves to clear and plant land in
Alabama, wrote back regularly with accounts of slave shirking and the discipline he administered. The hands he supervised seemed to have cared little for
the work or any of the crops. In a letter posted 8 July 1847, Skipwith reported
whipping Suky for not doing her corn planting, Isham for covering cotton
plants with a plow, and three others for failing to cut a sufficient number of
rows for oats. When he sent several slaves to plow the cotton, expecting each
of them to finish seven acres in a day, Skipwith found they had completed
only an acre and a half by midday "and gave them ten licks apiece upon their
skins."[10]

Resistance and physical punishment were not unique to Alabama or Mississippi frontier plantations, of course, but slavery there was somewhat different from the prevailing system in settled areas, at least initially. Planters had
to spare some of their best slaves from eastern estates as well as provide
expensive provisions without any initial return in order to open the new land,
restricting the fertile soils to all but the most substantial investors. Subsequently, the heavily indebted slaveowners organized their hands in gangs,
extended the work day, established higher work quotas enforced by harsh
discipline, and persistently contended with slaves to limit what had become
customary opportunities for independent production on their own time.
Slaves, on the other hand, often struggled to maintain their traditional rights
to garden and gather as well as hunt and fish, using the labor needs of the
planters as leverage. Many planters eventually gave in, realizing the benefits
this subsistence activity provided to them, if not for the supplement it made
to slave rations than for the contribution it made to social stability.[11]

As was the case in older, settled areas back east, many planters on the
frontier allowed their slaves to work small plots of land and keep a few
chickens, hogs, and cows, work that was relatively free of coercion.[12] Bondsmen and bondswomen cultivated their patches Saturday evenings, Sundays,
and sometimes nights after their fieldwork was complete, and they cared for
their animals in spare moments as well. The garden produce and the products
of their animal husbandry, it was usually understood by all, belonged to the

slaves to use, exchange, or sell as they chose, although some masters insisted that vegetables, chickens, eggs, and the like be sold directly to them.[13] Likewise, slaves used their own time to gather various plants, roots, and barks with medicinal and dyeing properties as well as many edible tree nuts. "When slaves was sick, dey went to de woods and got roots an' herbs ter doctor 'em wid," remembered Mississippi slave Fanny Smith Hodges, "If dey had runnin' off of de bowels, dey got red oak barks an' boiled it an' made 'em drink it. . . . If young gals had pains in dey stomachs dey made tea out'n gum bark and dat would bring 'em 'round."[14] This gathering, like gardening and animal husbandry, demonstrated a degree of independence from masters, as well as a good understanding of local flora.

Slave men also asserted their autonomy and familiarity with the landscape when they went hunting and fishing. On large estates there were often specifically designated slaves to perform these tasks, usually young men who had demonstrated particular interest and skill. "Mos' ever plantation kep' a man busy huntin' an' fishin' all de time," recalled former Natchez, Mississippi, bondsmen Charlie Davenport. "If dey shot a big buck, us had deer meat roasted on de spit. On Sundays us always had meat pie or fish or fresh game an' roasted taters an' coffee."[15] On those estates where masters allowed Saturday afternoons and Sundays to the slaves to use as they chose, however, almost any bondsman could venture off to the woods or nearby stream, provided he respect or successfully skirt restrictions on where, when, and how game and fish could be caught.

Former slave James Bolton remembered that slaves were prohibited from hunting at night as well as having guns or dogs of their own. But the night hours were the only time to catch possums, and, Bolton recalled, they caught plenty. His fellow slaves borrowed the master's dogs as well to catch rabbits during the day, and the game that could not be taken this way "we was right smart 'bout ketchin' in traps." To fish in the local creek they used hook and line as well as basket traps made by the plantation's carpenters. On the other hand, Henry Cheatem, born in Clay County, Mississippi, in 1850, claimed the slaves on his plantation were worked too hard and long to go fishing. This was probably uncommon, since many more slaves than not seemed to have exercised a fishing privilege or took the opportunity to fish without their masters' permission. It raises the important point, though, applicable to gardening, animal husbandry, and gathering too, that staple crop production was supposed to be the slaves' primary concern, demanding if not necessarily receiving most of their time. Other activities had to be done during the time left over and within certain limits that masters established to maintain slave subordination.[16]

One of the other typical restrictions on slave hunting was a demarcation of animal life in the woods that reflected southern antebellum social relations. According to historian Nicolas Proctor, by the 1830s there was an ever-clearer line through the terrestrial animal kingdom designating some species for whites and others for blacks. Like British aristocrats, American planter sportsmen distinguished themselves from those below by their reasons for hunting, and they chose their game accordingly. Black bear, deer, fox, ducks, and partridge, for example, typically provided more opportunity for recreation than raccoon or possum, which often simply treed and abruptly ended the chase. And even when black slaves did not always abide prescriptions against what they could trap or shoot, there was usually a notable difference between the hunting they did and the hunting their masters did. Former Missouri slave August Messersmith recalled how his father shot piles of pigeons from the backyard, which his mother fed to their hogs, and how they also killed ducks and geese "by tow sacks full, with clubs."[17]

For most slaves, independent subsistence activity was just that, a supplement to rations or, what was often the same thing, a means of producing items to trade or sell for other goods that satisfied basic needs. When Charles Ball had become accustomed to his new plantation home and decided to go hunting, he did it "to procure supplies of such things as were not allowed me by my master." The game he brought home to his family afforded them two or three meals a week, including a delectable Sunday dinner.[18] In addition to a weekly allowance of cornmeal, salt pork, and sometimes flour, slaves provided themselves with a more balanced diet by hunting rabbits, raccoons, and possums, catching shad and other fish, growing vegetables such as turnips, cabbage, peas, and collard greens, milking their cows, collecting eggs from their chickens, as well as gathering nuts and other fare in nearby woods. Although tainted by the hunger African Americans experienced during the 1930s, many of the Federal Writers' Project interviews as well as other sources suggest, in fact, that independent production often provided a considerable amount and variety of food.[19] "From the eighteenth century onward," Eugene Genovese claims, "many slaves had a better diet than rural whites simply because they made an effort to raise vegetables."[20]

Yet slaves received intangible rewards from their subsistence-oriented labors too. Those tasks often enticed them because they were less routinized and demanding than chopping or picking cotton and were relatively free of white oversight. To be sure, there is evidence that not all slaves were enthusiastic about doing more work even on their own time, no matter how much they might stand to benefit. One Mississippi planter complained that his chattel were "too indolent to cultivate their own crops in their own time" and advised that "a good overseer will always see that they do not neglect their own interest, any more than their master's."[21] Although this comment might be at least in part an expression of the planter's racist assumptions, Charles Ball recalled how many of his fellow bondsmen "were too indolent to go far enough from home to find good places for setting their traps." When his master charged him with heading up a fishing party, however, Ball admitted that he looked forward to it as "respite from the labors of the cotton field, and that I should not be doomed to drag out a dull and monotonous existence, within the confines of the enclosures of the plantation."[22]

As Nicolas Proctor explains, slaves' independent production, and the trade this sustained, promoted a spirit of resistance. "Whether weaving baskets, tilling their own gardens, or hunting game," he writes, "slaves who participated in the internal economy denied the totality of their owners' control over slave labor."[23] Bondswomen and bondsmen were subjected to what Stephanie Camp calls a "geography of containment," restricted in their movements by masters' prohibitions and slave patrols, and women even more so by a gendered division of labor that kept them closer to a plantation. They both participated, however, in creating a "rival geography" that was inherently subversive, materially and symbolically. Slaves redefined the landscape around them for their own purposes, and by permission or through truancy they escaped to woods, swamps, ponds, and streams where they could restore a sense of self and even cultivate a collective identity that was essential to continued defiance of masters.[24]

For slave men, hunting and fishing were also about asserting a version of masculinity. Unlike other work, including staple crop cultivation, these tasks were not shared with women, and culling game from woods and catching fish in streams provided bondsmen unparalleled opportunities for living out aspects of a gender role that masters and other whites typically denied them as part of their subordination. These activities allowed slave men to engage in distinctly male, self-directed, skilled labor that usually made a critical contribution to their family's well-being. "If my chillun ever et a moufful dat wasn't honest, dey et it somewhar else," recalled former Alabama bondsmen Josh Horn, "'ca'se us raised chillun fast, and us had a heap of 'em, sixteen, if I 'members right, and soon's I found out dat I could help feed 'em dat way, I done a heap of hunting. And everybody knows I's a good hunter. Alice [his wife] used to make me go every Friday night; den us always had a 'possum or two for Sunday."[25] Those slaves assigned to hunt and fish for the whole plantation population received a certain amount of authority and trust from their masters as well, signified in part by the chance to regularly leave the estate and the right to possess a firearm.[26]

Finally, while slaves might not have been aware of it, by engaging in independent production, making their living more freely from the natural world around them, they partly repaired the estrangement from nature at the heart of plantation cotton agriculture. In their garden patches, which slaves viewed as land that belonged to them either as property or by usufruct rights, they worked the soil to grow vegetables that nourished their bodies. This was different from laboring as chattel on land owned by a planter, growing cotton he sold, and receiving only a small portion of the crop's value on the market as in-kind payments such as cornmeal and coarse clothing. Likewise, in the woods or at streamside, spaces slaves seemed to have viewed as part of a commons, they edged toward the perimeter of their masters' control and proprietary claims over parts of the earth. Even when they sold or traded their garden produce, animal skins, or fish, treating them as commodities rather than consuming them directly, they exchanged products that had required much less alienated interaction with the natural world. "It is not likely that slaves were developing a neocapitalist mentality in the 1800s," historian Dylan Penningroth argues, because they labored under considerable restrictions on their time and credit and, just as important, because "property meant much more to them than acquisitive individualism."[27]

In the pocket of freedom where slaves' subsistence activity resided, their relationship with the physical and organic environment was largely unmediated by the ownership claims of white planters. This did not mean that they regarded the land, woods, and waterways without antagonism or fear—many traditional African American folk tales and songs attest to the difficulties and dangers that lurked beyond the cabin threshold—but even those sentiments can be viewed as evidence of connection, recognition of playing an intimate part in the local ecology. Some stories, such as "Why the Foxes' Mouth is Sharp, Why the Possum Has No Hair on His Tail, and Why the Rabbit Has a Short Tail and a White Spot on His Forehead," testify to close observation and a desire to understand the oddities of nature. Songs such as "Rabbit Hash," on the other hand, speak to the battle gardeners must do with the rest of the animal and insect world seeking to feed off their labor and the place human beings occupy in a natural order:

> Dere wus a big ole rabbit
> Dat had a mighty habit
> A-settin' in my gyardin,
> An' eatin' all my cabbitch.
>
> I hit 'im wida mallet,
> I tapped 'im wida maul.

Sich anudder rabbit hash,
You's never tasted 'tall.[28]

For a fortunate few, relying on the skills they had acquired from years of gardening, gathering, hunting, and fishing, the dark confines of forest and swamp also represented actual freedom, sheltering and feeding them as they took a break from the hated plantation or, more momentously, made their way north. That made an escape out of nature, though not of the romantic variety. Similarly, it invited slaves to identify wild animals as exemplars of free living. Talking to an interviewer in the 1930s, former Alabama slave Stephen McCray explained this with a story about the coon that met a dog, which apparently resonated with sharecropping blacks as well. The coon said to the dog, "Why is it you're so fat and I am so poor, and we is both animals?" The dog replied, "I lay round Master's house and let him kick me, and he gives me a piece of bread right on." With that the coon decided, "Better, then, that I stay poor." Drawing out a moral, McCray declared, "Them's my sentiment. I'm like the coon, I don't believe in 'buse."[29]

FREEDOM

Although the Civil War brought about the abolition of slavery, the peculiar institution's demise did not mean the end of black southerners' conjoined economic exploitation and alienation from nature. In the decades that followed, restoration of land to white planters, passage of restrictive "black codes," and promotion of wage labor and sharecropping contracts altered their use of the physical and organic environment for the worse. Still, just as they had during slavery, freedpeople attempted to carve out autonomous spaces, and a corresponding relationship with the natural world, in spite of the generalized exploitation of the prevailing economic system. In some cases they preserved customary rights to cultivate garden plots in their contracts with planters.[30] When that failed, or when they wanted to hunt or fish, they temporarily and sometimes permanently absented themselves from fields, willfully violating agreements that were supposed to define postbellum freedom. Black southerners acted in these ways to obtain the same tangible and intangible benefits independent production had provided during slavery. Without intending it, their gardening, hunting, and fishing also partially mended the rift with nature that wage labor and sharecropping perpetuated in the new era.

In Mississippi, as W. E. B. Du Bois explained, possession of the great black belt plantations along the river had hardly been disturbed by the war. The center of the commercialized cotton kingdom, the strip from Memphis to the Gulf was "the place where first and last Negroes were largely deprived of any opportunity for land ownership."[31] In November 1865, the state's white planters attempted to maintain their lockhold on the land, and to restore as much of the antebellum slave system as they could, with passage of so-called "black codes." These laws restricted freedpeople's rights to lease land, carry weapons, use the courts, consume alcohol, and preach. They prohibited blacks from withholding their labor from the market or otherwise being unemployed as well, defining this as vagrancy and requiring every freedperson to sign an annual labor contract. The codes' various provisions were designed not only to keep blacks landless but also to preserve them as a servile and poorly compensated labor force. Likewise, the legislation answered white concerns that blacks were simply incapable of self-directed labor and, for the good of everyone, needed to work under white supervision and control.[32]

With federal intervention, some of the worst provisions in Mississippi's black codes were repealed by the legislature in January 1867, and during the interim blacks came under the watch of seemingly sympathetic Freedmen's Bureau agents. But their dream of land ownership remained fleeting. Congress had established the bureau in 1865, to aid the South's war-ravaged white and black populations and facilitate reconstruction, and the first assistant commissioner of Mississippi, Col. Samuel Thomas, established his headquarters at Vicksburg in June of the same year.[33] Thomas and his successors believed wholeheartedly in free labor, work diligently performed for an agreed wage, which they set about implementing through contracts between white landowners and landless blacks. They saw this as progress, replacing chattel slavery with a fair means for laborers to work their way into land ownership and independence. But it did not take long for them to witness impediments to this vision. Reporting on the 2,000 freedpeople in his subdistrict around Philadelphia, Mississippi, Robert Gardner described them as "industrious and disposed to improve their condition," aspiring to landed independence rather than contracting with others. He saw that this was impossible, however, "on account of the strong prejudices existing against freedmen 'living by themselves.'"[34]

From the start of their work in 1865 and in the years following, agents also ran up against freedpeople's resistance to signing written contracts. "The freedmen are so suspicious and fearful that they will be again enslaved," reported one field agent from his post just above Natchez, "that great difficulty is experienced in inducing them to contract as they fear it may be signing them back to their masters as they expressed it." This caused significant problems with workers in the area, he said, because "there were no settled regulations to govern them until quite late." As antebellum slavery evolved into something else, former masters and former slaves negotiated with one another to protect what they saw as their still-contrary and irreconcilable interests. Freedpeople realized they lacked the advantage, and some of them hesitated to enter into written agreements for fear of bargaining away their few remaining customary rights. Reporting from his Delta subdistrict in Lauderdale County in September 1867, subordinate officer John Moore explained blacks' continued preference for verbal agreements. "The education and the superior knowledge of business matters possessed by the whites," he wrote, "are too often used to cheat and defraud the freedmen out of their just and lawful rights."[35]

Yet most freedmen were eventually coerced or persuaded to sign contracts with planters — men almost always represented freedwomen in any agreement — and these documents reveal an ongoing effort by both parties to shape the labor arrangement to their particular concerns. Initially, most of the year-long contracts established payment of a monthly wage to groups of laborers, between $10 and $20 for men and less for women and children, but over time more of them stipulated payment by a share of the cotton crop, and sometimes equal portions of the corn, peas, and potatoes. Wages did not vary greatly from one plantation to another, although there was some improvement in contract terms from 1865 to 1866, once freedpeople had demonstrated their willingness and ability to withhold some or all of their labor power as leverage against employers. Shares ranged from a quarter of a crop to half, changing like wages did depending on the fluctuating balance of power between landowners and freedpeople.[36]

The other parts of the contracts, which can be just as revealing of the transition from one labor system to another, dealt with hours of work and length of the work week and included provisions for housing and fuel wood, use of tools and draft animals, as well as access to garden plots. These sections in the agreements had a direct bearing on freedpeople's opportunities to carve out autonomous spaces for "living by themselves," and establishing a relatively unmediated exchange with nature, even within the confines of a new form of labor exploitation. Typically, a contract was for twelve months, required ten hours of field labor every day with the exceptions of half of Saturday and all of Sunday, and spelled out penalties for workers' who absented themselves before the agreement expired or otherwise failed to fulfill its terms. In addition, landowners granted plantation employees the rights to cut and haul wood to cook and heat their allowed living quarters, access to between half an acre of land or more per family to cultivate a garden, and use of the tools and draft animals needed to work both the estate land and the garden — also with punitive clauses should any harm come to stock at the hands of workers.

On his Lauderdale County plantation, for example, Wilson Henderson contracted with what were likely former resident slaves for the period from February 1866 to February of the next year. He agreed to pay portions of the corn and cotton crops to the two apparent heads of families and to provide sufficient quarters and fuel, healthy rations, and two sets of clothes for every laborer, as well as "to allot from the lands of said plantation, for garden purposes, to each family, not less than one half acre, if desired." The workday was set at ten hours in summer and nine in winter, with Sundays off, other than necessary chores. Hands received half of every Saturday as well, "if consistent with the interest of the farm, to enable them to cultivate the portion of land allotted to them for garden purposes." If laborers failed to fulfill their part of the contract, by permanently absenting themselves from the plantation, they forfeited all wages and would be discharged from employment. Any other lost time, except for bad weather, would be charged to the hands at the steep rate of fifty cents per day.[37]

There was, however, a certain amount of bargaining going on between landowners and freedpeople. Handwritten contracts differed from one estate to another, and most if not all of the standard, printed contracts, like the one Henderson used, were littered with modifications, deleting a clause here, adding new language there. And these changes were not often to the benefit of laborers. In the agreement S. G. Stovall made with hands on his plantation in Lauderdale County, the terms were largely a mix of both old and new advantages in his favor. The contract ran from the first day of February to the last day of December 1866, releasing him from any obligation to the landless freedpeople during the month of January. Cash wages would be paid on or before the last day of the agreement, and during the preceding months Stovall would provide "substantial and healthy rations" as well as fuel, medical care in case of sickness, and two sets of clothes. The clause allotting land for gardening and "reasonable use of tools and animals" was stricken out, as was the line allowing half of Saturday to cultivate the plots. At the end of the contract, Stovall also added a section that deducted the cost of any medical care from laborers' wages.[38]

In making the transition from slavery to free labor, landowners welcomed opportunities to legitimately disregard their workers welfare yet insisted on a degree of subservience and control as if they were chattel. They wanted and sometimes achieved the benefits of both labor systems. Even when contracts ran for a full twelve-month period, landowners occasionally dismissed workers in summer after the crops were laid by, or during the dead period in winter, on a false claim of the workers' failing to provide good and faithful labor.[39] Freedmen's Bureau agents spent a great deal of time attempting to settle complaints filed by freedpeople who had been put off land for some "trivial or fancied offense." In Natchez, for example, after the crops were laid by for the summer of 1865, Liza Jackson was discharged "without just cause," a situation remedied by payment of wages due and her return to work. Such breaches of contract, despite effective resolution, threatened to undermine the bureau's efforts and caused concern. "When freedmen are thus discharged they are invariably driven from their homes without pay for labor performed during the year," reported a subcommissioner in Jefferson County, "without their share of the crop being inured to them when it may be gathered and often without being permitted to reap the benefits of their own industry in raising for themselves small crops of corn, potatoes, peas &c." The injustice could breed distrust of whites, he feared, and lead freedpeople to "prefer any situation, any unemployment to . . . giving faithful hard labor on plantations."[40]

Still, there was also some truth to planters' claims that laborers were not fulfilling their obligations under contracts, certain patterns of behavior that they generally and typically characterized as "vagrancy." Even bureau agents sympathetic to freedpeople reported on the necessity of encouraging them to adhere strictly to their agreements and not go about "roaming over the County."[41] More than a few laborers took time off from cotton cultivation to do other things, or permanently left an estate, and the disputes that resulted could be complicated. When Peter Green made a habit of "absenting himself from his crop and neglecting it," landowner Hiram Harkelroad drove him away, prompting Green to file a complaint. The Hernando County subdistrict agents settled the disagreement by getting Harkelroad to buy Green's interest in the crop.[42] In numerous other cases freedpeople forfeited their wages or shares, requiring that they find another employer or some other means of making a living.

Dereliction of field work, however, did not necessarily mean former slaves were out visiting or wandering with no purpose in mind. Charlie Davenport recalled being bit by the "freedom bug," a condition that meant something like not having to chop cotton anymore, throwing down the hoe to go fishing "whensoever de notion strikes you." It also meant "us had to scratch for us ownse'fs."[43] Being absent from the plantation and violating a contract was not usually evidence of sloth or laziness on the laborers' part, as southern and some northern whites alike interpreted it. A few Freedmen's Bureau agents, less inclined to criticize freedpeople for working outside an evolving free labor system, suggested that they were, in fact, quite busy extracting a living from the land, although one comparatively unburdened by white coercion.

After noting the poor harvest of 1866 due to drought, William Walker reported that whites in the northeastern county of Tishomingo were in much greater need of aid than former slaves, "the colored people as a general thing being able to support themselves." Likewise, writing from his headquarters in the Delta, bureau official John Moore explained that most black residents in his subdistrict, including Tishomingo, had received neither wages nor a share of the poor crop in 1866, and their employers were indebted to them. Yet the "freed people are the more energetic and industrious," he wrote, "making every effort to sustain and support themselves."[44]

Many freedpeople took advantage of Mississippi's vast unsettled areas, using the "wilderness" that dominated the landscape from the Delta to the state's border with Alabama, or the abandoned clearings quickly reverting to woodland, for their own purposes. They knew how to girdle and fell trees, dig stumps and roots, and burn canebrakes to make way for corn, peas, cabbage, turnips, and other food crops, and they put this knowledge to use. Others simply tended gardens on white-owned estates, whether there was a cotton crop to speak of or not, as was their right either by custom or contract. And in many cases this gardening was the exclusive job of women. Noxubee County planter J. C. Colbert's contract with Joe Blythe and Harrison Atkinson in 1867, for example, granted them one-third of the cotton crop "and three acres of land for each of their wives."[45] That made a gendered distinction between cultivation of a staple crop destined for distant markets and garden produce for family use or local trade.

During slavery, both women and men had worked gardens, sometimes joined by the larger slave community at harvest time, although men frequently took full charge of the work when slave women had to finish their late-night sewing or weaving.[46] Throughout the postbellum era, families of freedpeople exercised their newly won liberty in part by trying to establish family production units organized according to the gendered spheres once reserved only for whites. In this arrangement the center of the women's world radiated outward from the home, becoming more circumscribed over time, while men's domain encompassed an ever-greater share of the space outside.[47] Yet after slavery more women cultivated nearby vegetable patches and increasingly took the opportunity to plant ornamental flower gardens while also keeping chickens, work that contributed to their families' nutrition, enhanced their homes, and sometimes provided a small income.[48] In some cases, as Sharon Holt explains, freedwomen's household labor produced a surplus that allowed for purchase of livestock and land, the settling of children, and "the development of an autonomous community life through churches, schools, charities, and other organizations."[49]

Hunting and fishing, on the other hand, continued to be the exclusive domain of freedmen. Sometimes they were primarily interested in leisure, like Charlie Davenport, but more often they were translating self-ownership into greater opportunity for independent production, with the benefits it once had during slavery. Rights to hunt and fish were not spelled out in new labor contracts, but both whites and blacks apparently continued to recognize them as privileges under a persistent southern paternalism.[50] As was the case during slavery, however, these privileges were not unlimited. And by the 1870s and 1880s, the "redeemed" white elite began passing enclosure or "fence" laws or more strictly enforcing existing laws against common use of unfenced land, not coincidentally starting in counties with high black populations. These restrictive measures gave landowners an absolute and exclusive right over everything on their property, including the wild animals in forests and meadows and the fish in streams and ponds, and making any uninvited hunters or fishermen trespassers.[51]

What also made postbellum hunting and fishing different, or gave them a new significance for freedmen, was the ongoing effort to establish a free labor system. Oftentimes when a Freedmen's Bureau agent reported laborers being absent from estates they specifically mentioned and dismissed the independent endeavors. At other times, freedmen's preference for the activities was implicit in observations about derelict laborers who "will not render faithful service according to contract."[52] This was the main reason for white objections, in fact, that hunting and fishing led freedpeople to violate their contracts with landowners and, with the food they raised in gardens or woodland clearings, allowed and encouraged them to live without relying primarily on some sort of wage, be it cash or a share of a cotton crop.

When former slaves did work diligently in the fields many Freedmen's Bureau agents still found reason to be critical because the freedpeople did not seem to understand the importance of steadily increasing control over nature for staple crop production, even if it did not benefit them directly. Observing the situation in his Louisville subdistrict during the fall of 1867, John Williams noted that some black residents had "sufficient corn &c" to make it through the year, while others were "very poor and will be dependent on the Planter." In any new contracts the latter should get a third of the cotton crop, he advised, along with the food they needed to prevent starvation. But the better-off freedpeople needed to be reigned in as well, by agreements that gave them half of the cotton crop and obligated them "to do all necessary work on the Plantation, during the year, so as to keep the lands in working condition, creeks attended to, fences repaired, &c." If they were not compelled to do this, he believed, it would not happen. "Freedpersons lack forethought, don't look beyond today, — the present," Williams explained, "they fail to know that their *future is* to 'till the soil' — to labor. They think only about *raising* and *gathering* crop, and are careless about the future of a plantation."[53]

To be sure, Williams felt the need to make a special plea because Winston County, unlike its neighbor Noxubee County or other parts of the state, was plagued by "barren soil." But he voiced a sentiment shared by many whites dedicated to the South's reconstruction, that blacks' garden patches supplemented by hunting and fishing were not enough. Extracting a meager existence from the land would not bring the new version of "progress." When Freedmen's Bureau agents and others looked around them they saw a landscape still in need of being subdued. "Scarcely 10 percent of Delta land had even been cleared in 1860," according to historian James Cobb, "and by 1865 the area was scarcely distinguishable from the frontier wilderness that had greeted the region's first settlers."[54] Transforming this wilderness would only happen with an unwavering dedication to large-scale production of an agricultural staple crop, such as cotton, by both black and white southerners.

By the 1870s, in fact, a wholesale remaking of the Mississippi landscape was underway, driven in part by large-scale migration. New groups of freedpeople began moving to the Delta and other parts of the Yazoo Basin from the older South, and later from within Mississippi, seeking to escape the dislocations of war and reconstruction and enticed by planters' promises of good land. "Agents jess kept comin after us," recalled Irene Robertson, "to get us to come to this rich country." At the time of the family's migration, her parents were working worn-out land in Tennessee, which required heavy use of guano fertilizer to raise a crop. When they came to eastern Arkansas, following their broke former master, they never saw the fabled "hogs jess walking round with knife and forks stickin in der backs beggin somebody to eat em," but the family did find land that was uncleared and fertile for planting.[55] Sustained by a burgeoning labor force, as well as improvements in flood control and railroad expansion, the center of the Cotton Kingdom shifted westward, to the fertile alluvial lands of Mississippi as well as Arkansas and Texas.

With the influx of black farmers to the Delta and renewed attention to commercial cotton production there, sharecropping contracts became the prevailing method of securing black labor. Having failed for the most part to become landowners themselves, or even tenants paying cash rent, freedpeople turned increasingly to share tenancy for the minimal independence it offered over wage labor. "What freedmen wanted most was self-direction in their work, the security of their families," explains Ronald Davis, "and the freedom to be unattached to persons and places other than themselves and their own farms." They realized this, however, in only a limited way. The sharecropping agreements black farmers made in the 1870s differed some-what from the contracts they made with white landowners in the years imme-diately after the war. Before, shares had been little more than a means for cash-poor white landowners to pay black laborers, who often worked in gangs and were provided with weekly rations, sets of clothes, and sometimes medical care, much like under slavery.[56] Increasingly, though, sharecropping evolved into a system in which black families worked separate plots of land, with much less white oversight, in exchange for a portion of the crop at harvest. In most cases, they were required by contract to grow cotton, and the typical share arrangement allowed the landowner to retain ownership of the crop or saw a planter-merchant make his claim by a crop-lien in exchange for credit. Yet freedpeople at least initially saw this as a better alternative to the so-called "free labor" they were being forced into in the 1860s.

This evolution of sharecropping during the waning years of Reconstruc-tion had a significant impact not only on the daily work experience of black farmers and their families but also on their relationship to the natural world. With greater control over their labor, blacks had more opportunity than ever before for gardening, hunting, and fishing, activities that had once provided some relief from the intense alienation inherent in plantation cotton cultiva-tion. The rights to work a patch of land, keep poultry and pigs, shoot or trap game, and catch a mess of shad lost none of their importance as alternative modes of using the physical and organic environment, largely unrestricted by landowners' claims of ownership and control. Even when black farmers and their families sold or traded garden truck or eggs as commodities, that was an exchange that took place outside of the sharecropping arrangement, as well as the world market that dictated cotton prices and the value of labor required to produce it.

CONCLUSION

When he was interviewed for the Federal Writers' Project in the 1930s, former Alabama slave William Henry Towns told a story, one that was meant to demonstrate the kindness of his old master, Mr. Young. One night, he re-called, a fellow slave, "Ole Caleb," was walking down the road with another slave from a different plantation, who might have been hired out, on their way home after a prayer meeting. The two men came across a possum and Caleb stopped to get the animal, but his companion told him not to bother with it. Caleb "wouldn't git none of him no how," he argued, "cause your ole master gwine take him jes' soon as you git hom wid him." Caleb explained that Mr. Young was not that kind of a man, and the two decided to catch the possum, which turned out to be very tasty. The next night even the other slave received a share of meat when the hands came in from the field.[57]

The story Towns told very likely blended elements of both fact and fiction, considering its form and some of the other things he had to say in his interview, but like many of the memories ex-slaves offered to their interviewers this one is nevertheless instructive. It demonstrates quite starkly the way the social relations of southern slavery shaped bondsmen's experience with the natural landscape and its inhabitants, beyond drudgery in the cotton fields. Hunting, as well as fishing and gardening, were never completely free and absolutely direct exchanges with the rest of nature, yet they occupied a space on the margins of the more oppressive endeavor of plantation staple crop production. Black slaves, particularly men, embraced these activities as opportunities to supplement their families' meager ration diet and demonstrate their masculinity, as well as escape white oversight. Not coincidentally, their hunting, fishing, and gardening also compared favorably to the estrangement from nature inherent in gang-labor cotton cultivation. Those activities represented varying occasions for a relationship with the physical and organic environment unmediated by white masters' claims of ownership over people and the land.

This multifaceted significance of independent production continued to resonate after slavery's demise. When he spoke to interviewers in 1938 about his brief childhood as chattel and his long life as a sharecropper, Henry Baker stressed the connection between the means for autonomy and the way people make a living. "As we is creatures we is 'bliged tuh live heah en we o'tta live wid great satisfaction by ownin' our own home," he said. "Ef er man is got his own home he kin do jes what he wants en whut not tuh plant. Ef yuh got your own home den yuh kin plant a plenty uv food stuff, all de corn, p'tatoes, oats, en rye en de things dat a farmer should plant."[58] But sharecropping never evolved into something that would allow the liberated existence Baker had in mind and, as the nineteenth century came to a close, the situation for black farmers and their families only worsened. The Populist revolt dissipated much like the dreams of Reconstruction, segregation became the law of the land throughout the South, voter disenfranchisement stripped most blacks and some poor whites of political rights, and unchecked extralegal violence increased. These developments became the push factors, matching the pull of employment, that brought millions of rural black southerners to the concrete ghettos of northern cities.

3 Men Alone Cannot Settle a Country

Domesticating Nature in the Kansas-

Nebraska Grasslands

As the stories of the Lowell mill girls and Delta slaves and freedpeople make clear, there were both similarities and differences in the ways changes in work affected how various groups of people thought about and used the environment around them. Gender mattered to both the Yankee white women and the southern black men, but race was perhaps a more significant factor for the latter, the reason for their bondage and their postemancipation exploitation. The two also experienced a severed connection with nature because of the labor they did and how it was organized, yet they responded to this separation differently, employing literary romanticism, turnouts, and turnover on the one hand, and stealing away to hunt, fish, and garden on the other.

Likewise, we can see parts of patterns as well as subtle differences in the case of women settlers in the Kansas and Nebraska grasslands, the subject of this chapter. Their lives were certainly shaped by gender conventions, which conditioned the labor they did, the form that their estrangement from nature took, and how they dealt with that sense of alienation. But in their minds much of the change that happened to them, from the latter part of one century to the beginning of the next, was willed and welcome. For these women, going west usually meant leaving behind established farms to encounter what often seemed like a wild and threatening landscape, one that they never really felt connected to, at least in the early years. Accordingly, they had a forward outlook rather than a retrogressive one, an attitude organized around turning matted sod into a productive farm and making a modern home.

When, for example, Sarah Anthony traveled to Kansas from New York in November 1875 to join a husband who had gone west six months earlier, she faced bitter disappointment. Her daughter, who made the journey as well, remembered that her mother often cried during the first few months. "These pioneer women [were] so suddenly transplanted from homes of comfort in the eastern states," wrote the daughter, "to these bare, treeless, wind swept, sun scorched prairies — with no conveniences — no comforts, not even a familiar face. Everything was so strange and so different from the life they had always known and with nothing to encourage them, but the thought of duty and that in proving faithful to its demands." What caused Anthony's discontent, at least in part, was an unfamiliar and alien landscape, as yet untouched by the civilizing hand of domesticity. With dedication and fortitude, however, settlers like her believed the place could be remade.[1]

By the early twentieth century, in fact, the initial struggle of settlement was becoming more distant memory than recent reality for the original pioneers and their children, and their opinion of the surrounding landscape was changing. After sixteen hard years on a Kansas farm, homesteader Anne Bingham lived out the rest of her life in town, and from there she described a place quite different from the one her family first confronted. "A ride out in the country," she wrote in the 1920s, "shows the results of early days in the glory of the trees, the fine farm buildings, modern and beautiful, and near neighbors and schools houses, country churches, orchards and paved roads to town and market." The grassland was transformed and homesteads improved, making the land a more habitable place.[2]

For Sarah Anthony and Anne Bingham, as well as countless other women and men on the Kansas-Nebraska plains, the first task at hand was to survive, which in their minds required bringing the natural world around them under control. Because the first couple of years after settlement were often so dire and critical, these efforts to make a living from the land necessitated that all members of a family production unit be willing to do various types of work. Gender mattered less than it previously had when it came to dividing labor. Even then, however, the primary way women contributed to subduing the grasslands was by imposing domesticity on them, and, over time, this became their exclusive form of interaction with the natural world. Near the turn of the century, their confrontation with the landscape coincided with campaigns to promote "domestic economy" and "scientific housekeeping." These refined ideals distinguished homesteaders' work from the endeavors of previous American settlers, and because labor is an inextricable part of people's relationship with nature, they also shaped the way women used and thought about the plains environment.

At the start of their new life on the plains, women homesteaders' attitude toward the land and its other inhabitants was usually an antagonistic one. Despite occasional recognition of beauty and expression of awe, they tended to think of nature as an impediment or willingly hostile adversary, something to overcome or tame through work. As the early years of settlement ended, the gendered division of labor became more rigid, and women's sphere was limited to the home and its surrounding area, their relationship with the physical and organic environment changed. The passing of the critical beginning period on the farm as well as the reassertion of more traditional gender roles happened at the same time many women began to adopt contemporary domestic economy ideals and embrace modern household conveniences. Consequently, early twentieth-century homesteader women and their daughters were separated from nature, but not in the same way they were before. Like the mill girls confined to a factory, they regarded nature as something beyond the threshold of the farmhouse or in the distant countryside, and they were more inclined to see it through the rosy lens of romanticism. They took this view, however, not so much as an indictment of their new lives or as an argument for returning to the old, but rather as evidence that they had prospered.[3]

FROM SODDIE TO FRAME HOUSE

Toward the end of the Civil War, a combination of factors pulled an increasing number of settlers to the mixed-grass region of the American plains. A drought ended in 1861 with several consecutive well-watered years, the Homestead Act of 1862 offered cheap land to the hardy and resilient, railroad lines made their way beyond eastern Kansas to create an integrated national market, and the Native American population was brutally exterminated or placed on ever-smaller reservations by force and the specter of starvation. These conditions enticed potential homesteaders beyond the more humid, wooded rim of the Illinois and Indiana prairie to a region once designated the Great American desert. In most of Kansas and Nebraska they found generally flat land covered in mid- and short-grass species, as well as a diminishing number of trees with every step west. The fertile soil with few obstructions promised good farming, but the open landscape also made for volatile weather and, as many settlers complained, a comparably dull existence.[4]

Some of the pioneer women who came to the Kansas-Nebraska plains in the postbellum period reported back to family and friends on the beauty and healthfulness of their new home. Most frequently, it seems, these were the ones who went to Nebraska. In 1887 a busy Sarah Gatch wrote to her sister's husband in Goshen, Ohio, from Wellsville, Nebraska, taking note of the good weather and sounding rather optimistic. "This is a beautiful country," she declared, and "all I ask is good health and good crops and I am sure I can make myself satisfied."[5] Other homesteaders remembered the profusion of wildflowers and variety of bird life. "It was a wonderful country to me," recalled one early settler who had ventured to the plains with her family as a little girl. "The most beautiful wild flowers bloomed and we school children wove great wreaths of them that reached clear around the room." Another, born and raised in a Nebraska dugout, recollected her pioneer life with great fondness. "So impressive were my childhood experiences," she explained, "that I have longed to return to the Muddy Valley once more to go fishing or wading, hunting wild roses, to the sandhills for choke cherries, or picking wild fruit along the banks of the muddy. In winter there was coasting, snow-balling or sleigh riding."[6]

A great number of homesteader women, however, especially those who went to Kansas, found the grasslands depressing and their families' prospects bleak.[7] Many of these settlers were not young girls when they arrived and were therefore more likely to have felt the full burden of survival at the time, or they recorded their experience before having the luxury to romanticize hardship. Viola Alexander could not help but feel discouraged in 1876, as she and her husband ventured to a new home near Milford, Kansas, with two small daughters in tow and the blue-stem growing so high around the wagon that they could only see the horses heads bobbing up and down. Likewise, Norwegian immigrant Helen Anderson accompanied her new husband to the plains and at least initially longed to return to her parents more ade-quately wooded homestead in Illinois. "It just seemed that the first year we were out here," she recalled, "the wind blew a gale every single day from the South and Southwest." Swedish transplant Anna Berg was so distraught at first that she fell apart, sitting down on a stump and weeping. And Adela Orpen's governess, a former slave from their native Virginia, also cried on first sight of their new plains home "because there was nothing beautiful to look at: everything was hopelessly ugly. . . . The vast measureless prairie with nothing but grass, unending grass, green in spring, dry brownish-yellow in summer, and burnt and black in winter; no trees, no rocks, no skyline even, only a hazy wobble in hot weather."[8]

These sorts of reports fit neatly with the descriptions Willa Cather in-cluded in several of her grassland novels, shaped by a childhood on the Ne-braska plains. Although sometimes overly sentimental, her plot lines also revealed the way some of the early settlers felt small and inadequate in their new environment. The "great fact was the land," Cather declared at the begin-ning of *O Pioneers!* "which seemed to overwhelm the little beginnings of human society that struggled in its somber wastes." The open question at that point in the story was whether or not people were an equal match for the landscape, capable of making any mark there at all. "It was still a wild thing that had its ugly moods," the protagonist's father remarks just before his death, "and no one knew when they were likely to come, or why." This was not a landscape made for humankind.[9]

Yet it was not only the tall grass, treeless expanse, unceasing wind, and heat waves that worked at the spirits of homesteaders. As they soon discovered, the grassland harbored many real dangers, often unpredictable and some potentially life-threatening. The women, in particular, seem to have lived in constant fear of one or another menace, from snakes and fleas to grasshopper clouds and prairie fires. Both Anna Olsson and her mother marveled at the beauty of "antelopes" running wild near their homestead, but they shuddered at the thought of the other creatures inhabiting the grassland. "Mamma is so scared she will step on a snake," Anna wrote in a diary, while her grandmother "goes down in the cellar and kills all the snakes she sees because she gets so mad at them." Her mother was also scared of wolves, or what might have been coyotes, and Anna recorded several stories to justify this fear, telling of a woman who was bitten on the arm, a neighbor who warned that wolves eat up little children, and an incident when the hired girl quickly slammed the door shut against a wolf trying to get inside.[10]

Pioneer women and girls had to be on guard against less ubiquitous but more dangerous, destructive, and unpredictable threats too. Their diaries, letters, and memoirs, as many historians have pointed out, are litanies of land-parching drought, howling blizzards, grass fires, and locust invasions. "The hardest period of my life was the years of drought," recalled Custer County, Nebraska, settler Elizabeth Sargent. In the summer of 1894, she remembered, "there was practically nothing. Corn, pastures and everything dried up. My husband killed prairie chickens and shipped them east and in this way was able to buy food for ourselves and our two children." Yet a bone-dry summer was not the only harsh card in nature's hand. Widowed when her husband was killed by lightning, Mary Robinson's mother struggled to care for her four children during the winter of 1888. That year a blizzard swept across their part of the grasslands, and she tied a rope around her waist to go out and feed the stock. Some of the snow drifts piled as high as the house, and many cattle froze to death.[11]

On several occasions fires swept across the plains, often consuming everything in their path and sometimes taking lives. Many of these were natural occurrences while others were due to carelessness. In one case, a fire possibly started by cattle ranchers trying to run farmers out nearly killed Baldwin Kruse's grandmother, recently arrived from Germany to Nebraska. Her husband had left to get supplies in Grand Island, and that afternoon a haze appeared on the southwest horizon. The woman quickly gathered their cow and brought her to safety in the lean-to, but the calf did not follow. Following the fire the calf was never seen again, and the family's haystack was burnt to ashes, but these were meager losses compared to what other settlers in the area experienced. In more than a few instances, in fact, quick thinking and bravery by women saved their homes. Mrs. Henry Hanson's mother, a Swedish pioneer, confronted a blaze during her first autumn when, like Baldwin Kruse's grandmother, the man of the house was away. The land around the dugout had not been plowed up so she started a back-fire, burning away the grasses surrounding the home.[12]

Although not posing the same danger to people's lives or homes, grasshopper hordes could wipe out a homesteading family's livelihood. Over and over again in memoirs, oral histories, and other sources, original settlers and their children tell about watching helplessly as a cloud of locusts filled the sky and chewed their way through field crops and garden plants, as well as anything else they could masticate with their scissor jaws. One visitation of grasshoppers in 1876 "injured the corn considerable," wrote Nebraska homesteader Mattie Oblinger, stripping the blades off, eating the silks, and nibbling the ends of the ears. "They were not so large nor did not eat near so fast as they did two years ago," she explained, so the local people would still see a small crop and escape complete destitution, but it "will not be near so good as it would have been." The ravenous insects also ate all of Mattie's cabbages.[13]

Then, too, there were the Indians, which many settlers, more often the women than the men, regarded as one more wild aspect of the unpredictable landscape. "My mother had always dreaded seeing Indians," recalled Berna Hunter Chrisman, "and here they came one evening, when she was along with my sister and me." When the forty families, "squaws walking with papooses strapped to their backs, braves riding their spotted ponies," asked for food rather than scalps, her mother was more than happy to oblige. Anna Olsson's mother was afraid of Indians as well but mustered more courage to talk to them when her husband was there with her. He thought such visits were fun, a sentiment likely due in part to knowing how weakened and reduced the remaining tribes had become through white encroachment, dwindling numbers of buffalo, and harassment by U.S. soldiers. Also, while Anna's father would perhaps have been no more able to defend the family against attack than his wife, her parents both drew on a long history of seeing men as protectors and buffers to perils beyond the home.[14]

Surveying the severe and threatening land around them, scorched by sun in summer, blasted by blizzard in winter, crawling with snakes and biting insects, subject to visits of ruinous locusts as well as devastating prairie fires, and populated by what they thought were murderous natives, women homesteaders could not help but feel overcome sometimes by nature. Still, just as men had an important role to play in protecting their families against dangers and transforming the grasslands, women were critical to taming the plains. "Men alone cannot settle a country," Adela Orpen insisted. "Therefore so soon as they have opened a way, however rough, the women and even little girls must follow quickly, else the way will soon choke up."[15] What female settlers brought to the great expanse was an essential ingredient to making a homestead and community, the attitude and skills of domesticity, which they wielded and applied in much the same way their male counterparts broke the land with steel plows.

In the lean years of initial settlement women's gendered role meant doing what they could to insure their families' basic survival and make their first home more livable. For those pioneers who homesteaded in the relatively treeless grasslands, at least for a while "home" was a structure literally of the earth, a rectangular "soddie" constructed from strips of matted roots and soil. Pioneers stacked these grassland bricks one on top of the other, leveled a row with mud, and secured each wall with a pole through the center. They left space for a door in the south wall and windows that opened to the south and east. Roofs were more sod laid on top of rafter poles, and floors were typically bare dirt, dusty at first but packed hard after repeated wetting and sweeping. The finished structure was not very big, perhaps between ten by twelve and fourteen by twenty-six feet, and it kept cool in the summer and warm in the winter.

One problem with the soddies, though, no matter how well constructed, was leaking roofs. After a week-long rainy spell, many remembered, the earthen ceiling was saturated and dripped, or worse. The walls, roofs, and straw spread on the dirt floors also harbored bedbugs and fleas. Wilbur Speer and his wife relocated to Custer County, Nebraska, from Wisconsin in 1889, moved into a soddie, and experienced this particular plague on the first night. The baby was fussy, his wife remembered, so she got up, lit the lamp, and discovered the place was infested with fleas.[16] Even when pioneers lived in a variation on the soddie, however, in a dugout or log cabin with grass roof or a true log cabin, there still were problems. Snakes were attracted to the rafters and often made a home there. "One time," remembered Berna Hunter Chrisman, "a large rattlesnake crawled through the roof of our dugout and fell behind the bed." She was only three or four years old at the time, but the memory was vivid. "My mother snatched sister and me from the floor where we played, and put us on the table. Then she seized the spade and dispatched the snake before it realized what was happening."[17]

Unlike the frame houses homesteading families had grown accustomed to back east, soddies and the rarer log cabins tended to be austere places of work with few comforts. "Home," explains historian Julie Roy Jeffrey, "was not the quiet and cozy retreat that nineteenth-century culture envisioned, but a busy center of endless chores and economic ventures."[18] When Melissa Genett Moore first arrived in Coffey County, Kansas, with her mother and father during the 1860s, she was fortunate to move into a newly constructed log cabin. But the cabin was sparsely furnished, and immediate needs dictated greater concern with function over form. "A goods box was made into a table," she remembered, and, lacking a stove, they cooked at the fireplace, "baking bread in a skillet."[19] Similarly, Adela Orpen's nearest neighbor in Kansas, Mrs. Weddell, "had reared her family of eight children quite successfully on the contents of one all-comprehending pot slung over an open wood fire." Once the family was fed, they left their one-room cabin for outdoors, where the children ran about and the mother puffed away at a corncob pipe full of tobacco. "With the Weddells," Orpen wrote, "life was reduced to its primary factors."[20]

Much like their female relations in Ohio, Indiana, Illinois, and other settled states, pioneer women cooked and preserved food, washed and mended clothes, and performed countless other daily, weekly, and monthly tasks. They did it on the open plains, however, where household labor had even greater significance and required more fortitude, resourcefulness, and ingenuity. "Just as men struggled to learn new farming techniques and modified existing economic institutions to meet new conditions," Sandra Myres notes, "women had to devise new domestic techniques to meet the challenges of frontier living."[21]

Disregarding traditional gender roles and spaces, both women and girls regularly went beyond their soddie or cabin thresholds to work, fetching water, tending a garden or orchard, foddering livestock, even planting and harvesting. Simply getting water for drinking, cooking, and washing could be an ordeal, one that required girls and women to shed any notion of being physically weak or irresolute. "In the morning," a sixteen-year-old Martha Farnsworth penned in her diary, "Belle + I hitched up old Barney + Prince to the wagon and hauled two barrels of water, about ½ mile from a nice Spring." The whole family had moved to Republican County, Kansas, but the sisters had no brothers, Martha explained, so "we have to Pa's 'boys,'" a role she seemed to relish. That same day, after dinner, she went riding with a cousin, bareback, "for we [are] two 'tom-boys.' "[22] Other activities initiated girls even younger than Martha into the necessary violence of farm life. Mattie Oblinger recalled in a letter how her young daughter pined to see her father kill an old sow, climbing to a window and never flinching at the sight. "I guess she would have stood right by him," Mattie wrote, "and I let her when I went to clean the entrails."[23]

Yet even when girls' and women's labor violated gender norms, it was usually directed toward the end of domesticity, or toward establishing a semblance of domestic order. Having followed her father to a Custer County, Nebraska, homestead, for example, Frances Reeder had put aside her books "and helped to dig into the sod and fashion fields in the new land." But she understood the point of all this work, beyond producing a marketable crop. "We plowed the sod for corn, planted an orchard and made the garden with a strawberry patch within," she recalled, "and tried, to the best of our ability, to transplant to central Nebraska the comforts and home environment of Iowa."[24] Likewise, most girls grew up and shed their tomboy ways, and nearly all women reasserted Victorian ideals they had partly discarded in their homesteads' more difficult days. "Even though frontier conditions forced them into manly pursuits and led them to modify some of their standards," Julie Roy Jeffrey argues, "they hardly pressed for a liberation from female norms and culture."[25] That sort of freedom came as the dubious freedom to work harder, and they turned their eyes instead toward a time when they had only traditional female tasks, fewer in number perhaps and lightened by improvements such as a windmill that drew water or a labor-saving sewing machine. The end toward which they labored, then, was also a partial retreat from the natural world into an increasingly well-furnished and well-equipped home.

Killing snakes, although demanding the conquest of fears more commonly associated with women of the nineteenth century, was one of many ways that homesteading mothers and wives paradoxically stepped outside traditional gender roles to make a more tranquil domestic sphere. Snakes were slithery embodiments of evil for the Judeo-Christian settlers, and when they found their way into soddies and cabins, roosting in the rafters or sluggishly resting in a cellar, they represented what needed to be changed about the plains to make a proper home there. Other wildlife posed a similar threat, often when men were away in the fields or on a trip to town, requiring decisive action on the women's part. "A skunk got into the milk room one day," recalled Mary Balcomb, "and mother grabbed it by the tail, carried it out, and killed it, but she would not advise another to try it." Another day, her mother "walked up to the den of a wildcat and watched it until her husband could go for a gun and shoot it." Similarly, Nebraska homesteader Berna Hunter Chrisman remembered how her mother chased down wild cats as they carried off chickens. She kept a club handy and on hearing a commotion would run outside to throw this at the cat, which released its prey in haste to escape. This event was usually followed by a chicken dinner.[26]

Women and girls engaged and changed aspects of the plains environment in countless number of ways, some of which over time fit more easily into the cultural framework pioneers brought across the one hundredth meridian than chasing down wild cats did. With few exceptions, from the outset of settlement all women kept a garden, a plot of land near the home, worked sometimes by men but regarded as primarily women's domain and responsibility. This was in keeping with a long-practiced gendered division of labor, one that divided a farm into delimited male and female spheres. In letters back home, for example, Kansas homesteader Mattie Oblinger made it clear simply by her pronouns that the outlying fields were her husband's sphere and the garden was primarily within her sphere. In 1874, with a year in the grasslands behind them, she wrote about how "Uriah got *his* Wheat & Flax sowed and considerable plowed corn," while "*I* have quite a nice lot of horse raddish & sage roots and Rhibarb" (my emphasis).[27]

Still, gendering labor and the land where members of the family production unit performed such labor, parceling out the tasks required for transforming the grasslands, did not necessarily lessen women's work load. Both the size of the gardens and the variety of plants women cultivated suggests garden plots demanded a great deal of their time and attention. Even when they lacked chairs to sit on, Adela Orpen remembered, they had a large garden. "There were rows upon rows," she said, "of peas, Lima beans, tomatoes, sweet corn, sweet potatoes, squashes, pumpkins, and melons — both sweet-scented and water-melons — by the quarter acre." Mattie Oblinger had a very similar mix of plants in her garden, including cucumbers, squashes, melons, beans, potatoes, cabbages, beets, and tomatoes. Having just arrived in 1873, however, she put the family's potatoes as well as their 130 cabbages in a neighbor's garden, because those did not fare as well in unturned sod.[28] Her plots, like the thousands of others scattered across the plains in the first decades of settlement, were not meant for dabbling, outlets for expression of a hobbyist's "green thumb."

Such large gardens required not only intensive labor but also a considerable amount of accumulated knowledge for planting, cultivating, and harvesting. Oblinger knew enough to plant her beans on a particular Friday, for example, and waited for the twins of Gemini to appear in the sky to plant her peas. She seemed less aware of the ways her polyculture method protected against the ravages of pests, yet was heartened nevertheless when a "striped bug" ruined only a few squashes and left her "vines" alone. Later, in the family's third year homesteading, she was surprised by winter's lingering into mid-April. She wrote to her family back in Indiana, explaining that she had not "made any garden yet" but wanted to if it did not snow all week, and that she hoped "we will have settled weather after this for the spring is very backward here."[29] Over time, Oblinger had to adjust some of her beliefs and practices as a gardener, to better suit the land and climate of Nebraska. This learning process, one that other women also experienced, kept her closely connected to the natural world.

Growing flowers around the house and yard demanded a refined understanding of what and how to plant as well. This activity, in particular, was unambiguously women's work and an important aspect of domesticating the plains. "In their efforts to make their surroundings homelike," Julie Roy Jeffrey points out, "women tried to soften what was often a sharp contrast between the world of nature and the world of family." While some women took a certain delight in the local flora and planted seeds they gathered from nearby, when it came to flowers, shrubs, and ornamental trees, they tended toward alien varieties. On a visit to distant neighbors, Mattie Oblinger got "a lot of Cottonwood and Willow cuttings to put out this spring," but she took some rose bushes, white and purple lilacs, and mountain currant too. This she added to the "forest shrubbery," peonies, "pinroes," and "dialetre" she had planted two years before. And her family back in Indiana had sent wine plant, which she had "divided in to five buds" and which was "comeing on nicely." Later, even as the family moved around, Mattie's daughter developed a winter ritual not unfamiliar to twenty-first century gardeners, flipping through her "2 catalogues from Buckbees' seed house" to prepare for spring planting. Other women were similarly enticed to import new flowers and shrubs to their respective corners of the grasslands.[30] They planted these seeds and slips along the exterior walls of their homes, on the borders of their vegetable gardens, and even in specially designated flower plots. One Belgian woman, though busy with her family and midwifery duties, kept a flower garden on her Nebraska homestead, protected against "the hot prairie winds" by a wall. "Once inside," a neighbor later recalled, "its bright blossoms, curving walks and shade trees were a treat indeed to a beauty-starved pioneer."[31]

Yet beauty was not the only tangible product of women's efforts to domesticate the land. From their gardens as well as the orchards they often helped plant and care for they gathered delectables to preserve for the rest of the year. This labor, both the gathering as well as the canning, brought a level of control over nature to the plains, ensuring a family's survival by bending the environment to the women's will. Baldwin Kruse's grandparents planted a variety of fruit trees on their Nebraska homestead in the Loup Valley, and the produce from these trees demanded a significant amount of attention during summer and fall. "The women of the household spent many days peeling and cutting up apples for canning and drying," he remembered.[32] Likewise, women boiled syrup out of pumpkins and squashes, made "a fine butter" out of the same, turned cabbage into sauerkraut and cucumbers into pickles, and created juices, jams, and jellies from grapes, wild plums, chokecherries, and currants gathered "in the hills" as well as "buckberries" that grew along riverbanks.[33]

Complementing the domesticating labor that women did outdoors on their homesteads, the jobs of building and furnishing a new home was another sure sign of transition to more refined, settled lives as well as the reassertion of more traditional gender roles. A family's move from soddie or log cabin to frame house indicated that the pioneer days had passed, the land was under at least a measurable degree of human manipulation, and some semblance of the cultural order men and women had known back East was reestablished there in the West. These houses were also not so obviously of the earth, which was part of what made them appealing. From building materials to furnishings to the way people lived inside them, frame houses introduced a new form of separation from the physical environment beyond the threshold. This was a large part of the "vernacular gentility" that, Andrea Radke argues, rural plains women used "to mark themselves against their harsh environments and thus reproduce the physical and ideological symbols of Euro-American civilization in the rural Great Plains." The homes and the more modern home life they represented were integral parts of a general shift toward a changed experience with nature.[34]

At least for some time, however, after the move from a temporary to a more permanent dwelling, much of the old life prevailed. This gradual change is nicely captured in the diary of Olive Capper, a Lincoln County, Kansas, homesteader. In the first part of 1895 she helped her family ready their new frame house, putting down carpets, moving the "millinery goods" over, and the like. As was the custom at the time, Olive frequently visited relations and friends, sometimes staying over through the night, and she was being courted by a young man who gave her a ring in proposal of marriage in early April. Sometimes with her beau and other times alone, Olive went to church, literary meetings, skating parties, and dances. Yet moving into a frame house and participating in various social activities did not necessarily represent a sharp break with a life organized around working the land. Olive performed the typical tasks of a young girl her age in the grasslands according to the day of the week and season, including washing and ironing, baking bread and making soap, as well as patching and sewing. From January to August she recorded various other activities as well, some of which required a direct, close relationship with the natural world outside the home.

As the weather warmed in the spring of 1895, Olive was busy helping plant the family's garden, and she was faithful about making note of the new season's arrival. On the second day of April she worked with her mother to put out most of the onion sets; about a week later she worked with both parents to "burn off the slough and cane patch"; and toward the end of the month she helped not only her own family but also neighbors with more planting. When the apple and peach trees were in full bloom Olive recorded that, and when she went to gather daises or other flowers with her sister or girlfriends she made a point to include those excursions in the diary too. "Myrtle & I gathered flowers," Olive wrote on May 29, "and I fixed my house plants & pulled weeds for pigs in afternoon." Later in the summer, entries noted when the family picked the first radishes, peas, sweet potatoes, or other garden vegetables for dinner.[35]

In nearly every diary entry for 1895 Olive also recorded the weather, and as the seasons changed and farm labor changed with them, she recorded when planting started, what crops her father planted, as well as what tools neighbors came to borrow. She paid particular attention to the direction and strength of the wind (e.g., "the wind blew tolerably chilly from W."), but sun as well as rain or snow were worthy of remarks too. One day in early April started out "lovely," but a west wind began later that morning, turned to the south around noon, and by afternoon was "a regular dust storm."[36] This sort of close observation, noting even the time when winds changed direction, was complemented by a refined understanding of farmwork and the tools required for various tasks. The same day that Olive helped her mother with the onion sets her sister went to a neighbor's place for a rake, her brother went to another neighbor's homestead to return a "jack-screw," and still another neighbor stopped by the Cappers' for the "feed rack." A month later, in early May, her father replanted the corn, with Olive's mother's help, and finished putting in the sorghum.[37]

DOMESTIC ECONOMY AND ROMANTIC NATURE

Although the shift from homesteading pioneers to settled farm family did not happen abruptly in the grasslands, even after the move from soddie to frame house, it did eventually happen, and a new home was an important part of that change. This shift was shaped, in part, by the concurrent spread of two advocacy movements in the late nineteenth and early twentieth centuries, one focused on "scientific farming" and another that promoted "domestic economy." These efforts to advance new ideas and practices were, in essence, born of primarily urban preoccupations, namely a greater concern for productivity and efficiency that an industrial transformation of the American economy entailed. As sections of the plains began to fill up, farmers consolidated their holdings, railroads made even more inroads, and market agriculture expanded, such urban-industrial concerns increasingly became farmers' concerns as well. Likewise, the girls and women of homesteader households were encouraged by home extension agents, farm journals, magazines, and mail-order catalogues to adopt new contemporary attitudes toward routine domestic chores and to embrace various modern household conveniences. When they did, it changed women's work, more sharply defined the gendered division of labor they performed, and altered their relationship with nature.

Scientific farming advocacy was ongoing throughout the nineteenth century, but it gathered considerable momentum in the 1890s. By various means and mediums farmers were advised to try different seed, alter crop rotation systems, improve livestock strains, and mechanize much of their arduous work, whether they were planting corn, harvesting wheat, or milking cows. Agricultural extension agents, farm journal editors, and others promoted the idea that farm families were capitalists, in need of rationalizing not only production but also marketing and distribution. These notions had a corollary in homemaker education, with its origins in the "scientific housekeeping" program of people such as Ellen Swallow Richards, which was designed to direct women toward various practices and conveniences that purportedly added to home life. "By rethinking basic work habits and learning to manage time and environment," Marilyn Holt explains, "women would be more effective and exert greater control over their labor and expenditure of energy."[38]

Domestic economy instruction was first provided to women through farmer's institutes such as the one organized by the Kansas State Agricultural College in 1906, probably the first such meeting in the state. An "experiment will be made this year in many counties," the organizers announced, "of having a separate meeting of women at the same time that the men are discussing some topic not of special interest to women." Later, with passage of the Smith-Lever Act, this kind of extension work was formalized and institutionalized. But as Marilyn Holt explains, new ideas and practices associated with the field reached women less through the few extension agents promoting domestic science and more by way of farm-based media, women's magazines, government publications, and eventually radio programs. In time women also formed clubs to disseminate information about making their rural home lives more modern.[39]

When farm institutes, magazines, and radio programs promoted scientific housekeeping or domestic economy, part of what they communicated was the need to adopt and use modern conveniences, new technology that supposedly would lessen women's labor and even help them do a better job. Besides giving greater importance to values such as efficiency and productivity, industrialization and the evolution of an integrated national market also had more practical consequences. Factories produced a bounty of products that had the potential to change the way domestic work was done. In some cases, such as the introduction of canned soup, industrial production simply absorbed labor that had been done in the home, leaving an opening for women to do other things or perhaps adding new importance to the work that remained. In other cases the products transformed a familiar and routine task.

This infusion of new goods and technology was certainly happening in Kansas and Nebraska in the late nineteenth and early twentieth centuries, and the domestic economy movement reinforced the products' appeal and impact. Coffey County, Kansas, pioneer Melissa Genett Moore recalled visiting her brother-in-law's home in 1876 and seeing the screened doors and windows, which so impressed her husband that he decided to install screens in their own home. Flies would no longer blacken the ceilings in the evenings and start up a loud buzzing early in the mornings. She declared, "The fly has been conquered." As bad as things got, Moore insisted, there was gradual improvement, marked in part by the purchase of sewing machines, washing machines, electric irons, and the like. "How many conveniences the young bride of today has that we of 1860 never dreamed of," she wrote in her 1924 memoir, "and as each new help came to us, it was an added joy."[40] After the Rebsch family constructed a cistern to catch rainwater and built a washhouse over it, for example, they purchased a gasoline-powered washing machine, ending the need for someone to manually turn the washer or wringer. Young Myrtle, born in 1902, was given the job of time-keeper in the wash house, making sure each cycle went for fifteen minutes, work she did not mind. "I could keep reading material to fill in the waiting time," she remembered, "and there was ample place to practice dance steps."[41]

It was not always true that new, so-called conveniences necessarily lessened or eased girls' or women's labor though. Sometimes they only changed the way work was done, and there was not always the required infrastructure to realize the full potential of the latest technology. With limited access to electricity, city water, and sewerage until the 1920s and 1930s, rural dwellers were often several steps behind urban dwellers and the domestic economy program. New consumer goods and modern technology did find their way into Kansas and Nebraska farm homes, however, and, in any case, the transformation of labor did have an impact on various aspects of daily life. For one thing, scientific housekeeping and the modern conveniences that went with it encouraged the retreat back to more traditional gender roles, away from fluid roles buttressed by the less rigid gendered division of labor of early settlement. Circumscribing women's lives, defining them more closely with the home, and inserting manufactured goods and technology between them and the world beyond the threshold also inevitably contributed to changing women's relationship with nature. Increasingly, the physical and organic environment was something "out there," known distantly or in the abstract, as a place to find beauty and the sublime.

Even when girls and women moved to a nearby town they continued to experience nature directly, particularly through work in their yards and gardens, and they persistently gave close attention to the weather as well as planting and harvesting cycles. Nearly all of the entries in the 1918 diary of widowed town dweller Emma Drew begin with a record of the high and low temperatures as well as general climate conditions, usually followed by a report of the work performed that day. A high of 83 degrees, for example, meant one March day was warm enough to make raking and trimming bushes in the yard a chore. Yet as spring approached and Drew planted a garden, it was more luxury than necessity, supplementing the groceries she purchased from a store in town, where she also went every month to pay gas, water, electric, coal, and phone bills. This was life without the ordeal of carrying water from a distant stream, cleaning clothes outdoors on a washboard, lighting a soddie with candles, or cultivating a garden to ward off starvation through the next winter.[42]

By the early twentieth century, in fact, both farm and town living with various modern amenities and a measure of security allowed original homesteader women to remember the early pioneer years with a considerable amount of romantic nostalgia. To one Kansas settler writing in the 1920s, the claim near Westerville that she came to with her parents in 1884 "was a wonderful country," colored by wildflowers that school children wove into great wreaths. In those pioneer days, she recollected, there were "dewy summer mornings, millions of prairie flowers everywhere, frogs croaking, prairie chickens booming and ducks quacking in that, their own country."[43]

Other women, perhaps more likely to be the ones who ventured west as adults, were somewhat ambivalent about the grasslands they had first encountered, although they were more certain about the merits of the landscape's transformation over the years. Rather than the "vast prairie" and "unsettled country" she came to in the 1880s, Viola Alexander insisted, "we now have beautiful homes throughout the country and a beautiful city with all its modern homes and every accommodation for its citizens." These improvements, she said, were "well worth all the hardships we 'Pioneer Women' had to endure to develop this vast and beautiful country of Clay County in 'Sunny Kansas.'" Taking a somewhat different view, Mrs. James Eddy remembered coming to Nebraska with her father at the turn of the century, recalling fondly how she used to pick raspberries and listen to song birds on walks in the nearby canyons. Yet she recognized that it was in spite of, rather than because of, "the hardships and troubles our parents lived through and the depressions and drouths we have gone through" that Custer County was such a special place to live.[44]

Still others even more distant from the pioneer experience seem to have imbibed romantic notions of the plains whole cloth. Olive Mitchell Staadt, for example, was born at the turn of the century and grew up on a farm in Franklin County, Kansas. After marrying in 1919, she kept busy raising a family, working as a bookkeeper and secretary for their seed farm, participating in home extension efforts, and serving various organizations, including the Garden Club, 4-H, and Franklin Historical Society. Later, in regular columns for the *Ottawa Times*, Staadt recalled the first decade of the century with hope that "the love of nature and the feeling of communion with the Almighty which was instilled into my soul as a child might be wakened to life in the reader." She wrote about the "gentle air of peace and tranquility" and "quiet beauty" among the hay mow in their old barn, the slow horse-drawn ride into town that allowed enjoyment of wildflowers and birdsong along the way, as well as transcendent walks around the farm and its environs. "Going forth on a Sunday morning stroll through the orchard," she said, "the peace and quiet of the day would sink deep into a the soul of a small child and bring those feelings of knowledge of a Creator who cared for His children." Undoubtedly, some of this carefree experience of the sublime, and particularly Staadt's writing about it decades later, had to do with her early literary influences, such as John Greenleaf Whittier. But it was a product of her family's settled, contemporary life as well. While Staadt's youth spanned the end of "the real horsepower age," she remembered various modern conveniences, from an egg incubator and cream separator to a gravity-flow water system powered by a windmill and a water heater connected to their large Majestic kitchen range. She never knew a time when their home did not have hot and cold running water in the bathroom and kitchen. Such amenities not only made work and daily rituals on the farm easier, at least ostensibly, but also enabled Staadt to take notice of transcendent qualities in nature.[45]

For those who lived in town or moved to a big city, the makings of a sublime sensibility were sometimes even more evident. Harriet Adams's parents had come to Kansas in 1856, caught up in the developing battle over slavery, and they first lived in a log cabin four miles outside of Leavenworth. By 1875, however, when Harriet was fifteen, they had moved to Topeka. She received an advanced education there, and this training, along with the estrangement from nature she felt as an urban dweller, are both evident in remarks she wrote about the Kansas countryside in 1908. "To us who love the field, the hillside and the woods and the sweep of the endless prairie," she began, "the recurring springs which clothe them as of old and yet anew, and the beauties of the flowers found in each are a source of perennial delight." Some of her earliest and most vivid memories, Adams claimed, were of "wind-swept prairie, and the odors of the earliest spring flowers, and of a little strip of wood every foot of which I knew, and a stream by whose banks I walked."[46]

And, of course, there were the likes of Willa Cather, who had moved away and wrote about the grasslands after living in Pittsburgh and New York City. "The blond cornfields were red gold," the narrator of *My Antonia* says, describing the sunset one evening. "The haystacks turned rosy and threw long shadows." Cather likened the red grass of the prairie at that hour to the burning bush of the Bible and, elsewhere in the book, compared it to the water of the sea, "with so much motion in it" that "the whole country seemed, somehow, to be running." In *O Pioneers!* Cather also portrayed the land that had initially appeared impossible to tame as an arcadian idyll. "There are few scenes more gratifying," she writes, "than a spring plowing in that country, where the furrows of a single field often lie a mile in length, and the brown earth, with such a strong, clean smell, and such a power of growth and fertility in it, yields itself to the plow; rolls away from the shear, not even dimming the brightness of the metal, with a soft, deep sigh of happiness."[47]

Women such as Harriet Adams, Olive Mitchell Staadt, and Willa Cather occupied a distinct place in a long history of Kansas-Nebraska grasslands settlement, one that fits in the history of evolving gender roles and changing work as well as the history of people's shifting relationship with the physical and organic environment. In fact, those narratives are inextricably linked. The women's foremothers moved to the region with a domesticating project in mind, later aided by a scientific housekeeping movement and the introduction of innovative home technology. By the turn of the century and the decades that followed, families that remained were measurably successful in transforming the plains into farms, taming some of the more alien aspects of the grasslands landscape, and making civilized havens from the wild natural world. This inevitably affected the way girls and women used and thought about nature, abetting adoption of more romantic notions about birds, flowers, streams, and even native grasses.

4

Degrees of Separation

Nature and the Shift from Farmer to Miner

to Factory Hand in Southern West Virginia

As was the case with many homesteading women and their male counterparts, and even more so with the children of homesteading families, the process of moving to the grasslands to make a farm was sometimes just a step on the road to a town or city. Family fortunes declined, forcing the abandonment of a quarter section and a search for new means to make a living, and family fortunes improved, allowing parents to offer their sons and daughters opportunities beyond their farms' surveyed boundaries. For these and other reasons, the rural-to-urban shift was also the story of millions more, in various parts of the country. Increasingly during the nineteenth century, from the era of Yankee mill girls to the beginning of African Americans' Great Migration, people left the land, often to labor in mills and factories for a wage. And this movement continued into the twentieth century, waxing and waning with the expansion and contraction of the economy during and following two world wars.

Yet the shift from agricultural labor in the country to factory labor in a town or city was not always a sharp break from one life to another. African Americans, for example, often took a circuitous route into the urban working class, going from plantation gang labor in bondage to comparatively freer sharecropping on former plantation lands to wage work and sometimes less intense racism in an auto plant or steel mill. The meaning of that transformation for black workers had a great deal to do with the starting point of racial slavery, but the experience of punctuated movement to a significantly different end was something many workers had in common, regardless of race. Native-born white residents of southern Appalachia, the subject of this chapter, also skipped their way from rural farms to urban assembly lines, only gradually separating themselves from the land and incrementally losing control over their labor and its products.

Before and even after the Civil War, most families in eastern Kentucky, east Tennessee, and southern West Virginia made their living by mixed subsistence farming. Toward the end of the nineteenth century, however, male heads of households began to supplement this agricultural labor with seasonal work cutting timber or mining coal. Later, they moved their families to company towns and went into the mines on a more regular basis, but even this was not an immediate wholesale change in their circumstances. A substantial amount of preindustrial life lingered in the coal camps. The men had a considerable amount of autonomy as miners, maintaining, as David Corbin put it, an "individualistic independence," one that squared with the freedom they were used to as subsistence farmers.[1] They continued to hunt on company land and fish in local streams as well, and nearly every family maintained a large garden and kept livestock.

Over time, coal mine operators in southern West Virginia and other parts of Appalachia established a repressive guard system to police the company towns, and they adopted factory discipline as well as new labor-saving technology underground. This provoked militant battles by miners for unionization, sometimes successful and sometimes not, and often forced the miners to rely on access to woods, streams, and open fields to keep their families fed during strikes. When the coal industry began to decline in the 1920s, however, and especially when production for the war in the 1940s enticed Americans to the urban factories, mountain people responded with out-migration, leaving for Akron, Cincinnati, Columbus, Detroit, Chicago, and other industrial cities. In these places resettled miners encountered a new, more potent combination of labor exploitation and alienation from the natural world.

During the course of several decades, mountain-born Appalachian coal miners experienced profound change in their work as well as their relationship with the physical and organic environment, as they moved from farm to mine to factory. Yet the period between the shift from hillside farm to coal camp needs closer inspection to ferret out persistent practices and ideas and to see that the movement to early mining was not necessarily a dramatic cleavage from another way of life, especially when set against the changes required by moving to auto plants, steel mills, and various other urban-industrial workplaces in the North. It was, rather, a story of continuity as well as change.

FARMER TO MINER

Before the advent of large-scale mining in Appalachia, life for mountain residents was not unlike that of the antebellum farm families in the Vermont, New Hampshire, and Massachusetts hills from which the mill girls hailed.

Most of the population was directly engaged in some combination of agricultural pursuits, raising crops for subsistence with a varying surplus for barter or trade, as well as keeping livestock for traction, food, and limited commercial exchange. But unlike the farm families of northern New England, the southern highlanders were less affected by the market revolution begun in the early national years. Especially on the Cumberland Plateau, including eastern Kentucky, east Tennessee, and southern West Virginia, where the steep ridges and narrow valleys made transportation difficult, mostly subsistence-oriented mixed farming continued even into the postbellum era.

As late as 1880, the average farm size in southern Appalachia was 187 acres, typically with 25 percent of the land cultivated, another 20 percent cleared pasture, and the rest left wooded. In the main fields, mountain residents planted corn as a staple crop, supplemented by wheat, rye, oats, and buckwheat, sometimes as part of a polyculture that included beans, melons, and squash. Male heads of household prepared the soil with simple tools, usually a bull-tongue plow, and other family members wielded hoes to help care for crops to harvest. In gardens, more clearly the work space of women aided by children of varying ages, the family grew vegetables such as onions, potatoes, and radishes. Most homesteads also had an orchard, with apple, pear, plum, cherry, and other fruit trees and a beehive for honey.[2]

Around and beyond their homes, farm families practiced animal husbandry, integrating livestock into their varied way of making a living from the land. Some of the corn a family grew was meant to fatten hogs—though some hogs were marked and let to roam the woods for mast—and those animals provided an important food source or, in some cases, an alchemic means to trade surplus crops and the wealth of the woods. Mules or oxen were kept to provide traction in the fields, and a horse or two might be kept as well to carry people along ridges and through hollows. Near the house was a poultry yard, with chickens for eggs and meat and geese for down to fill bed ticks and pillows. Beyond the homestead, sheep scoured the rocky hillsides and milk cows grazed in the cleared pasture. Wool from the sheep was carded, dyed, spun, and woven into homespun or turned into carpets for floors, and milk was usually churned into butter.[3]

The considerable woods and many streams in an area were reliable storehouses of provisions for people too. Roots such as ginseng were gathered for barter, while berry bushes and nut trees added to the mountaineers' tables in season. Deer, rabbits, squirrels, quail, and other game, along with fish from local creeks and rivers, were generally unfailing year-round sources of meat for families as well, at least before the passage of fish and game laws. And the woods satisfied a desire for beauty as well, complementing mostly women's efforts to spruce up the area around their cabins. "The mountain home had its flower garden, daffodils, lilies, dahlias, and sunflowers," historian Ronald Eller explains, "and in the spring nature provided a floral mosaic of dogwood, redbud, flag-lilies, larkspur, devil-in-the-bush, and hundreds of other wild-flowers."[4]

Settled on a hillside or nestled in a hollow with access to bottomland, mountain residents grew, raised, gathered, and caught their subsistence as part of family production units, based on an ideal of interdependence and a life lived close to the natural world that was directly and perceptibly around them. There was a division of labor, often by gender and age, but family members had a sense of their place and function, and their work was mean-ingful. When families owned their own land, as was typically the case, they could be nearly self-sufficient, and the products of their labor belonged to them, without an intermediary claiming a right of possession. Ultimately, however, this way of making a living was not sustainable. Farm families were large because children contributed essential labor and because kin mattered so much in the mountain culture, yet having so many children could not be reconciled with the demands of partible inheritance. In the years after the Civil War, the region's persistently high birth rate began to increase the popu-lation beyond remaining arable land, spelling doom for continued agrarian independence.

The demographic imbalance that became evident in the postbellum era was one of a number of factors that led to the spread of industrial wage work in the region. Speculators found many willing sellers for land and mineral rights among the increasingly strapped population, which then facilitated the process of railroad expansion and subsequently the advent of wide-scale com-mercial logging and coal mining. And mountain men became the labor force for the new extractive industries, cutting timber and digging coal at least initially as part of a strategy to stick with farming. They hired themselves out on a seasonal and temporary basis, not with a mind to suddenly and perma-nently make a separation from their preferred way of life, but this allowed capitalism to more fully penetrate the region and to begin its irreversible transformation.

In southern West Virginia, between the Tug Fork and Kanawha rivers, the industrial era was launched by construction and expansion of two major railroads, the Chesapeake and Ohio and the Norfolk and Western. This de-velopment was key to removing the natural resources of woods and coal-fields, although an extensive network of rail lines was late in coming to Ap-palachia in general and this part of the region in particular. In the immediate postbellum years, mining in the lower section of the state was still largely confined to Kanawha County, where the wide Kanawha River facilitated the slow shipment of coal to salt manufacturers and blacksmiths for at least six months out of the year. The lumber industry too had advanced only as far as major waterways and modest streams allowed rafting cut timber to local sawmills or distant railheads.[5]

The Chesapeake and Ohio started the process of industrialization in 1872, when the trunk line was finished and opened up the New River Field, including Fayette County. Within a decade that county had at least forty mines in operation and became the first in the state to produce more than a million tons of coal. By 1910, it had reached a prewar peak of more than 10 million tons. In the meantime, a branch line was built to adjacent Raleigh County in 1901, and the Guyandotte Valley extension opened Logan and Wyoming counties to mining in 1904.[6] The Norfolk and Western Railway, finished in 1893, ran parallel to the Chesapeake and Ohio between sixty and one hundred miles to the south, and it facilitated shipments from the coalfields along West Virginia's southern border, in Wayne, Mingo, McDowell, and Mercer counties. Between 1889 and 1910, in fact, McDowell County coal production increased from 246,000 tons to 12 million tons, making the county the largest producer in the state.[7] Concurrently, the main line railroads, feeder lines, and hundreds of smaller logging railroads opened forests to intensive commercial timber operations, which reached their peak by 1895. Yellow poplar, black walnut, chestnut, and other trees fell before the ax and saw, greatly shrinking what had been a large stretch of virgin growth across West Virginia, from 10 million acres in 1870 to a mere fifth of that by 1910.[8]

Behind all this feverish railroad building, timber cutting, and coal mining, of course, were land purchases as well as timber and mineral rights acquisition. By 1900, according to historian David Corbin, absentee owners had secured claim to 90 percent of Mingo, Logan, and Wayne Counties and 60 percent of Boone and McDowell. In 1923, he writes, "nonresidents of West Virginia owned more than half of the state and controlled four-fifths of its total value."[9] But logging and mining were sustained by the flow of labor into those operations as well, which ironically happened primarily because native mountain residents had a desire to continue making their own living from increasingly scarce land. Many of the men who felled timber or dug coal for a wage, at least initially, saw it as an accommodation to the realities of demographic imbalance, rising property taxes, and debts, or as a way to purchase land they had lost or never had. When they performed this labor it was a temporary means toward a more permanent end, and if they had a farm to return to their work was intermittent.

Well into the twentieth century, mine owners complained that native-born mountain residents were often an unreliable labor force because of their tendency to come and go according to a seasonal cycle. Although many local farmers took up a pick and shovel in the winter months, they left the mines for their fields in the spring and summer months, and again for harvesting in the fall. "Their shiftless methods of living have not accustomed them to continuous and sustained labor," Ronald Eller quotes one mining engineer as saying, adding a telling racial comparison that "they resemble the Negro in their desire for frequent periods of 'laying off.'"[10] From the other side, however, the "shiftlessness" made some sense. For most farmers and their families, actually, it was not an inherent indolence that kept them tied to the fields. They preferred a rural agrarian life and were attempting to preserve it through periodic bouts of wage work.

Crandall Shifflet argues that if agrarian mountain life had been appealing, farm families would not have left it. He lists the ways in which homesteads and the work there failed to measure up to coal camps and mining and insists that farmers willingly made the switch. "Mostly," he writes, "[farm] life was a cycle of endless labor. Roads, railroads, towns, stores, electric lighting, indoor plumbing, weekly garbage pickup, better medical and dental care, and other forms of 'modernization,' especially jobs, would have been welcomed by farm families to relieve the isolation, laboriousness, and misery of mountain life and work." This begs the question, however, why so many mountain residents attempted to have it both ways, farming most of the year and working only for a season.[11]

To be sure, various aspects of early mining did make that work less objectionable than it might have been and eventually became. Although digging at a coal seam in the dark and dank underground was significantly different from cultivating the soil in the open air, until the 1920s there was a certain amount of continuity in the organization of labor there, particularly in terms of the autonomy allowed. Although companies supplied prop timbers and track, miners owned their own tools and bought their own lamp oil, blasting powder, and other supplies. Underground, they had little or no supervision and developed a proprietary interest in the "room" they worked, retaining rights over it even when they were absent for a considerable amount of time. They controlled the length and pace of their workday too, paid on a piece-rate basis, and that meant they could quit when they had made enough money, a privilege they exercised with enough frequency to irritate production-minded operators. "The one point which is stressed most by the [owners]," complained a company vice president, "is the difficulty of operating a coal mine economically when the daily output is contingent upon the whims of the coal loader who works when, as long, and as hard as he pleases."[12] For the first few decades after the advent of coal mining in Appalachia, before the adoption of mechanical loaders and rationalization of work according to scientific management principles, miners retained an independence that squared with the freedom they were used to as farmers.[13]

Other aspects of mining also partly redeemed its industrial character. Even when mountain families finally left their homesteads or rented land, moving to one of the many company-owned settlements strung out in the hollows, they did not necessarily leave an agrarian experience behind. Herbert Garten's father, for example, farmed for a living while working "quite a bit in timber" and some in coal mines. Then around 1912 he moved the family from Summers County, West Virginia, to Terry. "There was better money in the mines," Garten explained, "and he had worked in the mines, off and on, you know, before he decided just to go in the mines."[14] Still, once in the coal camps, families like the Gartens perpetuated aspects of a traditional way of life by cultivating patches of land and keeping livestock, as well as hunting and fishing. Much like the miners' work underground, this mix of tasks was generally self-directed and autonomous. Unlike mining, however, the work above ground involved members of the entire family and provided regular contact with the daily and seasonal cycles of nature as well as a more direct experience with the ecological relationships between living things and the environment.

While the number varied over time and from county to county, a large majority of coal camp residents supplemented mining wages by cultivating a garden. Even in the mid-1920s the West Virginia Coal Association made the conservative estimate that 50 percent of the state's miners grew at least some of their own food, and a Children's Bureau survey found that even more families in Raleigh County made part of their living that way. Bureau representative Nettie McGill reported that 70 percent of the families interviewed had gardens, producing a variety of vegetables and fruits. Most families grew corn, beans, potatoes, tomatoes, and cabbage, she said, and a few also planted beets, onions, lettuce, watermelon, and cantaloupes. Some mining families cultivated orchard crops as well, including apples, peaches, plums, and cherries, mostly for canning and making wine and cider, and women planted flowers around their houses or in separate gardens.[15]

As part of welfare capitalism schemes, a few coal companies encouraged gardening by allowing use of available land, providing stable litter and lime fertilizer, and, at some mine operations, giving cash rewards for the best gardens and yards. In the summer of 1912, for example, the United States Coal and Coke Company, in Gary, West Virginia, paid a premium of ten dollars for the best garden and five dollars for the best-kept yard. "The vegetable patches," explained the (operator-friendly) trade journal *Coal Age*, "are almost invaluable to those who tend them for they assure them of fresh vegetables throughout the greater part of the year."[16] Companies ran the garden and yard contests, in part, because miners' gardening enabled them to keep wage rates down and yet still make a claim to benevolence. It was also a way to encourage beautification of the coal camps. Contest criteria often mentioned "neatness" in addition to "the kind and quality of crops raised" and "the natural advantages and disadvantages of the location," and judges made their awards in June and July, before gardeners would be harvesting significant amounts of produce. "The dull, gloomy look of the usual mining town disappears," *Coal Age* editors noted in writing about a McDowell County contest, "and in its stead rises the fresh, bright, sweet-smelling flowers; and the beautiful green lawns replace the clay and coal dirt."[17]

The garden and yard contests, intentionally or not, promoted a gendered division of labor as well. Companies gave most of the awards to men, although women were participants in competitions for flower cultivation and yard upkeep. The Weyanoke Coal and Coke Company, in Mercer County, West Virginia, annually gave coal camp residents both land and fertilizer for "their flower and vegetable beds," and awarded more than one hundred dollars in prizes to promote their use. But most of that prize money went to men for gardening, while "$5 was given to the lady having the prettiest flowers, and a porch settee to the lady whose flower display was next in order of merit."[18] Lula Lall Jones, an African American who came to a southern West Virginia mine from Kentucky with her husband, recalled how she won a flower garden contest — and a twenty-five dollar prize — five years in a row. "I had dahlias," she said. "I had bleeding hearts. I just had all kind."[19] Very likely, Jones was talking about a racially segregated competition, because many companies made separate awards for blacks and whites, and most if not all of them identified winners by ethnic group. At U.S. Coal and Coke's Gary operation, the winners in the yard contest were seven "Americans," one "Italian," one "Slavish," one "Colored," and one "German." In the garden competition the winners listed included two "American," two "Colored," three "Hungarian," one "Slavish," one "Polish," and one "German."[20]

Not every coal camp promoted gardening and yard upkeep with contests, which tended to be limited to the large "captive" mines and were rare at smaller, independent operations. Still, most mining families grew some of their own food and kept their yards tidy, even without the competitive encouragement, and in practice they followed a nuanced and mixed gendered division of labor adapted from previous lives on farms. Men, it seems, were largely responsible for tilling the soil and then taking care of staple crops such as corn, infrequently assisting other family members with morning or Sunday work in the rest of the garden. Recalling his boyhood, Fayette County miner Robert Forren explained how he and his father would come home in the evening, eat supper, "and go to the cornfield and hoe until nine and nine-thirty at night."[21] Women on farm homesteads worked gardens, helped by children, and this continued after families moved to the coal camps. One miner, according to David Corbin, boasted that his wife and daughter "worked harder in the fields than any man ever did and that's why we grew more stuff in the [company] towns than the farmers on their farms."[22] Young boys and more than a few girls were expected to contribute in this way too. "Every spring in Grays Flats my father planted a large garden to keep food on the table for our growing family," Robert Armstead recalled, and in the summer the children weeded and hoed. "I swatted flies and sweated hours of my childhood away," he said, "battling every kind of weed known to man."[23]

Animal husbandry was marked by even more mixed responsibility. Care of chickens, hogs, and cows fell to men and women as well as to children. Robert Armstead, who came from a larger family, remembered that the "boys fed hogs and chickens, cut wood, and piled coal up for winter," while their sisters "made beds, washed dishes, and helped with laundry." Robert Forren, who explained that only 30 to 35 percent of Fayette County coal camp residents had their own hogs, recalled children just released from school "visiting the different homes that did not have hogs, a'picking up the scraps from the tables and so on . . . to bring home to the family that did have a hog." Yet Concho, West Virginia, resident Ada Jackson remembered that women fed the various livestock in the evening and that "mostly the husband would feed them in the morning, because he would be up earlier." Among the tasks that filled her day, Jackson listed housework, taking care of children, sewing, cooking, feeding chickens and hogs, and working in the garden.[24]

Hunting and fishing, on the other hand, were almost entirely if not exclusively within the male domain. Ada Jackson's husband and his fellow miners, for example, caught blue cats and other fish from the New River, although she never joined them. "I'd go to the river every day," she recalled, "but I didn't fish." Likewise, Robert Armstead remembered only the males in his family fishing. "I saw men and boys standing next to Paw Paw Creek in all kinds of weather," he said, "some with just a stick and a string, trying to hook a few fish for dinner." Ames, West Virginia, resident Annie Kelly also recalled her brothers maintaining a "trot-line," a line that ran across the river, baited alternately with worms, stiff "doughballs," and fatback bacon pieces. In the fall, these same boys and their father, as well as nearly all the other male coal camp residents in the region, hunted for rabbit, squirrel, pheasant, deer, and bear. During time off or a slack period at a mine, they ventured out with shotgun or rifle in hand, and often a dog or two by their side, to take wild game on land that might have been owned by a railroad, coal, timber, or land company, but which local people treated as a commons.[25]

Coal miners and their various family members kept gardens, raised livestock, and hunted and fished in part because it was what they knew, particularly if they had migrated from a native homestead. Working the soil, caring for domestic animals, and harvesting some of their subsistence from the woods and streams, the miners had one foot still firmly planted in the preferred life they had left behind. At a very basic level, these subsistence activities were also essential, supplementing low wages and carrying mining families through the inevitable slow periods in an industry marked by an unchecked capacity for overproduction as well as fickle market demand. And this worked both ways, helping the miners as well as mine owners. The larger companies ran the garden and yard contests, as noted, because miners' gardening, as well as the animal husbandry and hunting they did on company land, enabled mine owners to hold down wage rates and yet still make a claim to benevolence. This is evident in what was likely a fictional but instructive story published by *Coal Age* during the recession prior to World War I. The plot has a corporate executive gone quail hunting who, looking around in a fit of good feeling, realizes the resource his company has in the recently logged hillsides. "I'm going to let our miners use the land," he tells the general manager the next day, "to help them make a living." In the story the company then divides the land into one- to five-acre tracts, moves houses from the coal camp, and constructs small barns and chicken houses. Workers who wish to till the land can move to one of the tracts and still be close to the mine — and, in fact, using the land is an obligation if workers want to "keep their places with the company."[26]

At one and the same time providing access to land could be a way for coal companies to establish miners' dependence on them as well as a means for those same workers to carve out a realm of independence. The latter was particularly important for miners in southern West Virginia, because nearly without exception they were required to live in company-run camps, take their pay in company scrip, and buy provisions in a company store.[27] In some places there were independent stores, but miners needed cash to shop there, and mining companies only changed scrip at a discount.[28] Either way, over-reliance on the company system would not necessarily keep a family well fed and could quickly lead a family into debt, so almost everyone made an effort to provide a good deal of their own subsistence. "We had to buy flour, sugar, salt, and stuff like that," remembered Ernest Carico, "but the rest we just raised."[29] Those who did not, or could not, work so diligently at making their own living might buy the eggs, chickens, ham, potatoes, apples, cabbage, and other meats and produce mining families raised in surplus and sold to a store for credit, which at least improved their lot.

Looking at coal company store ledgers, it is possible to get a glimpse of the multiple strategies mining families developed to get by, strategies that suggest they had not yet truly separated from an orientation centered on the farm, streams, and woods. Representative of such records are the daybooks kept by the managers of the Cannelton Coal Company's Store #2, which served the Cannelton coal camp in Fayette County, a few miles from the New River. Assessing two week-long periods in 1896, one during the month of April, before spring planting, and the other in August, when gardens were yielding produce, it appears that camp residents varied in their labors, but most cultivated a patch of ground, kept some animals, or at least fished. Although the daybooks are not a reliable window on hunting practices, because there are no entries in April, August, or any other month for the purchase of bullets or traps or for the sale of dressed wild game or skins to the store. This might mean that none of the men or boys in the camp hunted, but more likely it was an activity that they did somehow without leaving evidence in ledgers.[30]

In mid-April 1896 the most common purchases at the Cannelton company store were eggs, bacon, potatoes, sugar, coffee, beans, crackers, and candy, with transactions for nonfood items such as coal oil, fishing line, and scrub brushes or the cashing of scrip following close behind in recurrence. By the first part of August, there were many fewer visits to the store, and the most frequent transactions were a mix of cashing company scrip as well as buying lard, sugar, coal oil, soap, coffee, candy, eggs, cloth, tea, bacon, peaches, lemon, and tobacco, in that order. Examining the records for these two months it would seem that not everyone in the camp kept chickens or hogs or grew their own potatoes and beans, but that otherwise mining families purchased things they could generally not produce themselves. Other such items in the ledgers include slippers, paper, nails, baking powder, condensed milk, buckets, matches, tea, cloth, spices, salt, vanilla, vinegar, and needles. On the cusp of spring planting, a few mining families also purchased seed (radish, beet, etc.). By August, however, they were *selling* onion, corn, cabbage, and tomatoes in sizable quantities to the store, in addition to chickens, eggs, butter, ham, and rawhide, and a few were already buying canning jars.[31]

At the very least, the Cannelton ledgers and other daybooks show that mining families did not rely exclusively or always heavily on miners' wages. Coal camps generally allowed for persistent remnants of the agrarian life that many native-born mountain residents supposedly left behind when they moved, and this had implications for labor organizing there. Between the opportunities for satisfying their own subsistence needs while working at a mine and the ability of some residents to return to homestead and farm when they chose, many miners were reluctant to contemplate if not averse to struggle for unionization. According to David Corbin, when union organizer P. M. McBride toured Kanawha County in 1896 he associated much of his difficulty in recruiting miners to his cause with their capacity to take care of themselves. "Every available spot of ground seems to have received attention from the plow or spade," he wrote. "They raise all the vegetables they require and this assures them that the wolf shall be kept from the door."[32]

It was not only the basic fact of having an alternative means to satisfy material needs, however, that hindered United Mine Workers (UMW) campaigns in southern West Virginia. By gardening, keeping livestock, and hunting and fishing, miners and their families also minimized the degree of estrangement from nature required by the shift to industrial wage labor. They might have left their farms, but they did not have to separate completely from work on the land, to sever a relationship that fed them in more ways than one. Gardens provided vegetables in the winter months, and, just as important, explained Children's Bureau agent Nettie McGill in a report on Beckley-area coal camps, miners spoke of "the enjoyment which they derived from working in their gardens, especially as a change from work inside the mines."[33] Combined with the relative freedom miners experienced underground — before new technology and reorganization of work subjected them to the control and supervision most factory workers knew — this continued connection with the living things and landscape around them aboveground partly redeemed coal mining and life in coal camps. That made the men less willing to take the risks and endure the hardships of forming a union, demanding recognition, and securing a contract.

Yet changing circumstances held mining families' attention and eventually prompted male heads of household to take collective action. For one thing, the fit between agrarian life and coal mining was never seamless, and this disjuncture worsened and became more obvious over time. Persistent traditional subsistence practices began to run up against swelling populations and deteriorating housing in the coal camps, which were increasingly plagued by congestion and afflicted by inadequate or nonexistent systems for sewage and garbage disposal. Settlements were usually built in narrow hollows between two ridges, on either side of a railroad line and stream running through the valley, and there, among the hills, all manner of problems started to arise. When the mines were active, the influx of native-born residents, southern blacks, and immigrants was steady, and coal operators focused more intently on profits, while living conditions in the settlements declined. Although there were numerous experiments in benevolent capitalism to point to, those efforts did not always live up to their promise, and many companies simply balked at the large investments livability would require. Coal could not be mined economically, operators claimed, and anyway they had the right to use their property without interference.[34]

Throughout southern West Virginia, in every coal camp, families living close to the tipple were routinely showered with clouds of coal dust, "which turned everything a somber gray and frustrated the cleaning efforts of even the most meticulous housewife."[35] Garbage and refuse accumulated too, because companies did not make provisions for collection and removal. Some of it could be fed to hogs, but a good deal of it inevitably ended up dumped along roadsides or in nearby waterways, along with human sewage, making creeks unusable for drinking and fishing. "In some settlements," Nettie Mc-Gill wrote in 1923, "waste matter entered the creeks flowing through the center of the town, privies were tumble-down, and incredible amounts of garbage and rubbish lay on the ground." Wandering chickens, ducks, geese, and hogs, although important to miners for making a living, added "to the general disorder and unwholesomeness." Many families preferred to use water from shallow wells or springs, as they would have on their homestead, but in the company-run towns these were often polluted by privies situated above and "by chickens and stock, or by dishwater, drainage, and garbage."[36]

Belowground, the mining technology and the organization of mine work also underwent significant transformation in the first three decades of the twentieth century, changes that miners did not generally appreciate or welcome. Machines to undercut coal were introduced by operators as early as the 1880s, and at the turn of the century a quarter of the nation's coal was mined this way. In West Virginia, miners' picks were fast disappearing by 1905. There were only 141 cutting machines in Kanawha, Fayette, McDowell, Marion, and Tucker County mines in 1900, but five years later there were 1,158, and by 1910 nearly 2,000.[37] In terms of impact on work organization, however, this wave of mechanization had relatively little impact. Even after introduction of electric drills, better blasting powder, more efficient haulage, as well as the undercutting machines, miners still worked alone or with a partner in isolated rooms with a claim of proprietorship; they still set their own pace of production and determined the length of their work days; and they were still paid according to how much coal they loaded.[38]

What truly transformed the labor process and allowed for making mining more like factory work was the introduction of machine loaders. There were only a few of these machines scattered about the state's southern coalfields in 1910, but in the years that followed operators installed Myers-Whaley, Jeffrey, and other loaders in much greater numbers. The hand-loading era came to a quick end then, and by the middle of the 1920s, West Virginia led all other states in the production of machine-loaded coal.[39] Consequent to this change, operators implemented scientific management techniques, and miners lost the control they once exercised over the production process. Machine loaders addressed the problems caused by hand loaders who slackened their pace or decided to quit for the day, heralding the switch from piecework to a day rate of pay and adding some dependability to output. They concentrated operations as well, allowing closer supervision of the work force, which was reorganized into small crews under the watch of a foreman.[40]

Over time, as the quality of life in coal towns eroded and the freedom of mining was circumscribed, miners and their families became more receptive to unionization, though not without initial hesitation. Until the second decade of the twentieth century, the United Mine Workers had made little headway in southern West Virginia. They established a foothold in Kanawha County, during a 1902 strike, but miners there returned to work on a non-union basis after another strike two years later, and the union suffered another reversal in 1907 when it attempted to reorganize to fight a wage cut. During the years that followed, the UMW poured a considerable amount of money into regaining the lost ground, with scores of organizers spreading the union message; yet most miners failed to join, and those that did pay dues did so only grudgingly.[41]

What seems to have tipped the balance in the southern West Virginia coalfields was operators' use of a guard system that, ironically, they thought they needed to stop agitation. By 1910, Baldwin-Felts agents were present in nearly every company town in the state, and their brutish and arbitrary methods backfired, fueling miners' determination and willingness to act. When thousands of workers in Kanawha and Fayette County mines finally walked out in the spring of 1912, their demands in order of importance were recognition of the union, abolition of the mine-guard system, reform in the docking system, a check-weighman hired by the miners, the right to trade with any store they pleased, cash wages, and only lastly an increase in pay. They won their fight for recognition and received a modest improvement in wages, though they failed to remove the guards from their towns, maintaining the conditions for continued organizing and resistance.[42]

Several years later, World War I also fanned the flames of agitation by injecting the idealist rhetoric of fighting autocratic rule and saving democracy, sentiments that contrasted sharply with the reality of repression in company towns. With this inspiration, organizing efforts spread beyond the heart of the New River field to Raleigh, Boone, McDowell, Mingo, Logan, and other counties, yet without much lasting success. After the war, operators began to systematically break the UMW's tenuous hold in the region, starting with the defeat they exacted on miners at Blair Mountain in 1921. As a result, the share of union-mined coal in the southern West Virginia fields dropped from 65 percent in 1922 to 23 percent in 1927.[43] At the same time demand for coal began to decline precipitously, and many of the smaller operations started to close, years before the rest of the country was battered by depression. "By 1930," explains Ronald Eller, "unemployment, destitution, and despair stalked the coal fields."[44]

Still, miners were not without recourse to other means of subsistence. During the pre- and postwar labor battles as well as during the Depression they relied on persistent farming skills and access to land to feed themselves and their families. In 1919, David Corbin relates, one Kanawha County miner wrote to UMW president John Lewis that "we're not worrying about strike benefits . . . because we are killing hogs and gathering corn and other crops and squirrel hunting."[45] Usually during a strike miners were put out of their company housing and denied access to gardens, but even then there were mountain residents who had never relinquished their homestead or never gave up farming for mining, and they could help with land or provisions. There were still nearly 1,500 farms in Fayette County in 1920, many of which were located close to tracts of open range, and other counties had even more residents occupied exclusively by agriculture.[46]

Ellis Bailey's family had the best of both worlds, since they owned and farmed bottomland in Clear Creek, and he had a reliable cash income from digging ginseng as well as working in a UMW mine three or four days a week. On the farm they grew potatoes and corn and kept an apple orchard, and they willingly gave food to the miners caught up in the wildcat strikes near Cabin Creek after World War I. "When we got over there to sell our stuff," he remembered, "there was a Baldwin thug, and all the working men sitting out in the road with their furniture throwed out." Bailey and his father saw some hungry children too, and they started to pass out what they had brought, not expecting payment but taking in kind some of the mattresses and other household items the displaced miners no longer needed. Observing their actions, the Baldwin-Felts agents came over and told them to leave, threatening to shoot them if they looked back as they traveled down the road. Later, miners came to them. "Every miner wasn't working," Bailey recalled, "they'd come up here and I'd give them $10 every time they come, and they'd take about two wagon loads of grub."[47]

During the Great Depression, as the early decline of the coal industry stretched into another decade, miners who still had access to land also survived by relying on farming.[48] Herbert Garten's father, for example, lost his position at a Terry, West Virginia, mine and "went back up to the farm," the homestead they still owned near Clayton. Ernest Carico's father was laid off from a mine too, yet he managed to provide more than enough for the family to eat by working a patch on the old homestead. "He'd always raise enough to do us," Carico remembers, "and then what he had left over, potatoes and stuff like that, he'd just have to dump them out to the hogs or anything that would eat them. He couldn't sell them. . . . I saw him throw away several bushels of potatoes during the spring." Likewise, James Harlan Edwards had six children by the 1930s, but he could not recall any of them going hungry during those years. He cultivated three or four acres of ground, "making corn, beans, potatoes and everything," raised "an old calf or two" to sell for beef, and took to the woods to hunt the plentiful squirrels and trap groundhogs.[49] "Although the amount of land in farms remained relatively stable from 1930 to 1940," Ronald Eller explains, "the number of farms rose significantly during the depression years."[50]

MINER TO FACTORY HAND (TO MINER AGAIN)

Not everybody could or did respond to the coal industry's decline by reverting to full-time farming, however, and with the start of production for World War II, there was the added enticement of jobs up north to get people to leave. This marked another important change in the shift from farm to mine to factory labor, with correspondent changes in labor exploitation and alienation from nature, although this second part of the shift, like the first, was somewhat incomplete. In the latter half of the 1920s and throughout the 1930s, native-born mountain residents sometimes left Appalachia only to return as job prospects brightened and dimmed. They were, as Phillip Obermiller calls them, "shuttle migrants." Later, with the onset of war, a considerable number of southern highlanders began to leave for good, nearly 7 million of them between 1940 and 1960.[51] Even these migrants returned on frequent visits though, for weekends, holidays, vacations, funerals, reunions, and hunting seasons.[52]

Among the millions who left the mountains following the Depression years, 750,000 of them were from southern West Virginia, at least half of whom went to Ohio, and a good portion of those found their way to Akron. Recruiters for the rubber industry had been luring mountain residents to northern Ohio since the turn of the century, and many had come seeking the promised high wages, to save some money before returning home. By the 1920s, at least 80 percent of the employees at Goodyear were native born, and the number of workers who hailed from West Virginia and Kentucky was nearly equal to the number from Ohio. Like the coal industry, however, the rubber industry was "sick" even before the Depression, which caused a precipitous drop in employment at Akron factories and a brief period of reverse migration. Then war brought another boom, jobs in the city increased 41 percent, and West Virginia migrants made their way to the rubber center once more.[53]

Yet much like coal operators' perception in the late nineteenth century, rubber plant management did not always have a high regard for southern highlanders, particularly when they brought a disposition toward autonomy and self-determination to the shop floor. They lacked a familiarity with regular oversight, one industrial observer wrote in 1921, which created habits ill-suited to factory work. "The ex-miner resents all suggestion as to his working methods," he said, "resents all effort to compel continuous application, and assumes in general a hostile attitude toward supervision."[54] No doubt, when the tire and rubber goods manufacturers adopted new technology and scientific management methods, the regimentation and expectations of factory discipline clashed as much or more with the men's "individualistic independence" as it did in the coal mines back home. That explains, in part, why Akron saw so much labor upheaval in the 1930s, including the first sit-down strike. A large number of former miners stayed in the city during the rubber industry's downturn rather than return to the mountains, and they played key roles in organizing the United Rubber Workers. They drew on a general experience and set of values from working the land and mines of southern Appalachian, as well as a more particular experience and array of attitudes from dealing with recalcitrant operators and Baldwin-Felts thugs.

West Virginia migrants went to Akron and other northern industrial cities for the opportunities promised there, but they did not always look favorably on what they found. Organizing unions was one expression of this sentiment, a response to the labor exploitation they encountered inside the rubber plants. Outside the factories, in the increasingly crowded streets and ever-inadequate housing, conditions were also poor, although this was something they could do little to change. Before World War I, many Akron residents lived in neighborhoods of modest, single-family homes, with land enough for vegetable gardens, chickens, and cows. Consequent to a construction boom, however, neighborhoods were transformed, and newcomers lived in cramped apartments, plagued by traffic, street noise, and refuse. Escaping these conditions without leaving town became increasingly difficult. Workers in the city spent twice as much as the average American on recreation, the Bureau of Municipal Research claimed, "because of the limited opportunities afforded by Akron for free or inexpensive recreation, such as parks, playgrounds, and free band concerts."[55]

The West Virginia migrants' urban destinations did not always compare favorably with their coal camp homes, but there were trade-offs both ways, compelling reasons to move and nearly equally compelling reasons to return. "In a city you can get some money," recalled one of the new rubber workers, and "back there we got no money." The possibilities for making a living and the lack of opportunity in the mines were the deciding factors in his family's case. "I love the mountains," he said, "but look what goes with the mountains."[56] To make the choice to stay more agreeable, migrants developed other ways to escape the urban-industrial environment. By the post–World War II era, for example, more and more industrial laborers were taking to the woods and streams with gun and rod in hand, filling the ranks of a burgeoning community of working-class sportsmen. They found places for hunting and fishing within driving distance of Akron, Toledo, Detroit, and Chicago, and they began to join conservation organizations as well as form their own clubs to expand their options. Many of them also lived their old lives vicariously. This is the time, Chad Berry argues, when country music "began to include more songs of lonely migrants growing tired of urban life and lamenting Mom and Dad, and a lost way of life."[57]

Even in the mid-twentieth century, however, as the stream of migrants from southern West Virginia coal camps to northern factory towns became a flood, there were still people who decided to go back to the mountains. This was the story of Henry Garten, who left Terry, West Virginia, for Toledo, Ohio, in 1953, to work on the Baltimore and Ohio Railroad. During that time he returned to his home state frequently for long stretches, when the lakes froze and the younger workers were furloughed. In the end, he stayed in the North only three years. "It got to where I didn't get that time off, to where I had enough seniority to hold on year round," he explained, "so I had to make a decision." All the mines had long "panel lists," a line of laid-off ranked workers, but a friend of his acquired a small mine at White Oak and offered him a job. "I was waiting" Garten said, "for something like that."[58]

The irony is that men like Garten came back to a coal industry in flux, marked by corporate consolidations as well as organizational and technological changes that made mining still more destructive to the regional economy and local environment than it had been in the late nineteenth and early twentieth centuries. During the 1950s and 1960s large coal companies and energy conglomerates gobbled up small operations, while operators in various parts of Appalachia introduced "contour" and "auger" methods of coal extraction. Rather than dig a tunnel down or into a mountain to get at a coal seam, they ripped the "overburden" from a hillside to expose a seam of coal relatively near the surface and used bulldozers and giant drill bits to loosen and break it up for removal. This "strip mining" significantly lowered labor costs because it required many fewer miners per ton of coal mined, which exacerbated the technological unemployment that plagued the region. It ruined area farm land and groundwater as well, sending acid "spoil" down mountainsides to cover fields, orchards, and sometimes homes, burying whole streams or polluting the waters to make them unfit for aquatic life, and destroying large chunks of wildlife habitat. With little or no regulation, and poor enforcement of the few restrictions that states did impose, strip operators were able to displace responsibility for these environmental consequences and the costs of reclamation onto the general public.[59]

With the spread of strip mining across Appalachia, the mid-twentieth century saw the rise of protest, although the coal industry sometimes pitted mountain residents against one another. Many deep miners recognized what was happening and complained to coal operators, state legislators, and their own union leaders, arguing for the need to protect jobs as well as the environment. In southern West Virginia, these concerns were important in building an insurgency to end years of mismanagement and corruption in the UMW, and it was no coincidence that Miners for Democracy won control of the union by electing Boone County deep miner and strip mining opponent Arnold Miller as president in 1972. Yet even Miller was forced to temper his demands for abolition of surface mining by the growing membership employed at strip operations, most of whom adopted the same rationalizations for their work as the operators.

Wayne Keith, for example, defended surface coal mining as good for miners, the local economy, and even the land. He had left Wise County, Virginia, to work in a Sandusky, Ohio, foundry in the late 1960s, but returned to a job at a surface mine. "It gives people work," he said, "and the land that we strip is in 50 percent and a lot of times 100 percent better condition that it was when we came in there." On one job, he explained, they paid a man to mine a part of his property that "wasn't worth a plug nickel," leveled it off flat and sowed grass all over, "and now he's got a pasture out there." Other operations had created flat land for a college and an airport, which Keith believed to be a better use of the land. He also posed the classic "jobs versus environment" dilemma, wondering what mountain residents were supposed to do for work if strip mining was disallowed. "If you're going to say that you've got to quit strip mining because you're tearing up the land what's people going to do?"

he asked rhetorically. If the only alternative was welfare, "Why don't they let them go ahead and make a living?"[60]

By the mid-twentieth century, then, for those who stayed in the strip coalfields of Appalachia, or for those who left but returned when the cities did no suit them, life was something different from the values, concerns, and experience of nineteenth-century subsistence-minded mountain farmers. To most strip miners, at least, the earth was there to be scraped away and dumped in a "valley fill," while work was wage labor under someone else's control, merely "a job" that left no room for stewardship of the woods, fields, orchards, streams, and other parts of the landscape. This transformation in attitude and experience did not come suddenly, and it was always somewhat incomplete in the rural industrial context, but it ushered in a changed relationship with the natural world.

For those who made a permanent move, another form of alienation from labor and estrangement from the land prevailed. This is a story most aptly portrayed by Harriet Arnow Simpson in her 1954 book, *The Dollmaker*, which describes the trials and tribulations of the Nevel family as they move from southern Appalachia to Detroit during World War II, when the father takes a job in an auto plant.[61] For the fictional Nevels, and for other real-life Appalachian migrants, nature was noticeably in retreat in their new surroundings. Modern home conveniences, paved landscapes, regimented and monotonous work in the factories, and various other aspects of urban-industrial life contrasted sharply with traditional home chores, cultivating the soil, raising livestock, as well as hunting and fishing in the mountains of southern Appalachia. Still, despite the bleakness the Nevel family, like so many others, remain and adapt, and that is the subject of the next chapter.

5

A Decent, Wholesome Living Environment for Everyone

Michigan Autoworkers and the Origins

of Modern Environmentalism

Part of the power of Harriet Arnow Simpson's portrayal of the fictional Nevel family was its pointed accuracy. Like the family in *The Dollmaker*, many early twentieth-century autoworkers were migrants from rural areas, and they found a considerable amount of heartache and trouble when they made their journey to a city. Yet the move was not without at least a few good ends. Detroit and other large metropolitan areas gave migrants access to better schools, doctors, and hospitals, as well as cultural amenities such as movie theaters, amusement parks, and dance halls. Likewise, making advantage out of misery, migrants embraced the union organizing and collective bargaining that were often major steps toward an entire family's social mobility. In turn, by transforming their own consciousness and helping themselves, auto-workers changed the country's economic and political order. They built a key part of the foundation for a powerful industrial union movement that mea-surably altered the relationship between capital and labor, and they played a critical role in the consolidation of a Democratic coalition, one plagued by division but at least temporarily reliable for enacting a progressive, liberal agenda.

Although it might seem counterintuitive, the people who left hinterland homes for industrial cities in the interwar years and after, to make the cars that posed an increasingly potent threat to the environment, also helped forge a robust environmental movement. In Michigan, the geographic center of the auto industry, workers did this primarily through two sets of organizations, a collection of local and state sportsmen's clubs and the international and local chapters of a powerful industrial union, the United Auto Workers (UAW). In a myriad of ways, both the clubs and the union encouraged and aided growing concern by autoworker families for enhancing outdoor recreational opportunities, conserving natural resources, and controlling pollution. They spoke to and channeled autoworkers' desire to draw closer to nature, seemingly out of reach in the urban-industrial landscape, as well as their urgent need to clean up and protect local communities ravaged by gargantuan factories and sprawling cities. In the process, the organizations were the primary means by which Michigan autoworkers pioneered a working-class environmentalism, an important but somewhat forgotten foundation for the mainstream concern that blossomed across the country.

Starting in the 1920s a growing number of male autoworkers and other factory hands living in and around Detroit attended to a newfound sense of estrangement from the natural world by hunting and fishing. To support those activities they formed or joined local sportsmen's clubs, which held regular meetings and published monthly newsletters, and they established a state organization, the Michigan United Conservation Clubs (MUCC), which worked with existing conservation groups to lobby the legislature on fish and game laws. By the late 1940s and early 1950s, many working-class sportsmen began to develop a serviceable understanding of general ecological principles as well as a related, growing apprehension about pollution, particularly municipal sewage and industrial waste. These problems were increasingly common and troublesome around the main centers of car production, where autoworkers happened to live, and hunters and anglers put their clubs in the forefront of campaigns to bring about some redress. Not coincidentally, this interest in improving local environmental quality, as well as sportsmen's clubs' recreational orientation, complemented similar concerns of the UAW.

From the time it was founded in the mid-1930s, and especially after World War II, the autoworkers' union took a keen interest in expanding the leisure-time activities of the rank and file. By 1939 the union had a separate Recreation Department, which assisted local recreation committees to sponsor shooting clubs, ice-skating competitions, horseshoe leagues, and, perhaps most important for developing a working-class environmental consciousness, an annual summer camp at the union's labor center in Port Huron, just outside of Detroit. The idea, promoted and implemented by Recreation Department head Olga Madar, was to give autoworkers' children basic instruction in civic virtues and duties through group activities in nature, to "teach them how democracy works — in the down-to-earth way that living with others in the out-of-doors can provide." No doubt, this experience carried over into the lives of at least some campers during the rest of the year and, with other influences, shaped them for years to come, leaving a legacy of interest in open-air recreation and support for environmental controls.[1]

In fact, the UAW's summer camp was only one part of a larger effort by the union to nurture environmental awareness among autoworker families. Guided by Walter Reuther, an outspoken advocate of environmental reform, the UAW took the lead among American unions in mobilizing workers to pressure local, state, and federal governments to make "a decent, wholesome living environment for everyone."[2] Union leaders as well as the rank and file lobbied public officials, provided critical testimony at hearings, organized neighborhood groups, exercised their electoral power, picketed public meetings, and did all manner of other activities to expand and enhance outdoor recreational opportunities, clean up and protect area waterways, and improve air quality. By the late 1960s, most of this work was overseen by the Conservation and Resource Development Department, also headed by Olga Madar. In particular, she promoted autoworker participation in the Down River Anti-Pollution League and encouraged women autoworkers and male autoworkers' wives in forming United Active Women, both established to address industrial pollution problems in the Detroit River and River Rouge.

By the mid-1970s, much of the UAW-sponsored environmental activism had ceased. After Walter Reuther died in a plane crash on his way to see the UAW's new labor education center at Black Lake, the union struggled with waning support among organized labor for better regulatory legislation and improved enforcement of existing control laws. Higher unemployment, rising inflation, deindustrialization, and a growing effort on the part of corporate capital to break the social contract established in the New Deal era weakened the will and ability of bureaucratized unions to advance a broader vision and work with environmental organizations. It is important to remember, however, that before the denouement autoworkers had drawn on some of their many objections to urban-industrial life to play a key part in making a modern environmental movement.

ORGANIZING WORKING-CLASS SPORTSMEN'S CLUBS

Initially, before World War I, some labor in auto plants was seasonal, with local native-born workers coming and going depending on the needs of their farms, not unlike the first wage-earning coal miners and loggers in southern Appalachia. After the war, when auto manufacturing companies were attempting to rationalize production, a contingent of workers still tried to have it both ways, growing crops and assembling cars throughout the year. Howard Green, for example, continued to cultivate his land in Potterville, north of Lansing, as late as the 1920s and 1930s while working at Reo Motors. "He would come home from work, jump on the tractor and go out after work and run until dark," his son recalled, "come back up and milk cows by hand and milk those cows, go down to Reo, work all day and come back out." Apparently, many other Michigan farmers did the same, and more than a few periodically left their factories to assist immediate or not so immediate relations when crops needed planting and harvesting, especially during years of hardship.[3]

By the early twentieth century, however, farming in Michigan was undergoing considerable change. Overproduction, declining prices, soil exhaustion, and lower yields, as well as various pests, including the wheat midge and Hessian fly, all combined to shrink the number of farmers in the state and force those who remained to take new, sometimes expensive approaches. There was an increased commitment to specialized, commercial production, more emphasis on efficiency, greater effort to reclaim wetlands, as well as more interest in purchasing purebred livestock and arable land.[4] "Once the small intensively developed farms, which had evolved through mixed husbandry, reclamation, dairying, and experiments with novel plant forms, gained a foothold in the rural economy," Glenn Worth Britton explains, "they began absorbing abandoned farms, the property of land-poor farmers, and other lands owned by farmers who were ready to seek occupations elsewhere." After 1910, when the census reported an all-time high in the number of farms, there was a steady decline, and the state lost more than 10,000 farms by 1935. Meanwhile the number of milk cows rose from 564,000 to 951,000 between 1900 and 1945, but the number of farms reporting dairy cattle decreased.[5]

At the same time, an increasing number of the auto industry's labor force came from beyond nearby counties, and, like Michigan migrants who had to leave farming altogether, these new workers were less inclined or able to lead dual lives. Like other industries in the late nineteenth and twentieth centuries, auto manufacturing drew its share of immigrants, particularly from southern and eastern Europe, although World War I, subsequent immigration restriction, and the Great Depression stopped or at least limited movement across the Atlantic. To make up the difference, car makers relied even more on native-born migrants from distant farms in the Midwest and South, as well as miners from the Appalachian coal fields. Unless they wanted to make a much longer journey home, if there was some family land to return to, these men and women had to bear the full brunt of factory labor without an immediate rural escape at hand, going to work in Lansing, Flint, Detroit, and elsewhere, at auto plants that were the quintessence of modern industrial change.

Not too long after the automobile's introduction in the early twentieth century, manufacturers had transformed the car from an expensive, custom-built plaything for a wealthy few to a standardized machine that even farmers and workers could afford, largely by improving efficiency in production. They found this efficiency by arranging auto production in a progressive sequence, introducing a moving assembly line to that sequence, and deskilling the labor required for putting cars together, significantly altering work in their factories through the introduction and modification of scientific management principles. As late as 1910, notes industry historian Joyce Shaw Peterson, most jobs in auto shops were skilled work, but by 1924 skilled workers were only 5 to 10 percent of all auto workers, an "envied aristocracy of tool makers, experimental room hands, and draftsmen."[6]

To be sure, wages for semiskilled and unskilled workers at the modern auto plants were comparatively high, starting with Ford's introduction of a five dollar day, the industry standard by the 1920s. Hours were not inordinate, with most employees laboring nine hours a day, or an average of fifty hours per week, and Ford ordered his workers into three separate shifts of eight hours each as early as 1914. The ample pay and relatively short workdays were matched, however, by the drudgery of mass production. Work was repetitive, monotonous, and dull, allowing little if any opportunity for self-expression, individual satisfaction, or demonstrations of independence. The pace of labor was also brutal and filled the autoworkers' hours with tension. Car manufacturers and suppliers used the assembly line, outright belligerence, and in some cases promised benevolence to speed up production. Management instituted draconian and often petty work rules as well, prohibiting talking, sitting down, and smoking, all enforced by supervisors' ever-watchful vigilance.[7] And it was these conditions, combined with a corresponding sense of alienation from nature, that sent tens of thousands of common factory hands to woods, fields, streams, and lakes to hunt and fish.

Michigan autoworkers were not the first to seek sporting escape in the outdoors, and they were also not the first to turn newfound hunting and angling interests toward support for conservation. They were preceded, in fact, by sportsmen from the state's elite and middling ranks, who had begun to increase in numbers after the Civil War.[8] Responding to the various threats facing fish and game at the time, particularly expanded market hunting, timber cutting, and farming, and seeking to satisfy other needs that had to do with eroding definitions of manhood and blurring lines of social class, these men founded a statewide Sportsmen's Association in 1876, whose membership "contained many prominent citizens of the professions, of business and of industry of that day." They then used the organization and local clubs to enact conservation legislation, outlawing certain hunting and fishing methods, establishing hunting and fishing seasons, and setting fish and game limits. To improve enforcement that was initially lax and underfunded the state legislature created a Department of Conservation as well in 1921.[9]

Still, the work of new fish and game wardens was not easy, in part because they faced a growing number of sportsmen, most of them workers. By the 1920s, Detroit was the fourth-largest city in the country, and populations in the surrounding cities and towns were doubling and redoubling, swelling to fill the need for a massive labor force.[10] Meanwhile, not only were circumstances inside the auto plants motivating new factory hands to seek rural escape, but social, economic, and political changes were enabling them to act on this pursuit. One critical factor, already mentioned, was the advent of the mass-produced automobile, which put cars within reach of many more people by dropping the price of a Model T from $1,200 in 1909 to less than $300 by 1928. That affordability allowed even unskilled employees at Highland Park or River Rouge to have access to state or national parks and forests, the Great Lakes and other bodies of water, as well as private lands hundreds of miles away.[11]

Another important change in the lives of workers, adding to the practical significance of their increased mobility, was the expansion of leisure time, or rather a steady reduction in the length of workdays and work weeks as well as the extension of vacation benefits. Although available statistics are not entirely reliable, the average work week of a factory laborer probably fell from about sixty hours at the turn of the century to fifty-five hours on the eve of World War I, then dropped again to less than fifty hours by 1920, and still more during that decade and the next.[12] This reduction was due in part to worker organizing, as in the case of Worcester, Massachusetts, machinists who demanded an eight-hour day to have time enough "for thought" as well as "to feel the sunshine" and "smell the flowers."[13] It also happened because of calculated employer benevolence, part of a larger effort at "welfare capitalism" by companies trying to increase productivity as well as avert unionization, to make pay, hours, and conditions moderately better in the interest of greater profitability and continued exclusive control of the workplace. In a few cases these efforts included paid vacation benefits. Henry Ford's 100,000 workers in Detroit, for example, received a two-week paid vacation during the summer of 1930, and by the eve of World War II, as the economy recovered from the Great Depression, fully half of all industrial wage earners received some kind of vacation benefits.[14]

With cars to take them out of the cities and more time off, workers interested in outdoor recreation of some kind had an ever-growing number of places to go as well. During the 1920s and the 1930s the federal government funded a large amount of road building, continuing the expansion begun with the Federal Road Aid Act in 1916, and tripling the miles of surface roads between 1910 and 1940.[15] This was matched by projects to increase the number of camps, parks, and other sites across the nation for the general public. In 1924 and 1926, President Coolidge sponsored two important meetings of the National Conference on Outdoor Recreation, both of which emphasized "the rank and file" or, as Ethelbert Stewart, the commissioner of labor statistics, put it, "the factory girl and factory man" working on assembly lines in shoe factories and slaughterhouses, doing the same thing over and over, in desperate need of relief from "industrial fatigue."[16] This emphasis continued under President Hoover and, of course, with President Roosevelt's penchant for joining job relief and conservation, many New Deal work programs dealt directly with recreational development for common people.

In Michigan specifically, working-class hunters and anglers were directly aided by the Conservation Department, which established a public relations bureau in 1929 to educate the general public about use of outdoor recreation resources by way of press materials, radio spots, lectures, and films. Subsequently, between the end of the 1920s and the start of World War II, the number of deer hunting licenses increased almost fivefold, the number of small game licenses doubled, and resident rod licenses grew from just under 300,000 in 1933 (the first year they were put into effect) to more than 650,000.[17] With more and more licensed hunters and anglers in the state, the Conservation Department began creating game refuges and recreation areas too. By the end of World War II, in the downstate part of Michigan alone there were thirty-four public hunting grounds and thirteen recreation areas (most parts of which were open to hunting), along with the Allegan State Forest. This made for a total of 117,000 acres of land open to hunters, depending on the season.[18]

As with so many other aspects of American life, World War II was a watershed in the popularity of recreational hunting and fishing, and this was no less true in Michigan than in other parts of the country. At the end of the 1940s, nearly 1.5 million state residents took to the fields, forests, streams, and lakes with rifle, bow, rod, or traps in hand every year, at least according to license sales. In 1948 Wayne County residents — including line workers at River Rouge, Highland Park, Hamtramck, or one of Detroit's many other car plants — purchased 274,800 hunting and fishing licenses, an increase of 22,000 from the year before. Genesee County residents — many of them employees at General Motors in Flint — purchased 50,000 deer and small game licenses, putting them second to Wayne County in the number of state-sanctioned hunters. And Oakland County, just north of Detroit and including the city of Pontiac, was second in fishing licenses, with 59,000 sold.[19]

The greater popularity of hunting and fishing in Michigan through the interwar years and after was enough to sustain a vibrant network of sports-men's clubs. Although a few of these organizations dated back to the late nineteenth century, more were founded decades later. Some of them, like the Macomb County Sportsmen's Association and Genesee Sportsmen's Club, had membership lists in the thousands, and they published monthly newslet-ters with an even larger circulation. Most of them were also willing and able to marshal their numbers and resources to guard and advance the interest of hunters and anglers beyond the county level.[20] To that end, in 1937 thirty-two groups from different parts of the state joined together to form the Michigan United Conservation Clubs. This new organization was headed by Vic Beres-ford, secretary of the Wayne County Sportsmen's Club (based in River Rouge) and chair of the MUCC's antipollution committee. Within ten years, it had 250 affiliates and rivaled the Michigan Izaak Walton League as a powerful voice for the state's hunters and anglers.[21]

From the start, workers probably were the bulk of the membership of the different sportsmen's clubs, at least most of the ones established after the 1920s, as recreational hunting and fishing began to evolve from an elitist pastime to a common laborers' escape. One indication of the groups' make-up is the advertisements in their monthly newsletters, which promoted such anchors of working-class life as bowling alleys, hardware stores, filling sta-tions, and grocers, in addition to the requisite placements for guns shops and stores that sold ice-fishing supplies.[22] Similarly, various columns included items advising members to support proposed legislation that would end bans on Sunday hunting, a policy that still prevailed in a number of counties across the state. Only a little more than half of the downstate hunting areas were open on that particular day of the week, editors of the *Macomb County Sports-man* complained, even though it was "the only day when many hunters can go afield."[23] Another article, published in 1952, considered the threat posed by "wealthy individuals and private clubs" buying up available outdoor lands and closing them to public access, denying "the common man of moderate means" a place to hunt and fish. And the sportsmen's associations aligned themselves with workers' interests in other ways to encourage and enable the participation of working-class members. The Genesee Sportsmen's Associa-tion, for example, held mid-morning meetings for Flint autoworkers coming off the second and third shifts on the same day as the regularly scheduled evening meeting.[24]

Besides having a blue-collar base and orientation, most of the postwar sportsmen's clubs also had a largely male membership, tapping into a long history that linked hunting and fishing to definitions of masculinity.[25] Even when women did participate in club work, they did so through auxiliaries that kept a foot firmly stuck in the past, promoting older versions of what it meant to be a woman and, by inference, what it meant to be a man. At the beginning of 1949, for instance, the Barry County women's auxiliary arranged a dinner to hear a Michigan State College botanist talk about flower gardening, the sort of lecture Lowell mill girls or Kansas homesteading women might have heard a century or more before.[26] Even when women were edging their way into what was once men's sphere, it seems, there were limitations. This ambiguity is especially obvious in a 1949 cartoon by Oscar Warbach, who often did didactic but humorous drawings for the Department of Conservation. The cartoon jokingly portrayed how people experienced their time deer hunting, based on their jobs, social class, and gender. In it, a male "auto worker" sits with gun at the ready, expecting game "to come by like parts on the assembly line." Meanwhile, a "housewife" stands over the deer she killed, calculating the meat to be worth ninety cents a pound, because "she can't forget the budget." Although at leisure and in the woods, it suggests, a woman is (or should be) thinking of her work at home.[27]

Working-class sportsmen (and sportswomen) evidenced social and political concerns of the postwar era as well, by the way some hunters and anglers folded the evolving Cold War into the meaning of their outdoor activities, making conservation a patriotic pursuit, if not a viable means to thwart totalitarianism. Several of the sportsmen's clubs included a "Conservation Pledge" on the banner of their monthly newsletters, adding environmental stewardship to the duties of citizens in the free world. "I give my pledge as an American to save and faithfully defend from waste," it read, "the natural resources of my country, its soil and minerals, its forests, waters, and wildlife." This sentiment was in line with one expressed in a 1949 *Kent League Sportsman* article, by National Wildlife Federation president David Aylward, in which he claimed continued enjoyment of "our freedom and security" was contingent on safeguarding the nation's "fundamental resources through wise management."[28]

From a slightly different perspective, a 1950 article in the *Genesee Sportsman* held up hunting and fishing as bulwarks against Communist plans "to eliminate competition from the pursuit of livelihood." The author, a member of the traditionally conservative Izaak Walton League, acknowledged the rightness of removing or regulating some of the contest and struggle in life, "to save certain individuals and their dependents from serious suffering which they do not deserve, and over which they have not control." But the "game" of hunting and fishing provided necessary balance, he argued, and as "long as the stage for competition is not completely eliminated we have nothing to fear." Bringing the argument full circle, and adding an incongruous element, preserving competition required support by sportsmen for "preservation of our natural resources."[29]

Of course, the basic, immediate reason members of sportsmen's clubs supported conservation was because they wanted to hunt and fish, but as the class and gendered and Cold War elements of this inclination to outdoor recreation indicate, their desires and their satisfaction were not always a simple matter. Likewise, working-class conservation consciousness was neither one-dimensional nor static when it came to understanding nature. In fact, within a few years after the end of World War II, it evolved into an avowed ecological sensibility that recognized intricate connections between living things and their environment (seeing nature as a whole) and assumed there was such a thing as a "balance" in nature (a reigning scientific idea of the day). Yet while this ecological sensibility allowed for criticism of people who disturbed a supposed environmental integrity by logging, farming, or otherwise extracting natural resources, or for those who polluted the air and water with waste products, it never evinced anything like misanthropic preservationist advocacy for wilderness. Human beings belonged in nature, often to use or manipulate it in some manner or fashion, and the question was how.

To some extent, the development of ecological consciousness among hunters and anglers was quite intentional, a result of efforts by sportsmen to educate themselves by attending lectures or reading books such as the Conservation Foundation primer, *A Conservation Handbook*.[30] Improved environmental knowledge also followed from observation of fish and game management and concerted attempts by the Department of Conservation to explain the agency's work. Club newsletters regularly serialized articles by the state game commissioner that encouraged broad perspectives. "Change any of the land conditions," one of the articles explained, "and a change is brought through the whole range of life forms from the lowest bacteria to the highest mammal." Complementing this official rhetoric were club members' own stated views, grounded in recognition of other basic ecological principles. "While man can do much to remedy the current fox problem," the Jackson County newsletter editorialized in one case, "the solution will most likely be brought about by Nature itself." This conclusion was based on the assumption that when "a wildlife species stands at its peak population, it is flirting with danger," vulnerable to an epidemic or other control. Still, the editors continued, the swelling fox population was there and immediately in need of limitation by other "wildlife resources" at hand, namely "in the form of recreation through hunting and financial gain through both hunting and trapping."[31]

Oscar Warbach contributed to the developing conservationist consciousness as well, by depicting idealized nature that often included the hand of humankind in various cartoons, many of which appeared in sportsmen's club newsletters and local newspapers. One explained that pheasants were primarily seed eaters and that they used standing corn for cover during the winter, a scene followed by a second frame showing a chef mixing various ingredients — soil fertility, food, nesting cover, and winter cover — to feed to a pheasant holding a menu reading "Habitat Improvement." Another cartoon portrayed game numbers as a matter of interrelationships between wildlife, with a fox, pheasant, and rabbit in separate little buggies driving through peaks and valleys to convey connected population cycles.[32] This and other notions provided a foundation for a broadening of hunters' and anglers' perspective and understanding.

Motivated initially by their principal interests in maintaining adequate fish and game, and guided by increasingly refined notions about the ways of nature, working-class sportsmen (and sportswomen) eventually began to demonstrate growing interest in addressing various pollution problems. They were led to this by their clubs, which provided organizational support for political mobilization, as a 1949 *Kent League Sportsman* editorial suggests. Echoing the remarks of a speaker at a recent MUCC meeting, the newsletter counseled members to rise above their "selfish motives" and become more "mindful of the public welfare." Hunting and fishing clubs have outlived their usefulness, it insisted, "if they [are] organized merely for the stocking, feeding and protection of a single species, without regard to their obligation to the public, without respect to nature and science, without regard to human rights."[33]

Apparently, this kind of rhetoric resonated with hunters and anglers, and during the years after World War II clubs became particularly active in addressing municipal and industrial waste in streams, rivers, and lakes. In Genesee County, sportsmen became increasingly concerned with the more heavily degraded sections of the Flint River, off-limits to swimmers because of a high bacteria count from untreated sewage waste and likely contaminated with production waste as well. In response, the local sportsmen's club president established a Water Pollution Committee. Likewise, the Kent League Sportsmen called on the city to build a modern sewage treatment facility before pouring $15 million into a new Civic Center.[34] And various groups not only expressed concern but also started a petition campaign after a large fish kill in the Kalamazoo River, caused by Union Steel's repeated release of cyanide into the water. In fact, this became the first case settled under a new antipollution law, passed in 1949, with the critical support of sportsmen's clubs and the MUCC, despite opposition efforts of "industrial lobbyists."[35]

Yet there was still much to do to clean up Michigan waters, as the water resources commission established by the antipollution law explained in a comprehensive report. Large parts of at least twenty-five major rivers in the state were so fouled by municipal and industrial waste that they were hazardous for "recreational swimming and allied purposes." Not surprisingly, this included the Detroit River from downtown to Lake Erie, the River Rouge from Michigan Avenue to the Detroit River, much of the shoreline around Lake St. Clair, the full length of the Saginaw River, and the Kalamazoo River from Albion to Lake Michigan.[36] To clean up these and other waterways, and to begin to address the equally pressing problem of air pollution, sportsmen would need the assistance of other organizations, and eventually they got help of that kind from the United Auto Workers.

FORGING LABOR ENVIRONMENTALISM

Although Michigan autoworkers established and joined sportsmen's associations as early as the 1920s and 1930s, they were much slower in building a labor union. Even in 1936, a year after the American Federation of Labor chartered the UAW, membership was a meager 30,000 of the industry's half-million workers, and 70 percent of those members lived outside the state, in Indiana, Ohio, Wisconsin, and elsewhere. After Franklin Delano Roosevelt's first reelection to the White House, however, and prolabor Detroit mayor Frank Murphy's victorious campaign to take the governor's seat, the situation began to change. In the spring of 1937, a wave of sit-down strikes swept through Detroit and points beyond, including every Chrysler Corporation plant in the region, and organizers steadily built on the gains they made. Within a few years, after an expanded organizing effort at General Motors factories in 1940 and a particularly hard-fought battle at Ford's River Rouge in 1941, workers at all three of the major auto manufacturers (and many of their suppliers) officially labored in UAW shops.[37]

During the war years, Michigan auto plants and other factories saw still more upheaval, when workers feeling squeezed by heavy production demands and high inflation organized thousands of wildcat strikes. By the end of World War II, though, much of the shop-floor militancy that had won the UAW a dominant presence was replaced by a centralized, bureaucratic unionism, a variety of worker representation that fit neatly within the social contract offered by capital and the state. As the Cold War evolved and anticommunist hounding increased, the United Auto Workers leadership also made a Faustian bargain for labor in general. Walter Reuther won control of the UAW in 1946, following a major strike against General Motors the year before, and after reelection to the presidency in 1947 he led an anticommunist faction in taking control of the Congress of Industrial Organizations (CIO). As the decade came to a close, Reuther worked with allies to purge communist and unaffiliated radical union leaders as well as whole unions from the ranks, and they consolidated organized labor's alignment with the Democratic Party.

Yet Walter Reuther, his brothers, and many UAW leaders were old-style socialists, even if they were unable or unwilling to tolerate the presence of other activists pushing for fundamental change in the American economy. Drawing on their ideological background, they had no hesitation in supporting much of the battered but steadily advancing and evolving liberal program, heartily embracing various social issues of the day and steering the union beyond exclusive concern with wages and hours, doing what they could to establish the infrastructure for a caretaker-type union. This social democratic vision was what led the leadership to lend so much support to worker education and recreation, which helped establish a foundation for developing autoworkers' environmental consciousness, and it was what drove them to position the UAW as one of labor's foremost advocates for local, state, and national pollution controls.[38]

The union had promoted worker recreation from its start, initially through the Education Department, and after 1939 through a separate Recreation Department sustained by dues allocations. Then, at the 1953 convention, delegates increased the department's funding and voted to require local unions to establish recreation committees of their own. Those committees, working with the department, organized "hardball" and softball teams, bowling tournaments, shooting clubs, ice-skating competitions, horseshoe tournaments, and social dances, and they built public-use playgrounds. The various initiatives were overseen by the Recreation Department director, Melvyn West, until he was succeeded by his assistant, Olga Madar, who held the position from late 1946 to the 1970s, even after she was appointed to head the newly established Conservation and Resource Development Department as well in 1967.[39]

Like West, Madar had a complex view of recreation, which she outlined in a draft of an article for the department journal some time in the late 1940s. Recreation was not just loafing or playing, she wrote, though it might include things such as "lying on a river bank on a summer afternoon, looking at the sky." Even activities some might think of as work were actually recreation. "Anything you do because you want to do it, without the dollar and cents reward," she argued, "that's recreation." Planting a vegetable garden or hunting for deer could be done for fun and relaxation, though they might also garner material rewards. And it was particularly important for autoworkers to keep this in mind, she insisted, because labor on an assembly line was less likely than most to satisfy inherent "mental and spiritual cravings," needs that had to be fulfilled for people "to become complete and happy individuals." The man who inspected bearings hour after hour, day after day, and the woman who attached fasteners on doors all week long were both lacking the chance to be creative, and that necessitated thoughtful efforts at recreation. What a union member did with their "pocketful of leisure hours," Madar finished, "will mean much of the difference between being a good and useful satisfied citizen in our democracy, or being an inefficient, discontented grumbler."[40]

Madar extended her philosophy of recreation to cover young people too, believing that the children of autoworker parents needed at least temporary escape from urban-industrial life to become whole, well-functioning adults, and she expanded the Recreation Department's program accordingly, including an annual union-run summer camp. This fit with a general shift across the nation. Like hunting, fishing, and auto camping, children's summer camps became more and more popular over time, their number growing from fewer than a hundred at the turn of the century to over a thousand by the 1920s, each a chance for children to reconnect with the wild outdoors. Yet, as historian Michael Smith explains, by the 1930s summer camps were increasingly regarded by their operators, as well as developmental psychologists, as "laboratories for figuring out the kind of socialization necessary for modern life." The point was not so much to repudiate civilization but rather to use nature as a restorative space where kids could more fully internalize important social values and better learn to function in civil society.[41]

This change in thinking was certainly evident when the Michigan Department of Conservation piloted a summer camp program of their own in 1949, establishing sixteen group camps around the state that immersed children in the study of fish, game, and forest conservation in the field from the beginning of June to early September. The MUCC and affiliated sportsmen's clubs could give nothing but praise for the initiative. "Your summer camps won't be a drop in the bucket compared to this," a former MUCC president told a group of educators from around the United States, urging them to come to Michigan to learn about the program. "These children are learning that the soil and water and woods and wildlife that God gave so freely to this country are theirs to use," the assistant secretary of the Wayne County Sportsman's Club reported after the first summer, "but to use intelligently so that others may also use it." They were also learning to work together and live together, he said, "and it is with them that America's hope for the future rests."[42]

Civic and social purpose was an integral part of the Recreation Department's summer camp as well, originally proposed in a report at the 1941 UAW convention, though not established until after the war.[43] In the interim, the union ran recreation-oriented "summer schools," organized camping trips for girls in cooperation with the YWCA, and oversaw the recreation components of a training program for union officers at the Franklin Delano Roosevelt–CIO Labor Education Center, eight miles north of Port Huron in St. Clair County, on the Lake Huron shore.[44] In 1946, as veterans returned home and the nation's economy demobilized, the UAW used the labor center for its first summer camp, offering three- and six-week sessions to 160 children from the Detroit area, both girls and boys, white and black, most of them referred by a social services agency, and many with their expenses covered by the union. That venture was the basis for launching a full-fledged camp for autoworkers' children the next year, again at Port Huron.[45]

The Recreation Department ran the second annual camp for two weeks in July, with a capacity for 125 children ages eight to fourteen each week, at ten dollars per week. In promoting the program to UAW local recording secretaries via a letter as well as brochures to display in union halls, Madar listed a variety of organized activities that would be led by trained counselors, including swimming, tennis, overnight hikes, campfires, softball, and volleyball. The brochure's cover emphasized the affordability of the camp, announcing, "Now UAW-CIO Members Can Afford to Send Their Children to Camp Too," since typically at least part of the ten dollar fee was covered by a respective local union, while the International subsidized the operating expenses. Inside, the brochure described the buildings and grounds, with a large dining hall, working kitchen, stocked and staffed infirmary, and canteen, suggesting a site and landscape that was far from wild. But there were also two hundred acres of woods with plenty of trails, as well as a good beach, a long stretch of sand on the lake. The idea, Madar wrote, was to give children a space "to learn to live and play together the CIO way."[46]

After filling the Port Huron camp beyond its capacity during both weeks, in 1948 the Recreation Department partnered with Toledo UAW Local 12 to operate a summer camp at their site on Sand Lake, in Lenawee County, Michigan, sixty-five miles west of Detroit.[47] The International again underwrote part of the expenses, but by moving to Sand Lake the union could host 125 children a week from June 19 to August 14, allowing more than 1,000 girls and boys to attend. As at Port Huron, they would have ample opportunity for swimming and boating, hiking and nature study, as well as various recreational sports, in addition to training in handicrafts, folk dancing, drama, and music. The group activities, parents were assured, were meant to give the children "insight into democratic living."[48] Attendance was not what had been expected, however, due to some confusion over registration procedures, and the Recreation Department decided to move the International-sponsored summer camp back to the Labor Center, even while Local 12 continued to operate their camp as well.[49]

Throughout the 1950s, then, the Port Huron camp hosted hundreds of boys and girls for four weeks every summer, with a consistent emphasis on social and civic development. It was important for children to leave their cities and towns for life near woods, fields, marshes, and beaches, one report explained, "to develop in the boys and girls a love and appreciation of the natural aspects of the world." At the same time, the more natural landscape was meant to be a site for instruction in effectively navigating modern urban-industrial life. "The day has passed," the report noted, "when camping should be regarded as primarily a way of release from the harsh realities of city life." Instead, the staff was instructed to observe campers' patterns of thought and habit, to encourage those with "social value" and discourage those that were destructive to the individual and society. "It is possible and highly desirable," the report suggested, "to develop altruism and the best ideals of democratic thinking in camp."[50]

Later, in 1962, the same year the newly formed Students for a Democratic Society also used Port Huron to draft their radical statement of principles, the Recreation Department was still running the UAW's summer camp with the goal of promoting social democracy. "It is the 'togetherness' of nature and wholesome group living," the updated brochure read, "that make a camp vacation a never-to-be-forgotten experience." The program, it explained, provided young people with "the chance to practice some of the beliefs and principles for which our organization stands." Besides typical outdoor activities, boys and girls prepared their own newspaper and participated in a weekly Camper's Council, "to give the youngsters a chance to express their needs and interests . . . in the total organization of the program."[51] Not coincidentally, these were skills and attitudes that helped sustain UAW support and mobilization for industrial democracy, racial equality, an end to poverty, and environmental reform.

In fact, by the early 1960s, the UAW was becoming the leading proponent among organized labor for improvements in environmental quality. Along with several other unions, including the Oil, Chemical, and Atomic Workers (OCAW), the United Steel Workers (USW), and United Farm Workers (UFW), the United Auto Workers forged what might rightly be called "labor environmentalism," even in advance of changing perspectives and approaches within traditional conservation and preservation groups such as the Sierra Club and the Audubon Society. The UAW was among the first organizations, if not the first, to call attention to the contamination of air and water both inside and outside factory gates. In that way, it played a critical role in spurring the development of modern, mainstream environmentalism, a movement that blended growing concern for the effects of industrial production and city growth on human well-being with political campaigns and social protest.[52]

To be sure, throughout the second half of the twentieth century there were many unions that expressed only tepid and ultimately expedient support for regulatory controls, support that quickly dissipated when the relationship between labor and management shifted within an industry or the political and economic context changed to seemingly force a choice between jobs and environment. United Mine Workers (UMW) leaders, for example, sometimes used environmentalist rhetoric, but plagued by rampant corruption they often colluded with employers to prevent substantive state intervention that would protect both miners and the general public. Even after reformers democratized the union in 1972, the shift from underground to strip coal mining put the new leadership in a quandary, and they blocked federal legislation to stop stripping altogether, a measure that would have saved miners' jobs as well as streams, woods, and farm land.[53] Likewise, the Teamsters worked hand in hand with California produce growers to hinder the organizing of the United Farm Workers, signing sweetheart contracts with landowners that did little economically for migrant field hands and did nothing to deal with their frequent, harmful exposure to pesticides. Subsequently, the UFW's efforts in the fields fizzled, while the Teamsters neglected to maintain their own influence, distracted with other concerns.[54]

This was not the story for the United Auto Workers, however, which had a principled and sustained commitment to an environmental reform agenda, grounded in the sporting interests of members and the work of sportsmen's clubs. Hunting, fishing, and other outdoor recreational pursuits of the rank and file readied them to recognize the ways threats to ecological integrity could do harm not only to fish and game but also to human health. Even UAW president Walter Reuther pointed to a love for fishing as the particular concern that drove his commitment to environmental advocacy. He had moved to a neighborhood outside of Detroit in the mid-1950s in part because nearby Paint Creek was teeming with trout, he explained in a story he told many times, and even as late as 1960 he had managed to catch a twenty-four-inch German bream there. As the urban outskirts attracted more and more residents, however, the antiquated septic tank system of an upstream community started to overload the creek with pollution and smother the various aquatic life, including the fish. Reuther responded the way he would have on the shop floor, by organizing his neighbors into a conservation association, which he chaired, working through the courts to force the offending community to install a sewage treatment plant.[55]

Later, in 1963, when the MUCC hosted the annual meeting of the National Wildlife Federation (NWF) in Detroit, they had NWF executive director Thomas Kimball ask the UAW president to be one of the main speakers. Reuther agreed and delivered a talk that addressed the particular concerns of working-class sportsmen, starting with the lack of parks and recreation areas for poor and working people, citing ongoing battles to establish the Sleeping Bear and Picture Rocks National Lakeshore Areas in Michigan. "There is a feeling of utmost urgency," he said, "in the war against selfishness, greed, and apathy in meeting the ever-increasing needs of the people." Drawing from his own experience, he also pointed out that thousands of communities were in need of new or improved sewage treatment plants, and he railed against the slow and inadequate efforts to abate industrial water pollution.[56]

The next year, when President Johnson delivered his "Great Society" address at the University of Michigan, Reuther was invited to be on the stage, not only because the two men shared a commitment to ending poverty and insuring racial equality, but also because they had a common interest in natural beautification and environmental quality. Following the speech, the UAW president made a point to invoke Johnson's words when he opened a UAW-sponsored 1965 conference on clean water, an event attended by more than 1,000 delegates from both the United States and Canada representing a variety of labor unions, sportsmen's clubs, environmental organizations, recreational groups, and civic associations. "A great society," he quoted, "is a society more concerned with the quality of its goals than the quantity of its goods." Reuther argued for the need to reject the marketplace as the only measure of good and to adopt a new value system. "We look at something much more fundamental," he explained, "the enrichment and the growth and development of the human spirit, and yet, if we go on as we have been going on, we will destroy the kind of living environment in which the free human spirit can flourish." To avert disaster, he argued, there needed to be a grand crusade, with people mobilized at the community, state, and national levels to fight for clean water, pure air, and livable cities, challenging recalcitrant governments and irresponsible industry.[57]

Not too long after the clean water conference, the UAW created a Conservation and Resource Development Department, headed by Olga Madar. "This was done," she later explained, "because our members and their families are directly affected by the environment around them, both inside and outside of the plants in which they work."[58] Madar even testified before a Congressional committee considering stricter air pollution legislation, declaring the UAW's support for emission controls on cars, in contrast to auto industry obstinacy and despite possible adverse impacts on employment. Autoworkers, she said, were "first and foremost American citizens and consumers" who had "to breathe the same air and drink and bathe in the same water" as other Americans.[59]

The union also attempted to generate community action by helping union leaders and common members initiate various environmental campaigns. Perhaps the most ambitious project in the Detroit area was the UAW-sponsored effort to establish a Down River Anti-Pollution League (DAPL), encompassing Wyandotte, Lincoln Park, River Rouge, and Ecorse, where working-class residents had long complained about local industry's impact on air and water quality. In starting the group, the union hoped to address everything from people's burning eyes and asthma to peeling paint and "blighted" recreation. To this end, in September 1969 the International Executive Board approved funding for two interns, Roberta Bowers and Hillel Liebert, both enrolled in the University of Michigan's School of Social Work, and it assigned them a number of organizing tasks that would carry over into the spring of the next year. These included locating union members in the area, becoming familiar with environmental problems there, developing relationships with local and international union officers, as well as building a DAPL steering committee and arranging initial meetings.[60]

Bowers and Liebert began their work with a tour that started at the Detroit Sewage Treatment Plant, on the Detroit River, where they heard about overflow problems, smelled putrid odors from an adjacent soap plant, and observed heavy black smoke from nearby Detroit Edison smokestacks. From there they drove to see more polluters, including Great Lakes Steel, which pumped a "frightening" orange-red smoke into the air, as well as others such as Wyandotte Chemical, recently accused of putting waste products into the River Rouge. And they toured residential areas in each of the four towns, making note of the fact that River Rouge and Ecorse seem to be more heavily populated by blacks, while Lincoln Park and Wyandotte were more noticeably white. Then, at the end of the day, they finished with a trip to a small park on another part of the Rouge, surrounded by soot-belching smokestacks and directly across from piles of some nondescript industrial materials. Clearly, Bowers and Liebert understood, there were plenty of environmental problems to tackle in the city.[61] Recognizing that fact as well, Olga Madar gave them her full support and assigned Conservation Department staff member Charleen Knight to give them assistance.[62]

In mid-December the DAPL organizers held two separate meetings for the four different towns, representing seven UAW locals. Bard Young, the director of Region 1A and a member of the union's executive board, called on autoworkers to attend these meetings by explaining the threat pollution posed not only to waters used for fishing, swimming, and boating, but also to drinking water.[63] In response, over 200 UAW members attended the meeting for Lincoln Park and Wyandotte (it is not clear how many attended the other), and both gatherings produced recommendations that were then used by a steering committee to develop seven action projects. These included picketing the Michigan Water Resources Commission's February meeting to demand stricter enforcement of water pollution law and organizing opposition to construction of an incinerator in River Rouge.[64] In April of the next year, Lincoln Park resident Joyce Vermillion led a group of DAPL women in marking the first Earth Day celebration as well, by staging protests at the Great Lakes Steel blast furnaces on Zug Island in the Detroit River.[65]

By the end of the summer, the DAPL had nearly 700 members, published a monthly newsletter, and held regular meetings at local union halls in the area.[66] Building on this growing strength, the league conducted a "community environmental survey," canvassing Wyandotte, Ecorse, and River Rouge in door-to-door fashion with seventy interview teams of about six people each, asking open-ended questions specifically focused on air pollution. Their results revealed much of what the group already knew—that residents considered air and water quality, racism and racial conflict, and crime and economic difficulties to be the most serious problems in their respective towns, with slightly varied responses depending on the racial make-up and income levels of different neighborhoods.[67] The group also participated in Downriver clean-ups, one in September that was sponsored by the Michigan United Conservation Clubs and drew more than 400 volunteers, and another in the spring, to mark the second Earth Day, attended by 200 people despite a weeks-long strike and chilly weather.[68]

At some point during 1971, however, the DAPL ceased to exist. The fact that various other UAW-driven environmental campaigns were undertaken throughout the late 1960s and early 1970s, though, suggests that the league's demise was not for lack of interest or support by area residents. In May 1969, for example, the executive board mobilized the membership to clean up the Clinton River and Lake St. Clair, both popular recreational sites north of Detroit. Locals posted handbills produced by the Conservation Department on their respective plant bulletin boards, soliciting participation specifically from "hunters—fisherman—boaters" and including a general call for the help of "UAW Families" as well. The images the handbills used evoked postwar prosperity, men and women leisurely riding bikes, boys canoeing, and a family cooking out in a grassy park, a standard of living within reach but for the trash and oil slicks fouling the river and lake. And this was an appeal members were apparently receptive to, as it generated a sizable turnout of

1,500 people for the spring cleanup, after which the union sponsored another outing at the end of the summer with the same response.[69]

The next year, at the end of August, a group of (self-described) "UAW wives" met to form United Active Women, led by Winnie Fraser and Jessie Dillard and assisted by Olga Madar and Charleen Knight. Their main purpose was to get involved in various consumer and environmental affairs, and, working within a tradition of "municipal housekeeping," the women designated water quality improvement as their particular concern. In October, they established several committees, including a "Womenpower" committee to handle mobilization and recruitment, as well as a legislative committee to track germane developments in the law at all levels.[70] At first they worked on pollution from high-phosphate detergents, which the Detroit City Council banned in the early part of 1971. With that quick victory under their belt, the women's group arranged bus tours to give folks a close-up look at smoke and soot coming from area factory smokestacks, as well as the waste chemicals and sludge industrial polluters brazenly dumped into the Detroit River. "Be the first in your neighborhood," they wrote tongue in cheek in their monthly newsletter, "to breathe Down River's famous hydrocarbons, sulphur dioxide, and carbon monoxide." They did, in fact, provide this opportunity to more than one hundred people, but, like the DAPL, United Active Women did not last long and had disbanded by 1972.[71]

BLACK LAKE

In the time between the organization of grassroots environmental groups such as the Downriver Anti-Pollution League and United Active Women and their sputtering decline, Walter Reuther decided that the UAW needed a new labor education center. He had not always been so fond of the Port Huron camp, which he once referred to as a "recreational slum," but the programming they did there was an important part of social unionism and something he wanted to continue. Accordingly, Reuther initiated the construction of a new facility in the midst of 1,000 wooded acres at Black Lake, a retreat meant to be "a thing of beauty where man and nature can live in harmony." The area was quite remote from Detroit, however, known as a summer refuge for the city's elite, and construction costs quadrupled as the work proceeded, causing dissension on the executive board. Still, by the spring of 1970 Black Lake was almost finished, and Reuther arranged to fly out to the site with the architect, his wife, and a few others a little more than a week after speaking in Ann Arbor to University of Michigan students on the first Earth Day and while readying plans for a major environmental conference at the new center that summer. On the evening of 30 April, as the plane came in for a landing it clipped a stand of trees and burst into a huge fireball, killing everyone on board and giving pause even to Reuther's sharpest critics.[72]

The environmental conference went ahead as planned, and throughout the first half of the 1970s the UAW continued to work at winning more regulatory legislation as well as bringing labor unions and environmental and conservation groups together to develop a common agenda. Madar and the executive board remained steadfast after the Clean Air and Water Pollution Control Acts were passed, and they lent the union's support to improving these laws and enacting others. In the spring of 1976, the UAW also hosted another gathering at Black Lake, titled "Working for Environmental and Economic Justice and Jobs," cosponsored by the newly established Environmentalists for Full Employment and the Urban Environment Conference.[73] Leonard Woodcock, the union's president, opened the meeting with encouraging remarks, claiming an unprecedented level of "common cause between union members and environmentalists — between workers, poor people, minorities, and those seeking to protect our natural resources."[74]

Still, all was not well. While attendance at the second Black Lake conference was good, only 57 of the 300 participants actually represented organized labor, and more than half of those were affiliated with the UAW. Woodcock's heartening address fell flat as well, in part because he greatly overstated the level of cooperation between unions and environmental groups. During the conference, AFL-CIO executive assistant Tom Donahue even scolded Friends of the Earth leader David Brower, explaining that organized labor was primarily concerned with protecting workers' economic interests, and only secondarily could it get involved in "social unionism." This was a shaky foundation on which to build a movement that treated economic and environmental concerns as inextricably linked. Not surprisingly, by the end of the decade, the labor environmentalism that autoworkers had worked so hard to build was plagued by division and neglect.[75]

6

A Landscape Foreign
and Physically Threatening

Southern California Farmworkers, Pesticides,

and Environmental Justice

Although cooperation between organized labor and mainstream environmental groups was faltering by the late 1970s and early 1980s, those same years also witnessed events that set the stage for formation of an "environmental justice" movement. Starting in 1978, Lois Gibbs rallied her neighbors in a Buffalo suburb after they linked pervasive, chronic illness in the area to toxic chemicals dumped in the old Love Canal, which had since been filled and used for a school. Gibbs then went on to establish the Citizens Clearinghouse for Hazardous Wastes in 1981 and played a key role in the making of an antitoxics campaign that was community based and confrontational, attributes that came to define the environmental justice movement as a whole. About the same time, in Warren County, North Carolina, local people banded together to stop the siting of a hazardous waste landfill in their community, a years-long struggle that injected the question of racial disparity into the fight. This point, buttressed by the 1987 United Church of Christ Commission for Racial Justice report, *Toxic Wastes and Race in the United States*, became a guiding premise for environmental justice activists as well.

What was beginning to happen, however, was not disconnected from the past. In fact, the environmental justice movement was rooted in the labor environmentalism of preceding decades, to some extent the sort pioneered by the UAW but even more so the variety promoted by the United Farm Workers (UFW). That union, the subject of this chapter, focused primarily on organizing Mexican and Mexican American field-workers in southern California, conjoining community organizing with militant tactics to address racialized economic exploitation. Among the primary aims were higher wages, improved sanitation in the fields, and better migrant housing. By the late 1960s,

UFW leaders also had developed a profound concern for workers' and consumers' exposure to pesticides, initiating strikes and boycotts on grapes and lettuce to pressure growers into contracts that included provisions for eliminating or minimizing the use of various toxic agricultural chemicals.

Not surprisingly, the United Auto Workers supported the farmworker campaign from the very beginning, both financially and rhetorically. Walter Reuther especially recognized its significance in the larger struggle for social justice and found common ground with César Chávez in the effort to protect field hands from environmental hazards. When the UFW marched in December 1965 to galvanize the Delano grape strike that had begun that fall, Reuther stood side by side with Chávez and, just as important, brought a $10,000 contribution from the International, promising $5,000 more each month.[1] Later, the UAW bankrolled *Brothers and Sisters*, a documentary film about "the timeless issue of poor people fighting [for] a decent way of life," as a UFW organizer who was traveling around the country to win support for a grape boycott explained to Ontario autoworkers. And in the spring of 1969, as the strike and boycott continued, Reuther wrote to the leadership of all UAW locals, suggesting their participation in International Boycott Day that May. "Strong unions have a responsibility to help the small struggling unions," he contended, "to obtain recognition and win decent wages and working conditions."[2]

The UFW campaign resonated with autoworker leaders as well as the rank and file because California agriculture was thoroughly industrialized, defined by what Carey McWilliams had called "factories in the field" or, as the organizer introducing *Brothers and Sisters* put it, "open air factories."[3] Farming had changed significantly in the United Sates since young women left the hills and dales of New England to work in antebellum textile mills, and this was nowhere more true than in California's Central Valley. In Kern, Tulare, Fresno, and other counties, orchards and "ranches" were thousands of acres large, specializing in fruit, nut, and vegetable monocultures worked by migrants for low wages, using the latest pesticides, herbicides, and synthetic fertilizers. The crops produced were first and foremost commodities, little different from a car or steel rail, fashioned by alienated labor, while the land that grew them was an alien thing as well, doused with poisonous chemicals as if it were an inert adversary.

In many cases, field hands who came to the United States from Mexico were in worse health when they returned to their villages and subsistence farms than when they left, and they attributed this to the pesticides they were required to use by growers. "These workers located disease not within their own bodies as germs or viruses," historian Linda Nash explains, "but in a landscape they found foreign and physically threatening and one over which they had little or no control." Workers even began to associate certain illnesses with specific crops. "My daughter gets swollen hands and feet, and welts, when picking tomatoes," Nash quotes one migrant laborer saying, and "my husband gets very sick at the stomach when picking the lemons and Valencia oranges." It was difficult to feel connected to the land, and particularly to the fruits of the land, when labor there led to such discomfort and pain. And it was in this context that the farmworkers' struggle was born and temporarily thrived, and the contours of a new, alternative environmentalism were formed.[4]

To be sure, by the mid-1970s United Farm Workers organizing was losing ground. Some growers signed sweetheart contracts with the corrupt Teamsters, agreements that released them from what they saw as burdensome restrictions on the use of agricultural chemicals imposed by the UFW. Others, never organized by either union, took full advantage of weak, poorly enforced state and federal regulations to apply pesticides and herbicides as they saw fit. Yet despite this failure, the farmworker campaign left an important legacy for environmental justice activists. It established a model for understanding disparate exposure to environmental pollution and other threats to human health, calling attention to the role of racial inequality and economic marginalization in making those circumstances. The union effort also demonstrated the power of local organizing and social protest to aggressively confront environmental threats as well, employing methods and tactics that were revived again and again in the 1980s and 1990s in communities across the country.

CULTIVATING MIGRANT RESISTANCE

California's industrialized agriculture was born in the late nineteenth century of the large colonial estates left over from Spanish empire building, a process that mostly bypassed any stage of small, yeoman farms. When the territory was granted statehood in 1850, the average farm size there was already 4,000 acres, more than twenty times larger than the average farm in the rest of the United States. In the years following, westward-migrating settlers managed to acquire small parcels, so that by 1900 two-thirds of all farms in California were less than one hundred acres. But large landholdings also increased in number during the same period. At the beginning of the new century, there were 4,753 estates with 1,000 or more acres, and according to historian Craig Jenkins, these "contained almost two-thirds of all farmland, accounted for one-third of fixed farm capital, produced one-third of all commercial crops, and provided over one-third of farm employment."[5]

The extreme concentration of land ownership in California was the basis for land barons' inordinate economic and political power, power that was essential to their making a profit from cultivation of various crops, mainly wheat up to the 1880s and then increasingly citrus. And profit was, after all, their primary concern. Large landowners did not take up agriculture because they loved the soil and sought their virtue there, but rather because it seemed to hold promise as a lucrative commercial opportunity. By the twentieth century, growers were profoundly separated from the land, physically and mentally. It was not a live thing that they mixed with their own labor for the subsistence of themselves and their families. Instead it was capital, to be used by workers overseen by managers running the operation in a rational way, to make a commodity to be sold on the market for a hefty net gain.[6]

Earning a decent return on their investment was, in fact, the driving motivation behind growers' wholesale shift to specialized crop production, as they swept aside biological diversity for controlled cultivation of particular monocultures that seemed best suited to the "natural advantages" in a particular area. They did this largely by expanding fruit and nut crop acreage, accomplishing a six-fold increase during the interwar period, from a little more than half a million acres to more than 3 million acres. As a result, Steven Stoll notes, by the 1930s California was the nation's leading producer of apricots, prunes, plums, table and raisin grapes, lemons, figs, almonds, and walnuts. At the end of World War II, the state also grew 50 percent of the oranges Americans consumed. Underscoring the extent of specialization, two-thirds of these oranges as well as the state's entire harvest of lemons came from only four counties.[7]

Southern California's soil and climate were ideal for fruit and nut crops, feeding them a rich, dependable mix of various nutrients and warm sun. The region lacked adequate rainfall for most types of farming, however, and that necessitated drawing water from somewhere else. The state's agriculture was a "forced plant," Carey McWilliams observed in 1935, "the product of irrigation."[8] This was true early on, of course, but in the twentieth century it was a matter of scale. During the New Deal era and in the decades following, the federal government came to growers' aid with massive irrigation projects and subsidies, which growers willingly accepted, despite frequent demonstrations of a strong penchant for "free market" rhetoric. The Eden they cultivated in "the desert" was hard won, and state intervention played a critical role.

Actually, growers depended on government in many ways to deal with the attendant risks of specialized monoculture production, risks that were especially exaggerated by the southern California brand of industrialized agriculture. Fruit and nut crop cultivation was highly capitalized, requiring permanent plantings, housing for migrant labor, packing sheds, and processing plants. At the same time the production cycle was inordinately discontinuous, and fixed capital investments stood idle for a considerable amount of time each year, putting a squeeze on growers by lowering the average rate of profit. The nature of the crops also put pressure on the growers, requiring them to exercise unchallenged control over labor. The tasks involved in growing and harvesting lettuce as well as oranges, lemons, grapes, melons, and other fruits, especially, could not be readily mechanized. Yet workers were needed only for short periods of time, and on a small and tenuous profit margin they had to be forced to accept low wages and meager amenities.[9]

At least for a couple of decades the federal government aided southern California growers in securing a cheap, temporary labor supply primarily by maintaining their easy access to Mexican migrant workers and supporting their often belligerent responses to union organizing efforts. Mexican peasants had begun to cross the border for fieldwork in the North after the Revolution of 1910, well before there was a border patrol, and their numbers increased greatly during and even after the first World War. In the 1930s, these migrants were deported en masse, but labor upheaval caused by Filipinos and newly arrived "Okies" and "Arkies" led employers to consider other sources for workers. After independence from the United States shut down the supply from the Philippines in 1934 and production for World War II siphoned off Anglos, growers had no other choice. In June 1942, they petitioned the federal government to establish what became known as the "bracero program," which allowed thousands of Mexican laborers into the United States on a temporary basis.

On the other side of the border, the Mexican government touted the bracero program as a means to modernization for the country's workers and, through them, the national economy. Migrants working in the technologically superior United States, Deborah Cohen explains, "would learn modern agricultural skills and be exposed to 'modern' values and work habits." They would also return to buy farm machinery with the money they saved, initiating the process of change on their own land and starting a ripple effect throughout Mexican agriculture. By this measure, braceros were "field soldiers," participants in a war of a different kind, who defended and promoted the interests of their country by going north with machete in hand to harvest cotton, beets, lemons, and other crops.[10]

While making arrangements for the temporary worker program, a U.S. delegation also agreed to the demands of the Mexican government for certain guarantees protecting the participants, including a "prevailing wage." In practice, however, growers' associations set the prevailing wage on their own, in advance of the harvest, and this continued when the bracero program was made permanent, after the "wartime emergency" had passed. With a ready source of cheap, temporary, and vulnerable labor, defeating union campaigns became that much easier. When the National Farm Labor Union (NFLU) attempted to organize farmworkers at the end of the 1940s growers used both bracero workers and violence to undercut the effort. Subsequently, by the time the program had reached its peak in 1959, the number of braceros had steadily increased to become nearly a quarter of the total farm labor force, while wages for migrant agricultural workers had significantly declined, to less than half of average manufacturing wages.[11]

The role of the state began to change, though, when John F. Kennedy captured the White House in 1960, and organized labor used its influence with the new president and his Democratic Party to weaken the advantage growers gained by using bracero workers. At the urging of Walter Reuther, the AFL-CIO had created an Agricultural Workers Organizing Committee (AWOC) in 1959 to make another attempt at bringing a union to the fields and orchards of southern California. To create a different context for this campaign, the Kennedy administration began enforcing the protective statutes in the agreement with Mexico and ordered growers to remove braceros from strike zones. In response, growers relied more heavily on labor contractors and expanded their use of undocumented workers, or illegal immigrants. When the Department of Labor disallowed growers caught with "mixed crews" from using braceros in the future, many simply withdrew from the program. Then, in 1964, Congress abolished the bracero program entirely. Conditions were still not ripe for a union organizing campaign to succeed, however, and the AWOC also did not have the right approach for the task, so the effort suffered the same fate as the earlier NFLU attempt. Meanwhile the number of Mexican migrants continued to increase. "By the late 1960s," explains Craig Jenkins, "green carders and illegal immigrants had become the new seasonal labor base, making up over two-thirds of the seasonal labor force."[12] From the growers' perspective, the problem of finding a large pool of reliable and pliable workers seemed to be solved.

Yet orchard and ranch owners faced other obstacles as a consequence of adopting and expanding rigidly specialized monoculture production, most significantly worsening infestations of crop pests. By greatly simplifying the ecology of natural landscapes they created the conditions for an explosion of harmful insects, and by responding primarily with synthetic pesticides the growers made their situation worse, killing off the natural enemies of increasingly resilient pests.[13] This put them on an expensive and vicious treadmill, one they were continuously encouraged to run with support from agricultural agents, university scientists, and the chemical industry itself. After World War II, manufacturers introduced a slew of potent chlorinated hydrocarbon and organophosphate compounds, including DDT, parathion, and malathion. By 1963, Linda Nash explains, "more than 16,000 pesticides had been registered in California, and farmers had become increasingly reliant upon applications of multiple chemicals."[14]

Evidence of the detrimental impact all these pesticides had on the health and well-being of workers was not long in coming, leading to a more concerted effort to study the problem. One of the earliest catalytic incidents happened in 1949, when twenty-five pear pickers became ill after exposure to parathion. This prompted the California Department of Public Health (CDPH) to investigate cases of occupational disease attributable to agricultural chemicals throughout the state, which they found to be in the hundreds, including two deaths. The department continued to collect statistics in the years following, and during the 1950s the number of reported cases tripled. By the early 1960s, even though much pesticide-related illness was underreported, agriculture had the highest rate of occupational disease among all industries in California. Most of the reported cases were from the counties with the largest number of Mexican and Mexican American migrants, particularly Los Angeles, Fresno, Kern, and Tulare. The great majority were also young men, indicative of who was migrating from Mexico for work as well as a gendered division of labor that put women in less jeopardy for exposure.[15]

Clearly, many of the respiratory, skin, and other ailments migrant workers experienced were linked to agricultural chemicals, which field hands frequently encountered on the foliage of various crop plants, especially because little about fruit and nut cultivation was mechanized. But as CDPH investigators learned, it was sometimes difficult to determine exactly how certain pesticides made people sick and equally tricky to determine the full extent of poisoning. Fields and orchards were part of an unpredictable natural world, not laboratories under the controlled conditions that industrial hygienists favored. Climatic factors such as temperature, precipitation, wind, sun, and humidity, along with soil and crop type, were important environmental variables affecting migrant farmworkers' toxic exposures, and changes in these variables yielded a wide range of results even when pesticide application rates were the same. "Toxicity was not simply a quality of a given chemical," Linda Nash explains, "but a relationship between that chemical and the environment in which it was applied." There were significant human factors that made accurate assessments difficult as well, including work styles and personal habits, the type of clothing workers wore (or did not wear), and the mobility that sent hands from one place to another in quick succession. Adding to these difficulties was the unequal balance of power between employers and employees, which made both braceros and undocumented workers reluctant to speak up for fear of losing their jobs and being returned to Mexico.[16]

Ironically (although not surprisingly), the attention that the CDPH investigation and other toxic-exposure studies generated was used to avert the threat pesticides possibly posed to consumers, even though few people eating oranges, lettuce, almonds, or other crops from southern California evidenced signs of ill-health. Following a series of hearings around the country focused primarily on persistent organochlorine chemicals, Congress passed a bill in 1954 requiring the U.S. Food and Drug Administration to ensure that pesticide residues on food products posed no health risks to consumers. Several years later, the public debate sparked by publication of Rachel Carson's *Silent Spring* was still narrowly concerned with banning or limiting use of chlorinated hydrocarbon compounds such as DDT. In response, sometimes with the explicit or at least tacit support of environmental groups, growers were forced to increase their use of organophosphates. These chemicals, developed as biological weapons during World War II, were less likely to linger on food products shipped to a grocery store or market, but they were highly toxic, were rapidly absorbed through the skin, and posed a greater danger to farmworkers. As a result, occupational disease attributed to pesticides continued to increase, or rather the problem actually became worse.[17]

In August of 1963, there was another major parathion poisoning after growers ordered unusually heavy spraying to deal with the oriental fruit moth on their peach trees. More than ninety pickers sought medical attention — a third of those were hospitalized, and one farmworker died.[18] Other outbreaks followed, with thirty-seven workers poisoned in five different instances in 1966, another group of peach pickers poisoned in 1967, and nineteen orange pickers seriously poisoned in 1968.[19] Perhaps even more insidious, however, were the cases of workers made ill by pesticides in ones and twos and threes, sometimes going to the hospital but just as often keeping complaints to themselves and working with considerable discomfort. Joe Alejandro, for example, regularly experienced symptoms from exposure to the wet and dry sulfur compounds that he applied at a Delano vineyard. Itchy red splotches and blisters formed on his skin, which scratching only made worse, and his eyes became red and runny. "The effects of both of these types of spray," he insisted, "take about a month to go away." Likewise, Francisco Mendoza, a Tulare County resident, became sick every summer during the harvest. "I get pains in my stomach," he explained, "I throw up, and I get headaches. Sometimes I get chills and have itching sensation over my entire body." While

Mendoza did visit the doctor a couple of times and took several days off work to recover, he was also used to laboring in fields with low-level symptoms such as blurred vision.[20] In fact, when the California Department of Health did a survey of farmworkers, 71 percent of the 774 questioned evidenced some indication of pesticide poisoning. This suggested that official reports of occupational disease attributed to agricultural chemicals were extremely low.[21]

Besides toxic fields and orchards, Mexican and Mexican American agricultural laborers in southern California faced poor working and generally deficient living conditions too. Whether undocumented workers, permanent residents, or U.S. citizens, none of the migrants had the basic protections afforded by labor laws, including the National Labor Relations Act, the Fair Labor Standards Act, the Federal Unemployment Tax Act, and state supplementary unemployment, wage, and hour legislation, all of which excluded agricultural workers. Consequently, they labored between fifty and sixty hours a week for less than half the average factory wage, with no guaranteed overtime pay, without the right to organize unions, and with no right to unemployment insurance when the work ran out.[22] Employment was also often contingent on obeying certain rules, many of them reasonable, such as a ban on drinking or doing "habit-forming" drugs on the job, others vague enough to be used in an arbitrary fashion, such as an injunction against the "refusal to carry out instructions."[23]

Housing for the migrants varied, running the gamut from moderately acceptable worker-run camps and *colonias* to dilapidated corporation and contractor camps. Nearly a quarter of the labor force lived in colonias, which had emerged on marginal land in citrus towns during the interwar years. These were collections of simple structures, usually substandard, but they were the centers of communities, surrounded by churches, stores, and other businesses, with space to raise chickens, goats, ducks, and pigs as well as grow corn, squash, chilies, tomatoes, and lettuce. Most important, they were independent of grower control. "It can be said that workers who live in these farmworker communities are freemen," one report explained, "free to choose new employment, free to move where they please without fear of retaliation."[24] Many more workers, though, stayed in grower- or contractor-owned camps of varying degraded quality, with high rents deducted from their weekly pay. Made of wood or tin, with weak and rotting wooden or bare concrete floors, this housing was not always water tight and was plagued by extreme temperature changes in the day and night. Lighting was poor or nonexistent, and ventilation was hindered by sealed windows. Toilet facilities were unsanitary, regularly without toilet paper, soap, or wash towels, and mattresses as well as blankets were torn or soiled.[25] Additionally, the camp housing gave growers a means to more closely monitor and sometimes manipulate their workers, much like antebellum mill owners in Lowell and late nineteenth-century coal operators in Appalachia.

For migrant laborers who hailed from Mexico, the abysmal working and living conditions in southern California were tolerable only because they expected to return home. The field hands left their villages temporarily to earn cash wages that supplemented and sustained semisubsistence farming, the preferred occupation of many Mexicans even into the 1970s.[26] Generally, they cultivated small privately owned plots or *ejidos*, hacienda land that had been broken up and redistributed to peasants after the 1910 revolution. On these lands, they grew a corn-and-beans polyculture, a varying mix of squash and other vegetables, sorghum, wheat, and barley, as well as fruit trees, all with traditional methods and tools. They did their plowing with draft animals rather than tractors and relied little on the hybrid seeds, pesticides, or irrigation works introduced during the Green Revolution after World War II. To be sure, in the 1950s and 1960s many Mexican farmers began to use commercial fertilizer, yet that was primarily to increase yields of subsistence crops. Their main concern was feeding their families and livestock, and only secondarily did they produce a surplus to sell in a market.[27]

The ability of Mexican farmers to make a living on small private plots or ejidos was threatened, however, by familiar demographic pressures. Like other people who derived their subsistence directly from the land, the peasants had large families with numerous children who helped with farmwork but who eventually grew up and needed their own share of a village's finite amount of arable soil, which could be divided and parceled out only through so many generations. As the problem became more acute, and Mexico began to pursue an economic policy of import substitution that opened up industrial jobs in the cities, some rural dwellers left the countryside for wage work in Mexican factories, while others emigrated as braceros or undocumented laborers. "I have six children," declared Pedro Sandoval when he was caught by the border patrol in southern California. "Since 1951 I have found it necessary to leave my family and have sought work here in the United States for varying lengths of time."[28]

Mexican migration was usually like this, transitory and repeated, one part of a household economic strategy that enabled a new and growing family to survive with at least some of their independence and more traditional way of life intact. "While the migrants are gone," social scientists Lucia Kaiser and Kathryn Dewey explain, "the women, children, and older people maintain the subsistence plots." Their comparative study of villages in Guanajuato suggests that the *less* a particular community's farming was affected by modernization, the *more* likely it was that men and some women in that place

would seek out intermittent wage work in nearby towns or cities or to participate in seasonal migration across the distant northern border.[29] The peasants'
recurrent mobility, which brought them alienated labor in factories or industrial orchards and fields as well as estrangement from the natural world, was
paradoxically a form of resistance to the larger economic forces transforming
people's lives, both north and south.

The other way they resisted, or at least lessened the hardships of migrant
work, was by joining with Mexican American laborers to organize. In the early
1960s, despite the two previous failed efforts by the National Farm Labor
Union and the Agricultural Workers' Organizing Committee, César Chávez
initiated yet another attempt to establish a union in the fields and orchards of
southern California, with some reason to think he would be successful. A
trend toward more-consolidated landholdings and further crop specialization
was concentrating laborers in fewer places and making them easier to reach;
the increasing proportion of Mexican and Mexican Americans in the agricultural labor force was creating the potential for a cohesive social movement
among migrants; and the eventual demise of the bracero program left growers
without their traditional means of overstocking the labor pool and breaking
strikes. Chávez also started his work in Delano, a major residential center for
Mexican immigrants in the San Joaquin Valley and the hub of the table grape
industry. This anchored the union campaign among an ethnically homoge-
neous, moderately skilled, and relatively less-transient labor force, since many
workers could find prolonged employment in local orchards.[30]

For three years Chávez focused on community organizing, creating the
infrastructure, cultivating the leadership, and developing the popular support
that would be needed for the coming fight. Then, in the fall of 1965, the
National Farm Workers' Association (NFWA) he had so carefully and steadily
built declared a strike against the Delano grape growers. Two years later, in
1967, the NFWA merged with the AFL-CIO's Agricultural Workers' Organizing
Committee to make the United Farm Workers' Organizing Committee
(UFWOC), and in 1972 the UFWOC became simply the United Farm Workers
of America.[31] In the meantime, the incipient labor union rallied grape workers with community events, solidarity marches, and ethnic appeals. Leaders
trained organizers from among the laborers' ranks, and then fanned out to
convince and mobilize their own, initially around the basic issues of wages,
hours, housing, and sanitation in the fields.[32]

Midway through strike the UFWOC also decided to focus heavily on the
threat pesticides posed to farmworkers and consumers, in part because it was
a serious concern for orchard and field hands and in part because it would
enable the union to broaden the strike's appeal among the general public.

With encouragement from César Chávez, volunteer nurse Marion Moses assembled a group of health care professionals, known as the Health and Safety Commission, to collect data on working conditions, particularly the extent and consequences of farmworkers' exposure to toxic agricultural chemicals, and to educate organizers and others about what they found. In the early part of the next year, 1968, the UFWOC tapped California Rural Legal Assistance lawyer Ralph Abascal to work on the issue from a legal perspective as well, including circulation of application records, lab analyses, and updates on lawsuits.[33] To draw even more attention to the cause, the union initiated an international boycott of table grapes, establishing boycott committees in major cities across the country and calling on labor, community, and environmental leaders to lend their personal and organizational assistance.

Unlike mainstream environmental groups of the day, however, the farmworkers' union had an expansive understanding of the dangers pesticides posed.[34] By associating this concern with the fight for collective representation and changes in working conditions, the UFWOC coupled human health to environmental integrity and presented the protection of both as a matter of social justice. In the minds of Chávez, Moses, Abascal, Dolores Huerta, and others, growers' intensive, reckless use of agricultural chemicals was inextricably linked to the balance of power between classes and the subordination of Mexicans and Mexican Americans as an ethnic group. "Motivated by profit," declared one pamphlet on pesticides, "[growers] continue to subject our people to systematic poisoning." The best if not the only real means farmworkers had to change this situation, the UFWOC insisted, was to join and build a vibrant, militant labor organization that could negotiate agreements with employers. "Only with Union contracts," the pamphlet finished, "can our welfare be assured."[35]

During the summer of 1969, contract negotiations with twelve growers faltered when they obstinately refused to give up exclusive control over pesticide application. "The Union agrees that it will not harass any employer regarding the use of pesticides so long as the employer agrees to abide by the regulations heretofore referred to," the contract proposal read, and "it will not embark upon any program regarding pesticides that can in any way be detrimental or harmful to the industry which the employer belongs."[36] Following this impasse, Senator Walter Mondale convened a series of Congressional hearings on the status of migratory workers, at which southern California farmworker leaders emphasized the extent of pesticide poisoning, the fate of injured workers, growers' control of the state courts, and their refusal to negotiate. Yet the next month the UFWOC had its first tangible victory, signing a wine grape contract with Perelli-Minetti and Sons that included a historic health and safety clause. This provision established a health and safety committee composed of union and employer representatives, prohibited the use of DDT, aldrin, dieldrin, and endrin, restricted the use of chlorinated hydrocarbons, and required a cholinesterase test whenever workers used organophosphates.[37]

By the end of the next year, the UFWOC had managed to bring most table grape growers to the bargaining table and compel them to sign contracts, 150 in all, covering 30,000 workers. These contracts provided a modest wage increase, established a health and welfare program, secured seniority rights, set up a grievance process, and, just as important, included an improved version of the Perelli-Minetti health and safety clause, giving workers the power to approve use of organophosphates, refuse dangerous work, and determine reentry periods for workers laboring in sprayed vineyards.[38] Not coincidentally, in June 1971 the California Department of Agriculture, long the redoubt of industrial agriculture interests, finally developed standard reentry time intervals of its own. These intervals regulated workers' return to orchards and vineyards sprayed with any one of sixteen different organophosphate compounds, a carbamate pesticide, or sulfur. The agency also oversaw the continued phase-out of chlorinated hydrocarbons DDT and DDD, canceling most (but not all) remaining uses.[39]

With what seemed to be gathering momentum, the UFWOC turned its attention to organizing southern California lettuce growers in the Salinas and Santa Maria Valleys, but that campaign was not very successful. Some of the growers had anticipated the move by signing sweetheart contracts with the International Brotherhood of Teamsters (IBT). These contracts did little if anything to lift wages or bring improvements in working conditions, and yet they kept the UFWOC out and filled the corrupt Teamsters' coffers with dues payments. At the same time, violence perpetrated by IBT thugs, the hostility of local judges, and agricultural laborers' continued exclusion from state and federal legislation governing union organizing all made it quite difficult for the farmworkers' union to make any headway. Then, in 1972, Teamster president Frank Fitzsimmons declared the IBT's intent to go after the UFWOC's grape contracts, which had increased to 180 but would expire in the next year. Subsequently, by the end of 1973, the Teamsters had 305 agreements with Central Valley growers, covering 35,000 jobs, and the United Farm Workers had only 14 agreements covering 6,500 jobs. On the whole, this development was not good for agricultural laborers.[40]

Besides their deficiencies in protecting the economic interests of field, orchard, and vineyard hands, Teamster contracts put few meaningful restrictions on the use of pesticides. The Coachella Valley Grape agreement, for example, included a relatively short clause in the "health and seniority" section requiring the employer simply to follow existing state and federal law. And in practice, with little real enforcement, IBT contracts did not even require growers to do that much.[41] Not surprisingly, pesticide use increased through the first half of the decade, from 116 million pounds in 1971 to 183 million pounds in 1973, although harvested acreage changed little during the same period. Reports of occupational disease attributed to agricultural chemical exposure went up as well, with an average of 1,500 cases a year, most of them among "agricultural service workers." Organophosphates, the more acutely toxic but comparatively less persistent kind of pesticide, accounted for 18 percent of the reports over all and 68 percent of the systemic poisonings.[42]

Watching all of this happen, both the erosion of UFW power in the face of Teamster collusion with growers as well as the unrelenting suffering of migrants from exposure to agricultural chemicals, César Chávez and his staff tried to reach out to mainstream environmental groups for help. Shortly after Earth Day in the spring of 1973, UFW staff member Ramon Romero wrote Environmental Action to request a list of other like-minded organizations that were supporting the Oil, Chemical, and Atomic Workers (OCAW) in their battle with Shell Oil.[43] With that list in hand, Chávez began writing letters to the various environmental leaders, including Brock Evans, director of the Sierra Club's Washington, D.C., office. "The unity which the union movement can have with the environmentalists is crucial to our survival," he explained, "both in a spirit of justice and in the literal sense." The UFW's record of using contracts to restrict the use of pesticides, he also noted, was a basis for that unity to flourish. Evans replied with great sympathy for the farmworkers' cause and claimed that sentiment was shared by others in the Sierra Club, since many had recognized "that it is the workers who are usually most abused because of pollution." But the rhetorical support was never translated into organizational action.[44]

Even groups such as the Environmental Defense Fund (EDF), which had long been at the center of national efforts to reform pesticide use, clearly had some steps to take before making common cause with the United Farm Workers. Toward the end of the summer, UFW staff member Chris Meyer complained to the EDF newsletter editor, Victoria Hays, of the publication's utter failure to mention the union's campaign to protect workers from agricultural chemicals. "While there is much concern for those who will suffer the long term effects of indirect contact with pesticides on the consumer level," he wrote, "farm workers are dying every day from direct exposure in the fields." The union's answer to this, Meyer explained, was to win bans on the use of certain pesticides such as aldrin and dieldrin through contracts with employers, rather than the "sluggish" and unreliable strategy of lobbying the federal government to consider canceling permits for those same chemicals, as the EDF was doing. "Surely," he ended, "the fight for a balanced environment and the fight for social justice and dignity are not unrelated struggles." This was stating the obvious, of course, but the fact that UFW staff felt compelled to make the point suggests that in many people's minds the struggles were still separate.[45]

CONCURRENT DECLINE

Stymied in their efforts to develop a broad-based campaign against lettuce growers, the UFW leadership decided to equalize the contest with employers somewhat by securing legislative protection for farmworker organizing. They quickly won this battle in 1975 with passage of the California Agricultural Labor Relations Act, which gave agricultural laborers in the state the same rights to form unions, bargain collectively, and strike that other American workers had achieved in 1935. The law also established the Agricultural Labor Relations Board (ALRB), composed of members appointed by the governor, to oversee secret ballot elections and contract negotiations. In the following year the UFW put ALRB services to good use, winning 173 runoff elections, compared to only 41 won by the Teamsters, which convinced IBT leaders to finally call off their competing efforts.

The labor board was ultimately overwhelmed with the demands farmworkers put on it, however, and strapped for adequate resources to do its work. The agency shut down most of its operations for a brief spell for lack of funding and only limped along afterward when funding was restored. This once again slowed momentum that had been gathering for UFW victories. Then, when a Republican governor was elected in 1982, he stacked the board with progrower appointments and cut its funding by nearly a third. Farmworker organizing suffered accordingly. By the middle of the decade, only 10 percent of the agricultural labor force in California was unionized, and most field, orchard, and vineyard hands lacked the extensive protections from pesticides the UFW contracts had previously provided.[46]

Concurrent with the UFW's demise, labor environmentalism suffered a steady decline as well, due to a potent combination of factors. For one thing, with the UAW's Walter Reuther dead and the UMW's Arnold Miller compromised, with Chávez struggling to steer his union around a myriad of obstacles and Anthony Mazzochi having lost his bid for the OCAW presidency, there was a lack of progressive leadership in the American labor movement, at least at the top. This leadership vacuum conversely made it more difficult for the rank and file to use their unions as a means for cultivating environmental-minded activism, while mainstream environmental groups did very little if anything to address the problem. Aided by a lack of organized opposition as well as by a sinking American economy, corporations also had an easier time making the argument that the choice between jobs or the environment was a mutually exclusive one. The so-called energy crisis, coupled with the beginning stages of deindustrialization, caused rising prices and high unemployment and weakened the confidence common people needed to push a broad agenda.

Yet among the elements of organized labor that showed concern for environmental issues, the United Farm Workers especially left an important legacy, one that helped shape the emerging environmental justice movement. The union's grape and lettuce campaigns revealed the connections between economic exploitation, ethnic discrimination and subordination, and environmental degradation. Likewise, they demonstrated the importance of putting community organizing at the center of environmental campaigns, sustained with militant rhetoric and confrontational tactics designed to alter the prevailing balance of power. In various battles throughout the country in the next two decades, most of them waged at the local, grassroots level, these insights and lessons were quite evident.

Even isolated segments of organized labor seemed to have learned something. In the mid-1980s, for example, in a revival of labor environmentalism, the OCAW took on the chemical company BASF at its Geismar, Louisiana, plant, one of many in a stretch along the Mississippi River called "cancer alley." During a five-and-a-half year lockout, OCAW staff built an alliance between community activists, mainstream environmentalists, and workers. They helped establish some new alternative environmental groups as well, including African-American Ascension Parish Residents Against Toxic Pollution, Louisiana Workers Against Toxic Chemical Hazards, and the Louisiana Coalition for Tax Justice (which challenged tax breaks for companies that generated toxics). In the end the OCAW achieved a partial victory, with a new contract that kept the union and reinstated a third of the locked-out workers.[47]

Conclusion

In its most basic form work is the transformation of nature. To produce both food and shelter, as well as countless other goods and amenities as needs and wants evolve over time, human beings must change parts of the natural world around them. This continuous use of the physical and organic environment, and the remaking of self and communities that it necessarily entails, is the core element of human history, a materialist basis for change and continuity in the past. It conditions and is in turn affected by the evolution of social relations, technological innovations, demographic variation, and geographic mobility. "By producing their means of subsistence," Karl Marx and Friedrich Engels explained in *The German Ideology*, "men [and presumably they would now include women] are indirectly producing their actual material life." They are also, in early stages of social development, making the many diverse elements of culture. "The production of ideas, of conceptions, of consciousness," the two philosophers continued, "is at first directly interwoven with the material activity and the material intercourse of men, the language of real life."[1]

Yet what implications do these fundamental truths have for understanding people's relationship with nature? In the early nineteenth century, Henry David Thoreau had his own answer. "Fishermen, hunters, woodchoppers, and others," he wrote in *Walden*, "spending their lives in the fields and woods, in a peculiar sense a part of Nature themselves, are often in a more favorable mood for observing her, in the intervals of their pursuits, than philosophers or poets even, who approach her with expectation." By their work they were in a privileged position to know the streams and woods and their other inhabitants. "We are most interested when science reports what those men already know practically or instinctively," Thoreau claimed, "for that alone is a true *humanity*, or account of human experience."[2]

In these and other similar musings, Concord's famous eccentric might not have stated an absolute fact, but the underlying motive for his remarks was consistent and sound. The mills and factories appearing along the waterways of New England, and concurrent, related changes in farming, were transforming the ways his neighbors and distant countrymen knew and used the environment. Thoreau was very much worried about this, and it inclined him to idealize other ways of making a living, holding them up as a foil to condemn how the countryside, its inhabitants, and intercourse between the two were being altered. "By avarice and selfishness, and a groveling habit, from which none of us is free, or regarding the soil as property, or the means of acquiring property chiefly," he wrote elsewhere in *Walden*, "the landscape is deformed, husbandry is degraded with us, and the farmer leads the meanest of lives. He knows Nature but as a robber."[3]

The trends that inspired Henry David Thoreau to wax eloquent only intensified in the decades and century to follow. The transformation of labor power into a commodity, and sustained efforts to turn all of nature into the same, profoundly and adversely affected the content and purpose of various people's work as well as their relationship with the land, water, and air around them. This happened, of course, by twists and turns. Whatever the limitations of wage work and sharecropping, the lives of African Americans in the Mississippi Delta were certainly improved by emancipation from slavery. Homesteader women in Kansas and Nebraska, to cite another example, started the settlement process with generally antagonistic attitudes about the "wild" grasslands and did not fully develop a sense of connection to that landscape until they acquired the trappings of modern life and industrial notions about domestic economy. In many if not most cases, however, and perhaps even more so over the long run, industrial capitalism caused workers to suffer both economic exploitation and estrangement from the natural world. As the nineteenth and twentieth centuries progressed, many also found themselves living in environments polluted and poisoned by the very industries that gave them their jobs.

Through it all, textile mill operatives, coal miners, migrant field hands, and others devised means of accommodation and resistance, drawing on inherited traditions, values, and beliefs as well as developing new ones. Working-class literary romanticism gave expression to operatives' complicated longings for rural homesteads and soothed their dissatisfaction with the urban-industrial environment of Lowell and other antebellum factory towns. Hunting and fishing retained its social significance for freedpeople in the Delta and coal miners in southern Appalachia, while it became something more among Michigan autoworkers, who established and joined sportsmen's clubs that pioneered modern environmental reform. Workers also channeled their disquiet by organizing unions, mobilizing politically, and waging strikes. The Lowell mill girls made a first attempt at this during a couple of turnouts in the 1830s and 1840s, and, after a long interlude, in the twentieth century organized labor became at least a moderately effectual vehicle for addressing the environmental effects of industrial production.

Now, however, in the early twenty-first century, it is difficult for unions to play a leading role in mainstream environmentalism and the environmental justice movement. There are flashes of inspired cooperation, such as the Steelworkers' Redwood campaign and the "Teamsters and turtles" at the World Trade Organization protests in Seattle, but these are often born from the defensive posture of the American labor movement as much as anything else. Union density in the United States is at an all-time low of 12 percent of the nonagricultural labor force, down from 35 percent in the middle of the 1950s, and the situation becomes more dire every year. Even the Change to Win coalition, a set of unions that recently broke from the AFL-CIO, seems to lack a truly different vision, besides that of pouring more resources into organizing. In this present context, then, the future of labor environmentalism is uncertain.

Notes

INTRODUCTION

1 Henry Ford, *My Life and Work* (1922; reprint, New York: Arno Press, 1973), 1–2.

2 Ibid., 15, 103, 105.

3 "The Director's Corner," Folder "Recreation Reports, 1945–1948," Box 2, Recreation Department Collection, United Auto Workers, Archives of Labor and Urban Affairs, Wayne State University, Detroit, Mich. (hereafter cited as UAW Recreation Collection). See also Olga Madar, "What the UAW Is Doing about Recreation" (1959), Folder "History of the Department and Program Guides, ca. 1958–Mar 1960," Box 2, UAW Recreation Collection.

4 Lisa Fine, "Rights of Men, Rites of Passage: Hunting and Masculinity at Reo Motors of Lansing, Michigan, 1945–1975," *Journal of Social History* 33 (Summer 2000), 806.

5 Carl Hubert, "Bluntly Speaking," *Bowhunter* (September 1953), Folder 3, "Occasional Issues of Out-of-Print Periodicals Devoted to Michigan Sports and Conservation, 1933–1965," State Archives of Michigan, Lansing, Mich. (hereafter cited as SCP Collection).

6 Karl Marx, *Pre-Capitalist Economic Formations* (New York: International Publishers, 2000), 86–87.

7 Robert Gottlieb, *Forcing the Spring: The Transformation of the American Environmental Movement* (Washington, D.C.: Island Press, 1993); Jim Schwab, *Deeper Shades of Green: The Rise of Blue-Collar and Minority Environmentalism in America* (San Francisco: Sierra Club Books, 1994); Rosemary Feurer, "River Dreams: St. Louis and the Fight for a Missouri Valley Authority," in *Common Fields: An Environmental History of St. Louis*, ed. Andrew Hurley (Lawrence: University Press of Kansas, 1997), 221–41; Robert Gordon, "Poisons in the Fields: The United Farm Workers, Pesticides, and Environmental Politics," *Pacific Historical Review* 68 (February 1999): 51–77; and Gordon, "'Shell No!': OCAW and the Labor-Environmental Alliance," *Environmental History* 3 (October 1998): 460–87; ; Scott Dewey, "Working for the Environment: Organized Labor and the Origins of Environmentalism in the United States, 1948–1970," *Environmental History* 3 (January 1998): 45–63. See also Robert Gor-

don, "Environmental Blues: Working-Class Environmentalism and the Labor-Environmental Alliance," (Ph.D. diss., Wayne State University, 2004).

8 Andrew Hurley, *Environmental Inequalities: Class, Race, and Industrial Pollution in Gary, Indiana, 1945–1980* (Chapel Hill: University of North Carolina Press, 1995), xiv.

9 Laura Pulido, *Environmentalism and Economic Justice* (Tucson: University of Arizona Press, 1996); Chad Montrie, "Expedient Environmentalism: Opposition to Coal Surface Mining in Appalachia and the United Mine Workers of America, 1945–1977," *Environmental History* 5 (January 2000): 75–98; and Montrie, *To Save the Land and People: A History of Opposition to Surface Coal Mining in Appalachia* (Chapel Hill: University of North Carolina Press, 2003). See also Benjamin Heber Johnson, "Conservation, Subsistence, and Class at the Birth of Superior National Forest," *Environmental History* 4 (January 1999): 80–99.

10 Richard Judd, *Common Lands, Common People: The Origins of Conservation in Northern New England* (Cambridge: Harvard University Press, 1997).

11 Karl Jacoby, *Crimes Against Nature: Squatters, Poachers, Thieves, and the Hidden History of American Conservation* (Berkeley: University of California Press, 2001), 3.

12 White, Richard, "'Are You an Environmentalist or Do You Work for a Living?': Work and Nature," in *Uncommon Ground: Rethinking the Human Place in Nature*, ed. William Cronon (New York: W. W. Norton, 1996), 182. See also Richard White, *The Organic Machine* (New York: Hill and Wang, 1995).

13 Kathryn Morse, *The Nature of Gold: An Environmental History of the Klondike Gold Rush* (Seattle: University of Washington Press, 2003), 8, 14.

14 Laurie Mercier, *Anaconda: Labor, Community, and Culture in Montana's Smelter City* (Urbana: University of Illinois Press, 2001).

15 Thomas G. Andrews, "The Road to Ludlow: Work, Environment, and Industrialization, 1870–1915" (Ph.D. diss., University of Wisconsin-Madison, 2003); and Andrews, "'Made by Toile'? Tourism, Labor, and the Construction of the Colorado Landscape, 1858–1917," *Journal of American History* 92 (December 2005): 837–63.

16 Alan Derickson, *Black Lung: Anatomy of a Public Health Disaster* (Ithaca, N.Y.: Cornell University Press, 1998); Barbara Smith, *Digging Our Own Graves: Coal Miners and the Struggle over Black Lung Disease* (Philadelphia: Temple University Press, 1987). On workplace health and safety see as well Christopher Sellers, *Hazards of the Job: From Industrial Disease to Environmental Science* (Chapel Hill: University of North Carolina Press, 1997). This book made the case for the origins of environmental science in early investigations by industrial hygienists, contending that the scientific foundation of modern environmental consciousness has its roots in their attempts to address various workplace problems.

17 Karl Marx and Frederick Engels, *The German Ideology* (New York: International Publishers, 2001), 42, 49.

18 Bertell Ollman, *Alienation: Marx's Conception of Man in Capitalist Society* (Cambridge: Cambridge University Press, 1976), 98–99.

19 Stephen Meyer, *The Five Dollar Day: Labor Management and Social Control in the Ford Motor Company, 1908–1921* (Albany: State University of New York Press, 1981), 40; David Montgomery, *The Fall of the House of Labor: The Workplace, the State, and American Labor Activism, 1865–1925* (Cambridge: Cambridge University Press, 1987).

20 Donald Worster, *Dust Bowl: The Southern Plains in the 1930s* (New York: Oxford University Press, 1979), 7; Theodore Steinberg, *Nature Incorporated: Industrialization and the Waters of New England* (Amherst: University of Massachusetts Press, 1991), 12.

CHAPTER I

1 Sarah G. Bagley writing in *Lowell Offering*, December 1840, in Philip S. Foner, ed., *The Factory Girls: A Collection of Writings on Life and Struggles in the New England Factories of the 1840s* (Urbana: University of Illinois Press, 1977), 36–37.

2 Lucy Larcom, *A New England Girlhood: Outline from Memory* (1889; reprint, Boston: Northeastern University Press, 1986), 162–63.

3 The "mill girl" literature is extensive, but no historian has yet examined mill labor as part of the changing relationship between common people and the environment. For representative examples, three of the most important works, see Hannah Josephson, *The Golden Threads: New England's Mill Girls and Magnates* (New York: Duell, Sloan and Pearce, 1949); Thomas Dublin, *Women at Work: The Transformation of Work and Community in Lowell, Massachusetts, 1826–1860* (New York: Columbia University Press, 1979); and Theodore Steinberg, *Nature Incorporated: Industrialization and the Waters of New England* (Amherst: University of Massachusetts Press, 1991).

4 Harold Fisher Wilson, *The Hill Country of Northern New England: Its Social and Economic History* (New York: AMS Press, 1967), 19, 23–24; Richard Judd, *Common Lands, Common People: The Origins of Conservation in Northern New England* (Cambridge: Harvard University Press, 1997), 16–17, 32.

5 Norman W. Smith, "A Mature Frontier: The New Hampshire Economy, 1790–1850," *Historical New Hampshire* 24 (Fall 1969), 5.

6 Malenda Edwards to Sabrina Bennett, 18 August 1845, in Thomas Dublin, ed., *Farm to Factory: Women's Letters, 1830–1860* (New York: Columbia University Press, 1981), 85–86.

7 Alice Morse Earle, *Home Life in Colonial Days* (1898; reprint, Stockbridge, Mass.: Berkshire Traveller Press, 1974), 254–55.

8 Tryphena Ely White, 7 July and 19 July 1805, in *Tryphena Ely White's Journal* (New York: Grafton Press, 1904), 22, 25; Catherine Beecher, *A Treatise on Domestic Economy* (1841; reprint, New York: Schocken Books, 1977), 309, 327.

9 Earle, *Home Life*, 37–39; Beecher, *Treatise*, 306–7; Rolla Milton Tryon, *Household Manufactures in the United States, 1640–1860* (New York: August M. Kelley, 1966), 232.

10 Earle, *Home Life*, 166–74, 193–202; Lydia Maria Child, *The American Frugal Housewife* (Mineola, N.Y.: Dover Publications, 1999), 38–40; Tryon, *Household Manufactures*, 191–212.

11 Sarah Anna Emery, *Reminiscences of a Nonagenarian* (Newburyport, [Mass.]: William H. Huse, 1879), 7.

12 *New England Farmer*, 10 August 1822, 12; Olive Sawyer to Sabrina Bennett, 15 May 1839, in Dublin, *Farm to Factory*, 65.

13 Earle, *Home Life*, 257–59.

14 Sally Brown, 18, 19, and 21 March and 2 December 1832, in *The Diaries of Sally and*

Pamela Brown, 1832–38, ed. Blanche Brown Bryant and Gertrude Elaine Baker (Springfield, Vt.: William S. Bryant Foundation, 1970), 11.

15 4 June 1832, in ibid., 13; 26 June 1805, in White, *Journal*, 19.

16 Emery, *Reminiscences*, 28–29.

17 24 June 1805, in White, *Journal*, 18–19.

18 18 and 20 May 1819 and 20 May 1820, Anna Blackwood Howell Diaries, 1819–1839, Octavo Volumes "H," American Antiquarian Society, Worcester, Mass.

19 13 and 19 May and 26 June 1821, ibid.

20 Emery, *Reminiscences*, 28–29.

21 3 July 1805, in White, *Journal*, 20–21.

22 17 September 1832, in Bryant and Baker, *Diaries*, 21; Child, *American Frugal Housewife*, 25.

23 John Warner Barber, *Historical Collections* (Worcester, Mass.: Dorr, Howland, 1839), 404.

24 Rev. Henry A. Miles, *Lowell, As It Was, and As It Is* (Lowell, Mass.: Nathaniel L. Dayton, 1846), 12.

25 Steinberg, *Nature Incorporated*, 3, 52–61.

26 "Lucinda," "Abbey's Year in Lowell," *Lowell Offering* (1841), 1:1. The page numbers listed here and in other notes for the *Offering* refer to the bound volumes published in Westport, Connecticut, by the Greenwood Reprint Corporation, 1970.

27 Nell Kull, ed., " 'I Can Never Be Happy There in Among So Many Mountains': The Letters of Sally Rice," *Vermont History* 38 (Winter 1970), 52.

28 Harriet Farley, *Operatives' Reply to Hon. Jere. Clemens, Being a Sketch of Factory Life and Factory Enterprise and a Brief History of Manufacturing by Machinery* (Lowell, Mass.: S. J. Varney, 1850), 3, 9–10.

29 Mary H. Blewett, ed., *Caught Between Two Worlds: The Diary of a Lowell Mill Girl, Susan Brown of Epsom, New Hampshire* (Lowell, Massachusetts: Lowell Museum, 1984), 14.

30 Larcom, *New England Girlhood*, 182.

31 "Ella" [Harriet Farley], "A Weaver's Reverie," *Lowell Offering* (1841), 1:188–89. For a short list of pseudonyms used by *Lowell Offering* authors see *Lowell Offering* (1845), 4:1–3.

32 *Voice of Industry*, 3 December 1847, in Foner, *Factory Girls*, 92–93.

33 Permielia Dame to George Dame, 25 January 1835, Dame Family Papers, 1824–1951, New Hampshire Historical Society, Concord, N.H.

34 Dublin, *Women at Work*, 62, 64–65, 68.

35 *Voice of Industry*, 11 December 1846, 4.

36 Larcom, *New England Girlhood*, 162–64.

37 Patrick Malone and Chuck Parrott, "Greenways in the Industrial City: Parks and Promenades along the Lowell Canals," *Journal of the Society for Industrial Archaeology* 24, no. 1 (1998): 19–24, 27; Alan S. Emmet, "Open Space in Lowell, 1826–1886" (research paper, Center for Lowell History, 1975), 8–9; Maria Currier, "Shade Trees," *Lowell Offering* (1841), 1:233.

38 Lydia Sarah Hall, "Lowell Cemetery," *Lowell Offering* (1841), 1:186.

39 "V. C. N.," "A Morning Walk," *Operatives Magazine* 3 (June 1841): 47.

40 "E. C. T.," "Journey to Lebanon Springs," *Lowell Offering* (1842), 2:191.

41 Sarah Bagley, "Letter from Mount Washington House," *New England Offering* (November 1848): 171.

42 "Annette," *New England Farmer*, 11 August 1841, 42.

43 Harriet H. Robinson, *Loom and Spindle, or Life Among the Early Mills Girls* (1898; reprint, Kailu, Hawaii: Press Pacifica, 1976), 28, 40–41, 56–57.

44 Josephson, *Golden Threads*, 84, 91.

45 "Francine," "The Scenes of Nature," *Operatives Magazine* 2 (May 1841): 23.

46 "Anneline," "Evidence of Design in Nature," *Lowell Offering* (1842–43), 3:32–3.

47 "M. R. G.," "Address to Spring," *Lowell Offering* (1843–44), 4:159.

48 "Everes," "American Forest Scenery," *Operatives Magazine* 1 (April 1841): 1. This is from the first article in the first issue of the first number.

49 "J. S. W.," "Need of a Revelation," *Lowell Offering* (1843–44), 4:81.

50 Huldah J. Stone, "Improvement of Time," *Voice of Industry*, 7 August 1845, 2.

51 "Amanda," "Earth — A Scene of Pleasure," *Operatives Magazine* 4 (July 1841): 62.

52 "Adelaide," "Alone with Nature," *Operatives Magazine* 3 (June 1841): 37.

53 "Mary," *Voice of Industry*, 12 June 1846, 3.

54 Elizabeth Emerson Turner, "Childhood's Home," *Lowell Offering* (1841), 1:68–69.

55 Betsey Chamberlain, "Recollections of My Childhood," *Lowell Offering* (1841), 1:78–79.

56 "V.," "Love of Home," *Operatives Magazine* 2 (May 1841): 21.

57 "Clementine," "The Scenes of Nature," *Operatives Magazine* 2 (May 1841): 29.

58 "E. D.," "Thoughts on Home," *Lowell Offering* (1842–43), 3:280.

59 "T*****," "Factory Girl's Reverie," *Lowell Offering* (1845), 5:140.

60 Caroline Whitney, "My Mountain Home," *New England Offering* (September 1849): 205.

61 "S. A. M.," "My Mountain Home," *Operatives Magazine* 8 (November 1841): 115.

62 "The Lowell Factory Girl" in Foner, *Factory Girls*, 6–9.

63 J. R., *Voice of Industry*, 23 October 1846, 4.

64 Huldah J. Stone, *Voice of Industry*, 8 May 1846, 3.

65 Larcom, *New England Girlhood*, 88–89, 106–7.

66 Ibid., 186–87, 188–89, 194–95.

67 Josephson, *Golden Threads*, 23.

68 *Lowell (Mass.) Courier*, 4 April 1840, 2.

69 Malone and Parrott, "Greenways in the Industrial City," 19, 24.

70 *New England Farmer*, 23 July 1834, 16. For another example there is Knickerbocker's "Our Mountain and Valleys," from *New England Farmer*, 25 September 1839, 108:

> The mountains and valleys wide,
> Of our dear native land;
> In all their bright green loveliness,
> How gloriously they stand!
> The white clouds built on azure skies,
> Like palaces and towers,
> The spanning rainbow's brilliant arch,

Formed of the sun and showers!
The creeping breeze that floats in waves,
Far o'er the flowers rye,
And purple hills, with clover buds,
Reposing blushingly:
Rich are the fields with bearded grain,
Where the broad valleys run,
To meet the mountain ramparts blue,
Gilt by the cheerful sun . . .
'Tis God that gives the sun and shower,
The soil, and forest shade,
And husbandmen make joyful here, the lovely world He made.

71 "Letitia," *New England Farmer*, 25 August 1841, 61.

CHAPTER 2

1 Report by George W. Corliss, Pascagoula, Miss., 31 August 1867, 1, Roll 30, "Narrative Reports from Subordinate Officers, Aug 1865–Oct 1867," Records of the Assistant Commissioner for the State of Mississippi, Bureau of Refugee, Freedmen, and Abandoned Lands, 1865–1869, Record Group 105, National Archives, Washington, D.C. (hereafter cited as Freedmen's Bureau Records).

2 On this point see Mart Stewart's study of low-country Georgia: "Work, especially hard physical labor by the slaves, was the central activity on all North American plantations and the nexus of both social and environmental relationships. In labor on the land, in the development and maintenance of the plantation, and in the performance of the series of production tasks that made up the staple crop regimens, the relationships between owner, manager, and slaves, and between all of them and the natural environment, were expressed in concrete terms." Mart A. Stewart, *"What Nature Suffers to Groe": Life, Labor, and Landscape on the Georgia Coast, 1680–1920* (Athens: University of Georgia Press, 2002), 126.

3 Kimberly Smith addresses some of these points in an article on nineteenth-century black environmental thought, a variant of democratic agrarianism, which was developed and promoted by African American writers advocating abolition and racial equality. Black agrarians, she explains, focused on property rights as well as the status of labor and the exploitation of workers, and they "highlighted the importance of these issues to the community's and individual's relationship to the American landscape." See Kimberly Smith, "Black Agrarianism and the Foundations of Black Environmental Thought," *Environmental Ethics* 26 (Fall 2004): 267–86.

4 James C. Cobb, *The Most Southern Place on Earth: The Mississippi Delta and the Roots of Regional Identity* (New York: Oxford University Press, 1992), 7, 82.

5 Louis Hughes, *Thirty Years a Slave: From Bondage to Freedom* (Milwaukee: South Side Printing Company, 1897), 77; Cobb, *Most Southern Place*, 15.

6 J. William Harris, *Deep Souths: Delta, Piedmont, and Sea Island Society in the Age of Segregation* (Baltimore: Johns Hopkins University Press, 2001), 41–45; Hughes,

Thirty Years, 206–7. Cobb suggests that little more than 10 percent of Delta land had even been cleared in 1860, and after the Civil War it was hardly distinguishable from the land that had greeted the first black and white migrants. Cobb, *Most Southern Place*, 43.

7 Steven F. Miller, "Plantation Labor Organization and Slave Life on the Cotton Frontier: The Alabama-Mississippi Black Belt, 1815–1840," in *Cultivation and Culture: Labor and the Shaping of Slave Life in the Americas*, ed. Ira Berlin and Philip D. Morgan (Charlottesville: University of Virginia Press, 1993), 160–62; Hughes, *Thirty Years*, 77.

8 Cobb, *Most Southern Place*, 21; Hughes, *Thirty Years*, 26–32.

9 Miller, "Plantation Labor Organization," 164–65.

10 George Skipwith to John Cocke, 8 July 1847, in *Slave Testimony: Two Centuries of Letters, Speeches, Interviews, and Autobiographies*, ed. John W. Blassingame (Baton Rouge: Louisiana State University Press, 1977), 66–68.

11 Miller, "Plantation Labor Organization," 158–59, 163–64, 167; Dylan C. Penningroth, *The Claims of Kinfolk: African American Property and Community in the Nineteenth-Century South* (Chapel Hill: University of North Carolina Press, 2003), 59.

12 On independent activity among coastal slaves of North Carolina see David S. Cecelski, *The Waterman's Song: Slavery and Freedom in Maritime North Carolina* (Chapel Hill: University of North Carolina Press, 2001); among bondsmen and bondswomen on low-country rice plantations in South Carolina see Leslie Schwalm, *A Hard Fight for We: Women's Transition from Slavery to Freedom in South Carolina* (Urbana: University of Illinois Press, 1997); and among slaves on low-country Georgia cotton plantations see Betty Wood, *Women's Work, Men's Work: The Informal Slave Economies of Lowcountry Georgia* (Athens: University of Georgia Press, 1995).

13 "In the absence of legal protection, the claim a slave had to property seems to have depended on his or her long association with a thing, an association that had to be visible to as many eyes as possible. . . . What from a legal perspective might have seemed merely rights of use or possession translated over time into real claims of ownership." Penningroth, *Claims of Kinfolk*, 107.

14 Fanny Smith Hodges, Born in Slavery: Slave Narratives from the Federal Writers' Project, 1936–1938, Library of Congress, Manuscript Division, <http://memory.loc .government/ammem/snhtml/snack.htm> (hereafter cited as Born in Slavery), 2 (page numbers refer to individual interview transcripts). Historians familiar with the Federal Writers' Project "slave narratives" know the many reasons for handling those interviews with considerable scrutiny and care. Like other oral histories, their accuracy is marred by aging subjects' faulty memories as well as questioners' assumptions and prejudices. The remarks of the freedpeople are also heavily influenced by the pervasive poverty of the 1930s as well as lingering and newly borne fear of white abuse.

15 Charlie Davenport, Born in Slavery, 5.

16 James Bolton in *Remembering Slavery: African Americans Talk about Their Personal Experience of Slavery*, ed. Ira Berlin, Marc Favreau, and Steven F. Miller (New York: New Press, 1998), 186; Henry Cheatem, Born in Slavery, 2.

17 Nicolas W. Proctor, *Bathed in Blood: Hunting and Mastery in the Old South* (Char-

lottesville: University Press of Virginia, 2002), 129–30; August Messersmith in Berlin, Favreau, and Miller, *Remembering Slavery*, 11–12.

18 Charles Ball, *Fifty Years in Chains: The Life of an American Slave* (Indianapolis: Dayton & Asher, 1858), 195–96, 246–47.

19 See for example George Taylor, Born in Slavery, 1–2; Henry Walker, ibid., 1; and Charlie Davenport, ibid., 1–2. Davenport recalls that his mother even made a plentiful supply of dewberry and persimmon wine.

20 Eugene Genovese, *Roll, Jordan, Roll: The World the Slaves Made* (New York: Vintage Books, 1976), 535.

21 Miller, "Plantation Labor Organization," 168.

22 Ball, *Fifty Years in Chains*, 196, 205.

23 Proctor, *Bathed in Blood*, 148–9.

24 Stephanie M. H. Camp, *Closer to Freedom: Enslaved Women and Everyday Resistance in the Plantation South* (Chapel Hill: University of North Carolina Press, 2004), 6, 38.

25 Josh Horn, Born in Slavery, 1–2.

26 Ball, *Fifty Years in Chains*, 204; Proctor, *Bathed in Blood*, 155–57, 163.

27 "The evidence demonstrates that slaves were very poor. This may seem obvious, but it is worth emphasis because it is so tempting to see slaves as budding capitalists. They were not." Penningroth, *Claims of Kinfolk*, 76–77.

28 Langston Hughes and Arna Bontemps, eds., *The Book of Negro Folklore* (New York: Dodd, Mead, 1958), 8–9, 39–4. See also Elizabeth Blum, "Power, Danger, and Control: Slave Women's Perceptions of Wilderness in the Nineteenth Century," *Women's Studies* 31 (January/February 2002), 247–66.

29 B. A. Botkin, ed., *Lay My Burden Down: A Folk History of Slavery* (1945; reprint, Chicago: University of Chicago Press, 1969), 14.

30 Penningroth, *Claims of Kinfolk*, 131.

31 W. E. B. Du Bois, *Black Reconstruction in America* (1935; reprint, New York: Atheneum, 1992), 431.

32 Cobb, *Most Southern Place*, 51; Ronald F. Davis, *Good and Faithful Labor: From Slavery to Sharecropping in the Natchez District, 1860–1890* (Westport, Conn.: Greenwood Press, 1982), 4–5.

33 Colonel Thomas was succeeded by Gen. Thomas Wood in April 1866, followed by Gen. Alvan C. Gillem in January 1867, and Gen. Adelbert Ames in March 1869. Adelbert moved headquarters to Jackson and then supervised the closing of the office. His appointment was revoked in April 1869. From "Introduction," Freedmen's Bureau Records.

34 Report by Robert Gardner, Philadelphia, Miss., 31 October 1867, "Narrative Reports from Subordinate Officers, Aug 1865–Oct 1867," Freedmen's Bureau Records.

35 Report by Subcommissioner for Jefferson County, name illegible, August 1865, date unspecified, "Narrative Reports from Subordinate Officers, Aug 1865–Oct 1867," Freedmen's Bureau Records; Report by John Moore, Lauderdale, Miss., 21 September 1867, "Narrative Reports from Subordinate Officers, Aug 1865–Oct 1867," Freedmen's Bureau Records.

36 John Butts agreed to pay $10 for "first class men," $8 for "first class women," and "all others as they approximate the above classification." John Butts Contract, Solitaire

Plantation, no county stated, Mississippi, 8 June 1865, "Labor Contracts of Freedmen, Jan.–Jun. 1865," Freedmen's Bureau Records. Two years later A. Grayson Carter agreed to pay between $5 and $18 a month to each hand. A. Grayson Carter Contract, Washington County, Mississippi, 23 January 1867, "Labor Contracts of Freedmen, Feb. 1866–Nov. 1868," Freedmen's Bureau Records. For a representative example of a sharecropping agreement see S. D. Mangum Contract, Frogmore Plantation, Adams County, Mississippi, 12 January 1867, "Labor Contracts of Freedmen, Feb. 1866–Nov. 1868," Freedmen's Bureau Records.

37 Wilson Henderson Contract, Lauderdale County, Mississippi, 5 February 1866, "Labor Contracts of Freedmen, Feb. 1866–Nov. 1868," Freedmen's Bureau Records.

38 S. G. Stovall Contract, Kennedy Plantation, Lauderdale County, Mississippi, 1 February 1866, "Labor Contracts of Freedmen, Feb. 1866–Nov. 1868," Freedmen's Bureau Records.

39 Davis, *Good and Faithful Labor*, 9.

40 Report of Complaints, Natchez, Miss., August 1867, no date specified, "Narrative Reports from Subordinate Officers, Aug 1865–Oct 1867," Freedmen's Bureau Records; Report from Subcommissioner, Jefferson County, Miss., 1865, no date or month specified, "Narrative Reports from Subordinate Officers, Aug 1865–Oct 1867," Freedmen's Bureau Records.

41 Report by John A. Hynes, Member Board Registration, Sunflower County, Miss., 15 July 1867, "Narrative Reports from Subordinate Officers, Aug 1865–Oct 1867," Freedmen's Bureau Records.

42 Report of Complaints and Outrages for the Month of November 1867, Hernando County, Miss., "Narrative Reports from Subordinate Officers, Nov–Dec 1867," Freedmen's Bureau Records.

43 Charlie Davenport, Born in Slavery, 7.

44 Report by William Walker, President Board Registration, Tishomingo County, Miss., 12 July 1867, "Narrative Reports from Subordinate Officers, Aug 1865–Oct 1867," Freedmen's Bureau Records; Report by John Moore, Lauderdale, Miss., 21 September 1867, "Narrative Reports from Subordinate Officers, Aug 1865–Oct 1867," Freedmen's Bureau Records.

45 J. C. Colbert Contract, Noxubee County, 1 January 1867, "Labor Contracts of Freedmen, Feb. 1866–Nov. 1868," Freedmen's Bureau Records.

46 Genovese, *Roll, Jordan, Roll*, 535.

47 Jacqueline Jones, *Labor of Love, Labor of Sorrow: Black Women, Work, and the Family from Slavery to the Present* (New York: Vintage Books, 1986), 63, 87.

48 Diana Glave, "'A Garden So Brilliant with Colors, So Original in Its Design': Rural African American Women, Gardening, Progressive Reform, and the Foundation of an African American Environmental Perspective," *Environmental History* 8 (July 2003), 395–411. See also Richard Westmacott, *African-American Gardens and Yards in the Rural South* (Knoxville: The University of Tennessee Press, 1992).

49 Sharon Ann Holt, *Making Freedom Pay: North Carolina Freedpeople Working for Themselves, 1865–1900* (Athens: University of Georgia Press, 2000), xviii.

50 Charles S. Aiken, *The Cotton Plantation South Since the Civil War* (Baltimore: Johns Hopkins University Press, 1998), 27.

51 Penningroth, *Claims of Kinfolk*, 142. See also Shawn Everett Kantor, *Politics and Property Rights: The Closing of the Open Range in the Postbellum South* (Chicago: University of Chicago Press, 1998); and Steven Hahn, "Hunting, Fishing, and Foraging: Common Rights and Class Relations in the Postbellum South," *Radical History Review* 26 (October 1982): 37–64.

52 Report by Thad K. Preuss, Oxford, Miss., 31 August 1867, "Narrative Reports from Subordinate Officers, Aug 1865–Oct 1867," Freedmen's Bureau Records.

53 Report of John Williams, Louisville, Miss., November 1867, no date specified, "Narrative Reports from Subordinate Officers, Nov–Dec 1867," Freedmen's Bureau Records.

54 Cobb, *Most Southern Place*, 43.

55 Robert L. Brandfon, *Cotton Kingdom of the New South: A History of the Yazoo-Mississippi Delta from Reconstruction to the Twentieth Century* (Cambridge: Harvard University Press, 1967), 135–36; Irene Robertson, Born in Slavery, 2.

56 Davis, *Good and Faithful Labor*, 3–4, 89–90; see also Aiken, *Cotton Plantation South*, 19.

57 William Henry Towns, Born in Slavery, n.p., .

58 Henry Baker in Blassingame, *Slave Testimony*, 672.

CHAPTER 3

1 Mrs. Sarah Lindsay Anthony, Lilla Day Monroe Collection of Pioneer Stories, vol. 1, 1–2, Kansas State Historical Society, Topeka, Kans. (hereafter cited as Monroe Collection). Anthony was born in New York in 1847, moved with her family to Kansas, married in 1870, and died in 1924. This recollection was written by her daughter.

2 Anne E. Bingham, vol. 1, 4–5, Monroe Collection. Bingham lived on a Kansas farm from 1870 to 1886.

3 Approaching the study of frontier women in this way draws on but also extends and deepens the work of various other scholars. See Sandra Myres, *Westering Women and the Frontier Experience, 1800–1915* (Albuquerque: University of New Mexico Press, 1982); Julie Roy Jeffrey, "'There is Some Splendid Scenery': Women's Responses to the Great Plains Landscape," *Great Plains Quarterly* 8 (Spring 1988), 69–78; and Jeffrey, *Frontier Women: The Trans-Mississippi West, 1840–1880* (New York: Hill and Wang, 1979); Glenda Riley, "Women's Responses to the Challenges of Plains Living," *Great Plains Quarterly* 9 (Summer 1989), 174–84; and Riley, *The Female Frontier: A Comparative View of Women on the Prairie and Plains* (Lawrence: University Press of Kansas, 1988); and Andrea G. Radke, "Refining Rural Spaces: Women and Vernacular Gentility in the Great Plains, 1880–1920," *Great Plains Quarterly* 24 (Fall 2004), 227–48.

4 Carol Fairbanks and Sara Brooks Sundberg, *Farm Women on the Prairie Frontier: A Sourcebook for Canada and the United States* (Metuchen, N.J.: Scarecrow Press, 1983), 4–5, 23, 49.

5 Sarah Gatch to John Holmes, 20 March 1887, in Rebecca Winters Genealogical Society, *Families of the Pioneer: Early Settlers of Scotts Bluff, Morrill, and Banner Counties of Western Nebraska* (Scottsbluff, Neb.: Rebecca Winters Genealogical Society, 1985), 129.

6 Mrs. Floy Leach Cannon, "Custer in the Early '80s," and Mrs. Grace Jeffery Martin,

"Childhood Days in Custer County," in *Pioneer Stories of Custer County Nebraska* (Broken Bow, Neb.: E. R. Purcell, 1936), 85–86, 91–92. See also Otie Eubank Luce, "In the Wilds of Nebraska," 58, and Mrs. Cora Leech Lowder, "My Girlhood Days in Custer," 59.

7   Jeffrey, *Frontier Women*, 52–53, 77–78.

8   Mrs. Viola Catherine Alexander, vol. 1, 2–3, Monroe Collection; Helen Nelson Anderson, vol. 1, n.p., Monroe Collection; Mrs. Anna Pearson Berg, vol. 1, n.p., Monroe Collection; Adela Orpen, *Memories of the Old Emigrant Days in Kansas, 1862–1865* (New York: Harper & Brothers, 1928), 49–50. See also Myres, *Westering Women*, 12–36, for her chapter "The Pleasing Awfulness: Women's Views of Wilderness"; and Jeffrey, "'There is Some Splendid Scenery,'" 73–74.

9   Willa Cather, *O Pioneers!* (1913; reprint, New York: Quality Paperback Book Club, 1995), 15, 20, 29. Cather was born in Virginia in 1873, moved with her family at age nine to the Nebraska frontier, graduated from the University of Nebraska in 1895, and eventually made her way to New York City at age thirty-two, where she worked at *McClure's Magazine* for a time. She wrote *O Pioneers!* in 1913 and *My Antonia* in 1918.

10 Anna Olsson, *A Child of the Prairie*, trans. Martha Winblad, ed. Elizabeth Jaderborg. (Lindsborg, Kans.: privately printed, 1978), 1, 3.

11 Elizabeth Sargent and Mrs. Mary Taylor Robinson in *Pioneer Stories*, 10, 25.

12 Baldwin F. Kruse, *Paradise on the Prairie: Nebraska Settlers Stories* (Lincoln, Neb.: Paradise Publishers, 1986), 32–33; Mrs. Henry Hanson in *Swedish Pioneers in Saunders County, Nebraska: A Collection of Family Histories of Early Settlers in Nebraska*, ed. Albert Strom (Pittsburgh: n.p., 1972), 22.

13 Mattie V. Oblinger to Thomas family, 10 September 1876, Uriah W. Oblinger Collection, Library of Congress/Nebraska State Historical Society, <http://memory.loc .government/ammem/award98/nbhihtml/pshome.html> (hereafter cited as Oblinger Collection).

14 Berna Hunter Chrisman in *Pioneer Stories*, 144–45; Olsson, *Child of the Prairie*, 7.

15 Orpen, *Memories*, 4.

16 Kruse, *Paradise on the Prairie*, 27; Mrs. Wilbur Speer, *Pioneer Stories*, 46.

17 Berna Hunter Chrisman, *Pioneer Stories*, 144; Jeffrey, *Frontier Women*, 53–54.

18 Jeffrey, *Frontier Women*, 4, 60–61.

19 Melissa Genett Moore, *The Story of a Kansas Pioneer, Being the Autobiography of Melissa Genett Anderson* (Mt. Vernon, Ohio: Manufacturing Printers Co., 1924), 25.

20 Orpen, *Memories*, 15–16.

21 Myres, *Westering Women*, 146, and see the rest of her chapter, "New Home — Who'll Follow?: Women and Frontier Homemaking," 141–66.

22 Martha Farnsworth, 2 March 1884, vol. 1, Martha Farnsworth Diaries, 1882–1922, Collection 28, Kansas State Historical Society, Topeka, Kans.

23 Mattie V. Oblinger to Thomas family, 24 November 1874, Oblinger Collection.

24 Mrs. Frances Reeder Eddy, *Pioneer Stories*, 51.

25 Jeffrey, *Frontier Women*, 72–73.

26 Lydia Emily Goodno Balcomb, vol. 1, 1–2, Monroe Collection; Berna Hunter Chrisman, *Pioneer Stories*, 144.

27 Mattie V. Oblinger to Thomas family, 25 April 1874, Oblinger Collection.

28 Orpen, *Memories*, 19; Mattie V. Oblinger to George Thomas, Grizzie B. Thomas, and Wheeler Thomas family, 16 June 1873, Oblinger Collection.

29 Mattie V. Oblinger to Thomas family, 25 April 1874, Oblinger Collection; Mattie V. Oblinger to George Thomas, Grizzie B. Thomas, and Wheeler Thomas family, 16 June 1873, Oblinger Collection; Mattie V. Oblinger to Thomas family, 16 April 1876, Oblinger Collection.

30 Mattie V. Oblinger to Thomas family, 25 April 1874, Oblinger Collection; Mattie V. Oblinger to Thomas family, 16 April 1876, Oblinger Collection; Laura I. Oblinger to Uriah W. Oblinger, 22 January 1894, Oblinger Collection.

31 Jeffrey, "'There is Some Splendid Scenery,'" 75; Elizabeth C. Sargent, *Pioneer Stories*, 10.

32 Kruse, *Paradise on the Prairie*, 136–37.

33 Moore, *Story of a Kansas Pioneer*, 29; Wilhelmina Young Brown in Rebecca Winters Genealogical Society, *Families of the Pioneer*, 16.

34 Radke, "Refining Rural Spaces," 246.

35 Olive Capper, 11, 14, 18, 19, and 21 April 1895, and 29 May 1895, Olive Capper Diary, 1895, Kansas State Historical Society, Topeka, Kans. (hereafter cited as Capper Diary).

36 Olive Capper, 2 January 1895, Capper Diary.

37 Olive Capper, 2 April 1895 and 6 Mary 1895, Capper Diary.

38 Marilyn Irvin Holt, *Linoleum, Better Babies, and the Modern Farm Woman, 1890–1930* (Albuquerque: University of New Mexico Press, 1995), 24, 40.

39 Ibid., 43, 58, 67.

40 Moore, *Story of a Kansas Pioneer*, 44–45.

41 Myrtle Brunkow Rebsch, *Coming of Age in 1920's Kansas* (Universal Biorhythm Company, 1993), 1–2; see also Laura I. Oblinger to Uriah W. Oblinger, 24 July 1887, Oblinger Collection.

42 Emma Drew, 13 March 1918, Emma Drew Diaries, 1918–1924, Collection 332, Kansas State Historical Society, Topeka, Kans.

43 Mrs. Floyd Leach Cannon, *Pioneer Stories*, 85–86.

44 Mrs. Viola Catherine Alexander, vol. 1, 7, Monroe Collection; Mrs. James W. Eddy, *Pioneer Stories*, 79.

45 Olive Mitchell Staadt, *Gentle Memories: Kansas, 1900–1910* (n.p., n.d.), 2–3, 6, 41–42, 93.

46 Harriet Adams, vol. 1, n.p., Monroe Collection.

47 Willa Cather, *My Antonia* (1918; reprint, Boston: Houghton Mifflin, 1988), 28, 12; and *O Pioneers!*, 76.

CHAPTER 4

1 David Alan Corbin, *Life, Work, and Rebellion in the Coal Fields: The Southern West Virginia Miners, 1880–1922* (Urbana: University of Illinois Press, 1981), 38.

2 Ronald Eller, *Miners, Millhands, and Mountaineers: Industrialization of the Appalachian South, 1880–1930* (Knoxville: University of Tennessee Press, 1982), 16–18.

3 Ibid., 19; Donald Edward Davis, *Where There Are Mountains: An Environmental History of the Southern Appalachians* (Athens: University of Georgia Press, 2000), 126.

4 Eller, *Miners, Millhands, and Mountaineers*, 19.

5 Corbin, *Life, Work, and Rebellion*, 2; John Alexander Williams, *West Virginia: A Bicentennial History* (Morgantown: West Virginia University Press, 1976), 112; Jerry Bruce Thomas, "Coal Country: The Rise of the Southern Smokeless Coal Industry" (Ph.D. diss., University of North Carolina, 1971), 30–31.

6 Phil Conley, *History of the Coal Industry of West Virginia* (Charleston, W.Va.: Education Foundation, 1960), 209–10, 250; J. T. Peters and H. R. Carden, *History of Fayette County* (Fayetteville, W.Va.: Fayette County Historical Society, 1926), 298.

7 Corbin, *Life, Work, and Rebellion*, 5.

8 Ronald Lewis, *Transforming the Appalachian Countryside: Railroads, Deforestation, and Social Change in West Virginia, 1880–1920* (Chapel Hill: University of North Carolina Press, 1998), 46; Williams, *West Virginia*, 112.

9 Corbin, *Life, Work, and Rebellion*, 4.

10 Eller, *Miners, Millhands, and Mountaineers*, 166–67.

11 Crandall A. Shifflet, *Coal Towns: Life, Work, and Culture in Company Towns of Southern Appalachia, 1880–1960* (Knoxville: University of Tennessee Press, 1994), 7–8.

12 Keith Dix, *What's a Coal Miner to Do?: The Mechanization of Coal Mining* (Pittsburgh: University of Pittsburgh Press, 1988), 5–7, 13.

13 Corbin, *Life, Work, and Rebellion*, 38.

14 Herbert Garten, interview by Paul Nyden, 6 September 1980, written transcript, C290, Interviews, Appalachian Oral History Project, West Virginia and Regional History Collection, West Virginia University, Morgantown, W.Va. (hereafter cited as Interviews WVRHC).

15 Nettie McGill, *Welfare of Children in the Bituminous Coal Communities in West Virginia*, Children's Bureau, U.S. Department of Labor (Washington: Government Printing Office, 1923), 53; Corbin, *Life, Work, and Rebellion*, 33; Ada Wilson Jackson, interview by Paul Nyden, 13 December 1980, written transcript, C312, Interviews WVRHC; Lula Lall Jones, interview by Paul Nyden, 13 December 1980, written transcript, C313, Interviews WVRHC.

16 *Coal Age* 2, no. 6 (1912): 201.

17 *Coal Age* 3, no. 15 (1913): 580; *Coal Age* 12, no. 20 (1917): 856.

18 *Coal Age* 4, no. 2 (1913): 389.

19 Lula Lall Jones, interview.

20 *Coal Age* 2, no. 6 (1912): 201. See also a report on the contest at the Taylor Coal Company, in eastern Kentucky, which made awards to "white" and "colored" separately. *Coal Age* 3, no. 15 (1913): 580.

21 Robert Forren, interview by Paul Nyden, 24 and 25 September 1980, written transcript, C294, Interviews WVRHC.

22 Corbin, *Life, Work, and Rebellion*, 33.

23 Robert Armstead, *Black Days, Black Dust: The Memories of an African American Coal Miner* (Knoxville: University of Tennessee Press, 2002), 23.

24 Ibid., 24; Robert Forren, interview; Ada Jackson, interview.

25 Ada Jackson, interview; Armstead, *Black Days, Black Dust*, 24; Annie Kelly, interview by Paul Nyden, 23 October 1980, written transcript, C301, Interviews WVRHC; E. H. Phipps, interview by Paul Nyden, 16 October 1980, written transcript, C299, Interviews WVRHC.

26 *Coal Age* 6, no. 23 (1914): 935.

27 "Numerically and proportionally (94 percent), more miners in West Virginia lived in company towns than did miners in any other state. Since the percentage figure includes northern West Virginia, where many miners lived in commercial towns, the proportion for southern West Virginia was probably about 98 percent." Corbin, *Life, Work, and Rebellion*, 8.

28 E. H. Phipps, interview.

29 Ernest Carrico, interview by Ray Ringley, 6 December 1973, Tapes 62 and 63, Transcript No. 79, Appalachian Oral History Project, Emory and Henry College Oral History Collection (hereafter cited as OHP-EH); Ada Jackson, interview; Corbin, *Life, Work, and Rebellion*, 34.

30 See also, for comparison, the Cedar Grove Mining Company Ledger, 1883–1885, A&M No. 2936, West Virginia and Regional History Collection, West Virginia University, Morgantown, W.Va.

31 Cannelton Coal Co., Store #2, Daybooks for 1896 and 1897–98, Series 4, New River Field Coal Co. Records, 1878–1956, A&M No. 2570, ibid.

32 Corbin, *Life, Work, and Rebellion*, 34.

33 McGill was actually talking about the few mining families who were able and allowed to live on the outskirts of coal camps, but the sentiment applies to camp residents as well. When combined with the fact that mountain residents overwhelmingly preferred farming to other ways of making a living (even in the late 1920s, according to her report, some miners still left in the summer to work homestead land), it is clear that people were getting various forms of satisfaction from agricultural labor. McGill, *Welfare of Children*, 76.

34 Thomas, "Coal Country," 304.

35 Eller, *Miners, Millhands, and Mountaineers*, 138.

36 McGill, *Welfare of Children*, 10, 15; Eller, *Miners, Millhands, and Mountaineers*, 185–86.

37 Dix, *Coal Miner*, 6–7; Conley, *History of the Coal Industry*, 36–37.

38 Dix, *Coal Miner*, 77–79.

39 Conley, *History of the Coal Industry*, 37.

40 Dix, *Coal Miner*, 82–83.

41 Corbin, *Life, Work, and Rebellion*, 49–50.

42 Ibid., 50, 32–33, 116–17.

43 Testimony of Percy Tetlow, acting president of District No. 17, United Mine Workers of America, in Senate Committee on Interstate Commerce, *Conditions in the Coal Fields of Pennsylvania, West Virginia, and Ohio*, vol. 2, 70th Cong., 1st sess. (Washington: Government Printing Office, 1928), 1445–60.

44 Eller, *Miners, Millhands, and Mountaineers*, 157–58.

45 Corbin, *Life, Work, and Rebellion*, 34–35.

46 Peters and Carden, *History of Fayette County*, 303.

47 Ellis Bailey, interview by Bill Taft, 1974, no date or month specified, written transcript, C163, Interviews WVRHC.

48 Eller, *Miners, Millhands, and Mountaineers*, 238–39.

49 Herbert Garten, interview; Ernest Carrico, interview; James Harlan Edwards, interview by Ray Ringley, 1 October 1973, Tapes 180 and 181, Transcript No. 77, 8, OHP-EH.

50 Eller, *Miners, Millhands, and Mountaineers*, 238–39.

51 Phillip J. Obermiller, Thomas E. Wagner, and E. Bruce Tucker, eds., *Appalachian Odyssey: Historical Perspectives on the Great Migration* (Westport, Conn.: Praeger, 2000), xi–xii.

52 Carl E. Feather, *Mountain People in a Flat Land* (Athens: Ohio University Press, 1998), 3.

53 Susan Johnson, "West Virginia Rubber Workers in Akron," in *Transnational West Virginia: Ethnic Communities and Economic Change, 1840–1940*, ed. Ken Fones-Wolf and Ronald Lewis (Morgantown: West Virginia University Press, 2002), 299, 305–11; Phillip Obermiller, "Appalachian Odyssey," in Obermiller, Wagner, and Tucker, *Appalachian Odyssey*, xi–xii.

54 Quoting H. A. Haring, "Three Classes of Labor to Avoid" from *Factory and Industrial Management* (1921), in Johnson, "West Virginia Rubber Workers," 304.

55 Quoted in Daniel Nelson, *American Rubber Workers & Organized Labor, 1900–1941* (Princeton: Princeton University Press, 1988), 73.

56 Quoted in Johnson, "West Virginia Rubber Workers," 299.

57 Chad Berry, "Southern White Migration to the Midwest, an Overview," in Obermiller, Wagner, and Tucker, *Appalachian Odyssey*, 14

58 Herbert Garten, interview.

59 Chad Montrie, *To Save the Land and People: A History of Opposition to Surface Coal Mining in Appalachia* (Chapel Hill: University of North Carolina Press, 2003).

60 Wayne Keith was a son-in-law to Robert Hamm and was present when Hamm was interviewed, interjecting at times with his own views about coal mining in southwestern Virginia. Robert W. Hamm, interview by Ray Ringley, 30 September 1973, Tapes 186 A & B, Transcript No. 81, 7, OHP-EH.

61 Harriet Arnow Simpson, *The Dollmaker* (1954; reprint, New York: Harper Collins, 1972).

CHAPTER 5

1 Olga Madar and August Scholle to All Recording Secretaries of UAW-CIO Local Union in Michigan, 14 May 1947, Folder "Camps, Childrens Camp, 1948," Box 1, Recreation Department Collection, United Auto Workers, Archives of Labor and Urban Affairs, Wayne State University, Detroit, Mich. (hereafter cited as UAW Recreation Collection).

2 Reuther Address, Folder 6, "Speeches; Water Pollution Control Federation, 25 Sept 1968," Box 559, President's Office, Walter P. Reuther Collection, United Auto Workers, Archives of Labor and Urban Affairs, Wayne State University, Detroit, Mich. (hereafter cited as UAW President's Office Collection).

3 Glen Green quoted in Lisa Fine, "Rights of Men, Rites of Passage: Hunting and Masculinity at Reo Motors of Lansing, Michigan, 1945–1975," *Journal of Social History* 33 (Summer 2000): 810.

4 Glenn Worth Britton, "'Improving' the Middle Landscape: Conservation and Social Change in Rural Southern Michigan, 1890 to 1940" (Ph.D. diss., University of California, Los Angeles, 2005), ix–x, 94–95.

5   Ibid., 372–73.

6   Joyce Shaw Peterson, *American Automobile Workers, 1900–1933* (Albany: State University of New York Press, 1987), 31, 36–37.

7   Ibid., 42, 50; Kevin Boyle, *The UAW and the Heyday of American Liberalism, 1945–1968* (Ithaca: Cornell University Press, 1995), 12.

8   S. E. Sangster, "Tentative Outline for proposed 'History of Michigan Fish & Game'" (1941), 1–3, Folder 3, Box 1, Michigan Writers' Project, Department of Natural Resources, State Archives of Michigan, Lansing, Mich. (hereafter cited as MWP-DNR Collection); Richard Bailey, "Outline of Fur and Game History" (ca. 1941), 5–7, Folder 3, Box 1, MWP-DNR Collection.

9   S. E. Sangster, "Fish and Game Laws" (1941), 4, 6–8, Folder 8, Box 1, MWP-DNR Collection; Richard Bailey, "Outline of Fur and Game History," 6–7, Folder 3, Box 1, MWP-DNR Collection; See also John Reiger, *American Sportsmen and the Origins of Conservation* (Norman: University of Oklahoma Press, 1975).

10 S. E. Sangster, "Fish and Game Laws" (1941), 4, 7–8, Folder 8, Box 1, MWP-DNR Collection.

11 Paul S. Sutter, *Driven Wild: How the Fight Against Automobiles Launched the Modern Wilderness Movement* (Seattle: University of Washington Press, 2002), 23–24.

12 Daniel T. Rodgers, *The Work Ethic in Industrial America, 1850–1920* (Chicago: University of Chicago Press, 1979), 106.

13 Roy Rosenzweig, *Eight Hours for What We Will: Workers and Leisure in the Industrial City, 1870–1920* (Cambridge: Cambridge University Press, 1983), 1.

14 Cindy Aron, *Working at Play: A History of Vacations in the United States* (New York: Oxford University Press, 1999), 205, 248.

15 Peterson, *American Automobile Workers*, 5; Sutter, *Driven Wild*, 4.

16 Sutter, *Driven Wild*, 44–45.

17 S. E. Sangster, "Tentative Outline for proposed 'History of Michigan Fish & Game'" (1941), 3, Folder 3, Box 1, MWP-DNR Collection; S. E. Sangster, "Fish and Game Laws" (1941), 11–12, Folder 8, Box 1, MWP-DNR Collection.

18 "Southern Michigan State Game Areas and Recreation Areas, 1949–1950," Box 6, Folder 3, RG-68-6, State Archives of Michigan, Lansing, Mich.; *Kent League Sportsman* (October 1949), 9, Folder 6, Box 1, "Occasional Issues of Out-of-Print Periodicals Devoted to Michigan Sports and Conservation, 1933–1965," State Archives of Michigan, Lansing, Mich. (hereafter cited as SCP Collection).

19 *Genesee Sportsman* (December 1949), 4, Folder 4, Box 1, SCP Collection.

20 *Macomb County Sportsman* (January 1949), Folder 7, Box 1, SCP Collection; *Genesee Sportsman* (September 1950), Folder 4, Box 1, SCP Collection; *Jackson County Sportsman* (February 1947), Folder 1, Box 1, SCP Collection; *Kent League Sportsman* (March 1949), Folder 6, Box 1, SCP Collection.

21 Fine, "Rights of Men," 809. The two organizations tried to repair the division between them in 1949 when the Izaak Walton League's head invited the MUCC to attend their annual convention in Grand Rapids, which they voted to do, and to continue to work together on conservation issues. It is not entirely clear what specifically caused this division, but it might have something to do with either the class background of their respective membership (the Izaak Walton League was older by

almost a decade and a half and included more elite sportsmen in its ranks) or the more aggressive political approach the MUCC took to address conservation and environmental issues. *Kent League Sportsman* (June 1949), Folder 6, Box 1, SCP Collection.

22 *Afield and Afloat in Jackson County* (February 1947), Folder 1, Box 1, SCP Collection; *Barry County Sportsman* (February 1949), Folder 2, Box 1, SCP Collection; *Macomb County Sportsman* (January 1949), Folder 7, Box 1, SCP Collection; *Genesee Sportsman* (January 1949), Folder 4, Box 1, SCP Collection.

23 *Afield and Afloat in Jackson County* (February 1947), Folder 1, Box 1, SCP Collection; *Macomb County Sportsman* (October 1949), Folder 7, Box 1, SCP Collection.

24 *Northern Michigan Sportsman* (January 1952), Folder 11, Box 1, SCP Collection; *Genesee Sportsman* (January 1949) and (September 1950), Folder 4, Box 1, SCP Collection.

25 Fine, "Rights of Men," 809. On the inclusion of women in recreational hunting in the late nineteenth and early twentieth centuries, see Andrea Smalley, "'Our Lady Sportsmen': Gender, Class, and Conservation in Sport Hunting Magazines, 1873–1920," *Journal of the Gilded Age and Progressive Era* 4 (October 2005): 355–80.

26 *Kent League Sportsman* (March 1949), Folder 6, Box 1, SCP Collection; *Barry County Sportsman* (February 1949), Folder 2, Box 1, SCP Collection; *Genesee Sportsman* (September 1950), Folder 4, Box 1, SCP Collection; see also Vera Norwood, *Made from This Earth: American Women and Nature* (Chapel Hill: University of North Carolina Press, 1993).

27 Apparently, a few working-class women did go hunting and fishing alongside men. Some newsletters featured advertisements for women in need of the proper clothing for outings, including plain-cut wool pants and coats, durable boots, and thermal underwear. In one *Genesee Sportsman* ad, a pencil-drawn model walks cradling a gun in her arms, promoting a notion of woman's place and proper behavior that clashed somewhat with traditional ideas. Newsletters also reported on the work of women's auxiliaries to promote fishing contests, in columns such as the "Sportswomen's Club Chatter." *Genesee Sportsman* (January 1949) and (September 1950), Folder 4, Box 1, SCP Collection; *Barry County Sportsman* (June 1949), Folder 2, Box 1, SCP Collection; Oscar Warbach Cartoon, "Nov–Dec 1949," Box 2, Department of Natural Resources—Conservation Division, Series 2, State Archives of Michigan, Lansing, Mich. (hereafter cited as DNR Warbach Collection).

28 *Macomb County Sportsman* (January 1949), Folder 7, Box 1, SCP Collection; *Barry County Sportsman* (June 1949), Folder 2, Box 1, SCP Collection; *Genesee Sportsman* (October 1949), Folder 4, Box 1, SCP Collection.

29 *Genesee Sportsman* (September 1950), Folder 4, Box 1, SCP Collection; *Kent League Sportsman* (February 1949), Folder 6, Box 1, SCP Collection.

30 *Barry County Sportsman* (February 1949), Folder 2, Box 1, SCP Collection.

31 *Afield and Afloat in Jackson County* (February 1947), Folder 1, Box 1, SCP Collection. A similar but less anthropocentric version of this way of thinking appeared in a 1953 issue of the *Bowhunter*, published in Wisconsin. "One thing is certain," the president of the bowhunter's association wrote in his monthly column, "long before the present herd of deer came into existence the eternal laws which govern such things were already in existence. They have functioned the same as they have always functioned. It

is obvious that the cycle has passed the peak and is now going down. . . . The herd will continue to fall until the forces of nature acting upon it have again become stabilized, after which the same process will again repeat itself, subject, of course, to natural conditions of habitat which then prevail. That is the law of nature and puny man is not going to change it." *Bowhunter* (January 1953), Folder 3, Box 1, SCP Collection.

32 Oscar Warbach Cartoons, "Nov–Dec 1949," Box 2, DNR Warbach Collection.

33 *Kent League Sportsman* (January 1949), Folder 6, Box 1, SCP Collection.

34 *Genesee Sportsman* (October 1949), Folder 4, Box 1, SCP Collection; *Genesee Sportsman* (June 1951), Folder 4, Box 1, SCP Collection; *Kent League Sportsman* (January 1949), Folder 6, Box 1, SCP Collection.

35 The 1949 legislation was part of a set of bills, some of which dealt with hunting and fishing while others updated the state's water pollution control policy, unchanged since 1929. That earlier law had prohibited discharge of any waste that could harm fish or injure the public health, but it was not enforced, and pollution of rivers and lakes went unabated. After enactment of the new legislation, some companies were hurriedly proactive in at least appearing to control their discharge. That same year, for example, Ford's River Rouge spent $1.5 million to deal with waste waters, waste oil, steel pickling liquors, and coke-oven waste. *Macomb County Sportsman* (September 1949), Folder 7, Box 1, SCP Collection; *Afield and Afloat in Jackson County* (February 1947), Folder 1, Box 1, SCP Collection; *Kent League Sportsman* (February 1949), Folder 6, Box 1, SCP Collection; *Saginaw Valley Sportsman* (January 1949), Folder 15, Box 1, SCP Collection.

36 *Saginaw Valley Sportsman* (July 1949), Folder 15, Box 1, SCP Collection.

37 Nelson Lichtenstein, *Walter Reuther: The Most Dangerous Man in Detroit* (Urbana: University of Illinois Press, 1995), 56–57, 63.

38 Ibid., 300–308; Kevin Boyle, "Little More than Ashes: The UAW and American Reform in the 1960s," in *Organized Labor and American Politics, 1894–1994*, ed. Kevin Boyle (Albany: State University of New York Press, 1998), 217–21, 230–31; Boyle, *Heyday of American Liberalism*, 11, 34–36.

39 "The Origin of the Recreation Department of the UAW," ca. 1959, Folder "History of the Department and Program Guides, ca. 1958–Mar 1960," Box 2, UAW Recreation Collection; "UAW Recreation," ca. 1959, Folder "History of the Department and Program Guides, ca. 1958–Mar 1960," Box 2, UAW Recreation Collection; Olga Madar, "What the UAW is Doing About Recreation," 1959, Folder "History of the Department and Program Guides, ca. 1958–Mar 1960," Box 2, UAW Recreation Collection.

40 Draft of article for "The Director's Corner," n.d., Folder "Recreation Reports, 1945–1948," Box 2, UAW Recreation Collection.

41 Michael Smith, " 'The Ego Idea of the Good Camper' and the Nature of Summer Camp," *Environmental History* 11 (January 2006): 73, 77–80.

42 *Saginaw Valley Sportsman* (November 1949), Folder 15, Box 1, SCP Collection.

43 "The Origin of the Recreation Department of the UAW," 1959, Folder "History of the Department and Program Guides, ca. 1958–Mar 1960," Box 2, UAW Recreation Collection.

44 Inter-Office Communication, R. J. Thomas to Melvin G. West, 27 December 1945, "July 1945–December 1945 Recreation Report," Folder "Recreation Reports, 1945–

1948," Box 2, UAW Recreation Collection; Melvin G. West to Mr. George Addes, 19 June 1945, "Recreation Reports, 1945–1948," Box 2, UAW Recreation Collection; National Institute for Local Union Officers, August 22–September 4, 1948 (Printed Program), Folder "Camps, FDR Camp, 1948," Box 1, UAW Recreation Collection; Inter-Office Communication, Melvin G. West to Frank Winn, "Quarterly Report — Recreation Department — March, 1946–June 1946," 10 July 1946, Folder "Recreation Reports, 1945–1948," Box 2, UAW Recreation Collection.

45 The referral agencies included the Department of Public Welfare, Down River Consultation Service, Family Service Society, Psychological Clinic of the Detroit Public Schools, Jewish Social Service Bureau, Warren Township Family Service Society, Children's Center, and others. "Detroit Group Project — Camp Season 1946," Folder "Camps, Childrens Camp, 1948," Box 1, UAW Recreation Collection.

46 Olga Madar and August Scholle [president, Michigan CIO Council] to All Recording Secretaries of UAW-CIO Local Unions in Michigan, 14 May 1947, Folder "Camps, Children's Camp, 1948," Box 1, UAW Recreation Collection; "The FDR-CIO Labor Center Camp for Children," 1947, Folder "Camps, Children's Camp, 1950," Box 1, UAW Recreation Collection. The union filled the camp to capacity both weeks, but the camp still operated at a loss. They collected $1400 in fees the first week and $1430 the second to generate, with additional revenue, a gross income of $3054; but $3706 in expenses resulted in a net loss of $652. "Profit and Loss Statement," 19 July 1947, Folder "Camps, Children's Camp, 1948," Box 1, UAW Recreation Collection.

47 The year before, in 1947, there were 321 camps in Michigan, three of them associated with organized labor: the one run by the Michigan UAW near Port Huron, another operated by Toledo UAW Local 12 on Sand Lake, and a third sponsored by both AFL and CIO unions in Muskegon County, on Lake Michigan. "1947 Directory of Summer Camps for Children, Michigan State Department of Social Welfare," Folder "Camps, Children's Camp, 1948," Box 1, UAW Recreation Collection.

48 Walter Reuther to Olga Madar, 25 February 1948, Folder "Camps, Children's Camp, 1948," Box 1, UAW Recreation Collection; "Michigan Department of Conservation — Division of Parks and Recreation — Seasonal Group Camp Application and Permit," Folder "Camps, Children's Camp, 1948," Box 1, UAW Recreation Collection; "Children's Camp" Press Release, 14 June 1948, Folder "Camps, Children's Camp, 1948," Box 1, UAW Recreation Collection.

49 "Report of the Recreation Department Activities, November 1947–October 1948," Folder "Recreation Reports, 1945–1948," Box 2, UAW Recreation Collection.

50 "Report of F.D.R. C.I.O. Camp for Children," n.d., Folder "Camps, Children's Camp, 1948," Box 1, UAW Recreation Collection.

51 Brochure for FDR-AFL-CIO Children's Camp (1962), Folder "Camp Folders; 1958, 1960–62," Box 2, UAW Recreation Collection.

52 See Scott Dewey, "Working for the Environment: Organized Labor and the Origins of Environmentalism in the United States, 1948–1970," *Environmental History* 3 (January 1998): 45–63. On labor environmentalism in general see also Robert Gordon, "Environmental Blues: Working-Class Environmentalism and the Labor-Environmental Alliance" (Ph.D. diss., Wayne State University, 2004).

53 Chad Montrie, *To Save the Land and People: A History of Opposition to Surface Coal*

Mining in Appalachia (Chapel Hill: University of North Carolina Press, 2003); and "Expedient Environmentalism: Opposition to Coal Surface Mining in Appalachia and the United Mine Workers of America, 1945–1977," *Environmental History* 5 (January 2000): 75–98.

54 Chris Meyer to Victoria A. Hays, 24 August 1973, Folder 21, "Environmental Action," Box 3, Work Department Collection, United Farm Workers, Archives of Labor and Urban Affairs, Wayne State University, Detroit, Mich.; Laura Pulido, *Environmentalism and Economic Justice* (Tucson: University of Arizona Press, 1996), 121; See also J. Craig Jenkin, *The Politics of Insurgency: The Farm Worker Movement in the 1960s* (New York: Columbia University Press, 1985); Linda Nash, "The Fruits of Ill-Health: Pesticides and Workers' Bodies in Post–World War II California," *Osiris* 19 (2004), 203–19; and Robert Gordon, "Poisons in the Fields: The United Farm Workers, Pesticides, and Environmental Politics," *Pacific Historical Review* 68 (February 1999): 51–77; and "'Shell No!': OCAW and the Labor-Environmental Alliance," *Environmental History* 3 (October 1998): 460–87.

55 Walter Reuther to Stewart Udall, 2 March 1965, Folder 1, "Interior Dept. of Stewart Udall, Secy., 1964–67," Box 377, UAW President's Office Collection; Clean Water Conference Speech, 6 November 1965, Folder 3, "Speeches; Clear Water Conference, 6 Nov 1965," Box 555, UAW President's Office Collection; Notes for Speech, Folder 6, "Speeches; Water Pollution Control Federation, 25 Sept 1968," Box 559, UAW President's Office Collection.

56 Otha Brown [secretary to Walter Reuther] to Thomas Kimball, 11 January 1963, Folder 4, "Speeches, Mar. 1963," Box 552, UAW President's Office Collection; Thomas Kimball to Walter Reuther, 7 February 1963, Folder 4, "Speeches, Mar. 1963," Box 552, UAW President's Office Collection; *Detroit News*, 1 March 1963, Folder 4, "Speeches, Mar. 1963," Box 552, UAW President's Office Collection; Rachel Carson was also scheduled to speak at this meeting, but she canceled after she was diagnosed with breast cancer and her doctor advised against traveling.

57 "Brief History of UAW Environmental Leadership," Folder "Conservation & Recreation Depts. History, policies & operations, 1930s–1970s," Box 11, Conservation and Recreation Departments Collection, United Auto Workers, Archives of Labor and Urban Affairs, Wayne State University, Detroit, Mich. (hereafter cited as UAW Conservation and Recreation Collection); Dewey, "Working for the Environment," 51–52; Walter Reuther, Opening Speech, Folder 3, "Speeches; Clear Water Conference, 6 Nov 1965," Box 555, UAW President's Office Collection.

58 Madar was made acting director of the Recreation Department in 1946, and she became the permanent director in 1947. She also received an appointment to the UAW Executive Board at the same 1966 convention where the Conservation and Resource Development Department was created. "Recreation Department Collection Guide" and "Brief History of UAW Environmental Leadership," Folder "Conservation & Recreation Depts. History, policies & operations, 1930s–1970s," Box 11, UAW Conservation and Recreation Collection.

59 Dewey, "Working for the Environment," 52.

60 Membership in the Downriver area was represented by Locals 2, 15, 22, 157, 174, 387, and 600. Summary Report, 18 November 1969," no author, Folder "Down River

Anti-Pollution League; Corres & reports, 1969," Box 2, UAW Conservation and Recreation Collection; Report on Reviving DAPL, likely written by Olga Madar, n.d., Folder "Down River Anti-Pollution League; Corres & reports, 1969," Box 2, UAW Conservation and Recreation Collection; John Yolton to Harold Johnson, 23 December 1969, Folder "Down River Anti-Pollution League; Corres & reports, 1969," Box 2, UAW Conservation and Recreation Collection.

61 Liebert included a map of area polluters with his report, based on an unspecified Lake Erie report from August 1968. In the Detroit River Basin the main culprits included Revere Copper & Brass, Great Lakes Steel*, Wyandotte Chemical*, Pennsalt Chemical*, Firestone Tire & Rubber, Chrysler, Dana, E. I. du Pont, McLouth Steel*, Mobil Oil, and Monsanto Chemical*. In the Rouge River Basin, there was Allied Chemical*, Scott Paper*, American Cement, Associated Spring, Haller, Ford Motor-Rouge*, Darling & Co., Seaway Cartage, Trilex, Evans Products, and Burroughs. The asterisks denote the companies with the worst of the worst records for dumping pollutants. "Summary Log for Sept 10–Nov 8, 1969: Hillel Liebert," Folder "Down River Anti-Pollution League; Corres & reports, 1969," Box 2, UAW Conservation and Recreation Collection; "Industrial Wastes in Our Rivers," 19 November 1969, Folder "Down River Anti-Pollution League; Corres & reports, 1969," Box 2, UAW Conservation and Recreation Collection.

62 Inter-Office Communication, Olga Madar to Bard Young, 20 October 1969, Folder "Down River Anti-Pollution League; Corres & reports, 1969," Box 2, UAW Conservation and Recreation Collection.

63 "Summary Report," 18 November 1969, Folder "Down River Anti-Pollution League; Corres & reports, 1969," Box 2, UAW Conservation and Recreation Collection; Bard Young, Phillip Terrana, and Olga Madar to UAW Member and Spouse, 25 November 1969, Folder "Down River Anti-Pollution League; Corres & reports, 1969," Box 2, UAW Conservation and Recreation Collection.

64 UAW Press Release, 10 December 1969, Folder "Down River Anti-Pollution League; Corres & reports, 1969," Box 2, UAW Conservation and Recreation Collection; Water Resources Commission Meeting Picketline Flier, Folder "DAPL Flyers, 1970–71," Box 2, UAW Conservation and Recreation Collection; Peter Naccrato and Charleen Knight to Community Leader, 16 March 1970, Folder "Down River Anti-Pollution League; Corres & reports, 1969," Box 2, UAW Conservation and Recreation Collection.

65 *Mellus News*, 15 April 1970, Folder "Down River Anti-Pollution League; Corres & reports, 1969," Box 2, UAW Conservation and Recreation Collection; *Detroit News*, 21 April 1970, Folder "Down River Anti-Pollution League; Corres & reports, 1969," Box 2, UAW Conservation and Recreation Collection.

66 The group published their newsletter from March 1970 to at least July 1971. *DAPL News*, vol. 1, no. 2 (27 July 1970), Folder "DAPL Newsletter, 1970–71," Box 2, UAW Conservation and Recreation Collection; Ted Pankowski to Roger Battaglia, 17 July 1970, Folder "DAPL corres. & reports, Jun–Dec 1970," Box 2, UAW Conservation and Recreation Collection.

67 "Environmental Inventory: Wyandotte, Ecorse, River Rouge, Fall 1970," Folder "DAPL corres. & reports, Jun–Dec 1970," Box 2, UAW Conservation and Recreation Collection.

68 *Free Press*, 20 Sept 1970, Folder "DAPL corres. & reports, Jun–Dec 1970," Box 2, UAW Conservation and Recreation Collection; Inter-Office Memo, Dave Czamanske to Olga Madar et al., "Summary of Activities February 1 thru April 24, 1971," Folder "Downriver Anti-Pollution League, corres. & reports, 1971–72," Box 2, UAW Conservation and Recreation Collection.

69 UAW Handbill, May 1969, Folder "Clinton River Cleanup, 1969–71," Box 8, UAW Conservation and Recreation Collection; UAW Handbill, August 1969, Folder "Clinton River Cleanup, 1969–71," Box 8, UAW Conservation and Recreation Collection.

70 Winnie Fraser to Wives of UAW Officers, Board Members and Staff, 10 August 1970, Folder "United Active Women: UAW Wives Group," Box 8, UAW Conservation and Recreation Collection; Outline of Organization, 6 Oct 1970, Folder "United Active Women: UAW Wives Group," Box 8, UAW Conservation and Recreation Collection; Bus Trip Down River, Folder "United Active Women: UAW Wives Group," Box 8, UAW Conservation and Recreation Collection.

71 *Distaff Notebook*, August 1971 (vol. 1, no. 1), Folder "United Active Women: UAW Wives Group," Box 8, UAW Conservation and Recreation Collection.

72 Lichtenstein, *Walter Reuther*, 436–37.

73 Robert Gottlieb, *Forcing the Spring: The Transformation of the American Environmental Movement* (Washington, D.C.: Island Press, 1993), 291.

74 Gordon, "Environmental Blues," 214–16.

75 Ibid., 217.

CHAPTER 6

1 "Join the Non-Violent Strike for Justice," handbill, 1970, Folder 14, "United Automobile Workers (UAW) Walter P. Reuther Memorial, 1970," Box 75, Office of the President Collection, United Farm Workers, Archives of Labor and Urban Affairs, Wayne State University, Detroit, Mich. (hereafter cited as UFW President Collection); Maralyn Edid, *Farm Labor Organizing: Trends & Prospects* (Ithaca, N.Y.: ILR Press, 1994), 36–37.

2 Speech to introduce *Brothers and Sisters*, n.d., Folder 8, "Speech File, n.d." Box 46, United Farm Workers Information and Research Department Collection, United Farm Workers, Archives of Labor and Urban Affairs, Wayne State University, Detroit, Mich. (hereafter cited as UFW Information and Research Collection); Walter Reuther and Ken Morris [Region 1B Director] to Local Presidents, Recording Secretaries, Financial Secretaries, CAP and Education Committee Chairmen, 22 April 1969, Folder 13, "United Automobile Workers (UAW), 1969–1970," Box 75, UFW President Collection.

3 Carey McWilliams, *Factories in the Field: The Story of Migratory Farm Labor in California* (1939; reprint, Santa Barbara, Calif.: Peregrine Publishers, 1971); Speech to introduce "Brothers and Sisters," n.d., Folder 8, "Speech File, n.d." Box 46, UFW Information and Research Collection.

4 Linda Nash, "The Fruits of Ill-Health: Pesticides and Workers' Bodies in Post–World War II California," *Osiris* 19 (2004): 213.

5 J. Craig Jenkins, *The Politics of Insurgency: The Farm Worker Movement in the 1960s* (New York: Columbia University Press, 1985), 37–39, 44.

6 Steven Stoll, *The Fruits of Unnatural Advantage: Making the Industrial Countryside in California* (Berkeley: University of California Press, 1998), 32; Douglas Cazaux Sackman, *Orange Empire: California and the Fruits of Eden* (Berkeley: University of California Press, 2005), 121.

7 Steven Stoll, *Fruits of Unnatural Advantage*, 2, 4; Nash, "Fruits of Ill-Health," 206.

8 McWilliams, *Factories in the Field*, 5–6.

9 Ellen Casper, "A Social History of Farm Labor in California, With Special Emphasis on the United Farm Workers Union and California Rural Legal Assistance" (Ph.D. diss., New School for Social Research, 1984), 15–16; Jenkins, *Politics of Insurgency*, 30.

10 Deborah Cohen, "Caught in the Middle: The Mexican State's Relationship with the United States and Its Own Citizen-Workers, 1942–1954," *Journal of American Ethnic History* 20 (Spring 2001): 113.

11 Casper, "Social History of Farm Labor," 88–90, 49; Jenkins, *Politics of Insurgency*, 77–79.

12 Edid, *Farm Labor Organizing*, 34–35; Jenkins, *Politics of Insurgency*, 80–82.

13 Steven Stoll, *Fruits of Unnatural Advantage*, 94.

14 Nash, "Fruits of Ill-Health," 205.

15 Ibid., 205, 207; Laura Pulido, *Environmentalism and Economic Justice* (Tucson: University of Arizona Press, 1996), 77, 81; "Domestic Agricultural Migrants in the United States (1965)," Public Health Service Publication No. 540, Folder 1, "Farm Labor Migration Patterns, 1965–69," Box 13, UFW Information and Research Collection.

16 Nash, "Fruits of Ill-Health," 208–9.

17 Ibid., 215; Pulido, *Environmentalism and Economic Justice*, 103; Robert Gordon, "Poisons in the Fields: The United Farm Workers, Pesticides, and Environmental Politics," *Pacific Historical Review* 68 (February 1999): 56–57.

18 Affidavit of Dr. Irma West, n.d., Folder 18, "Pesticides, 1968–73," Box 21, Administration Files Collection, United Farm Workers, Archives of Labor and Urban Affairs, Wayne State University, Detroit, Mich. (hereafter cited as UFW Administration Files Collection).

19 Nash, "Fruits of Ill-Health," 214.

20 Affidavit of Joe Alejandro, n.d., Folder 18, "Pesticides, 1968–73," Box 21, Central Administration Files Collection, United Farm Workers, Archives of Labor and Urban Affairs, Wayne State University, Detroit, Mich. (hereafter cited as UFW Central Administration Files Collection); Affidavit of Francisco Mendoza, n.d., Folder 18, "Pesticides, 1968–73," Box 21, UFW Administration Files Collection.

21 Gordon, "Poisons in the Fields," 58.

22 Casper, "Social History of Farm Labor," 77; Statement of Faustina Solis in Senate Committee on Labor and Public Welfare, Subcommittee on Health, *Hearings on S. 2660, to Extend Provisions for Migrant Health Services . . . October 21st and 22d, 1969*, 91st Cong., 1st sess. (Washington: Government Printing Office, 1969), 104; "Summary of the Orange Grand Jury Report on Labor Camps in Orange County, CA." in Folder

2, "Housing, Farm Labor, 1974," Box 17, UFW Information and Research Collection.

23 "Di Giorgio Fruit Corporation, Ranch and Packing House Rules," Folder 18, "Workers Statements, 1967," Box 14, UFW Central Administration Files Collection.

24 Henry P. Anderson, "The Bracero Program in California, with Particular Reference to Health Status, Attitudes, and Practices" (University of California, Berkeley, 1961), 59; Sackman, *Orange Empire*, 175; Gregorio Mora, "New Directions in the Chicano History of California," *Mexican Studies/Estudios Mexicanos* 14 (Summer 1998), 460; "Special Report on Seasonal Farm Worker and Company Housing," March 15, 1966, Folder 6, "Housing, 1966," Box 36, UFW President Collection.

25 "Summary of the Orange Grand Jury Report on Labor Camps in Orange County, CA.," Folder 2, "Housing, Farm Labor, 1974," Box 17, UFW Information and Research Collection; "Monterey County Labor Camps Report," Folder 2, "Housing, Farm Labor, 1974," Box 17, UFW Information and Research Collection.

26 The percentage of the population living in rural areas of Mexico (settlements with less than 2,500 inhabitants) had declined from 65 percent in 1941 to 41 percent in 1970, but in absolute terms it had increased from 12.7 to 20 million during the same period, and nearly half of the nation's labor force still worked in agriculture. See Lucia L. Kaiser and Kathryn G. Dewey, "Migration, Cash Cropping and Subsistence Agriculture: Relationships to Household Food Expenditures in Rural Mexico," *Social Science and Medicine* 33, no. 10 (1991), 1116; Rodrigo A. Medellin, "Productivity and Employment in Subsistence Agriculture: An Experimental Case Study in Mexico" (thesis prospectus, Harvard University, 1974), 8.

27 Medellin, "Productivity and Employment," 11–12; Scott Swinton, *Peasant Farming Practices and Off-Farm Employment in Puebla, Mexico* (Ithaca, N.Y.: Cornell University, 1983), 14–15, 26–34; Barbara J. Williams, "Subsistence Agriculture and Wage Labor: A Mexican Case Study of Man-Land Relationships in a Changing Economy" (working paper, University of Wisconsin–Madison, 1968), 47–50.

28 Medellin, "Productivity and Employment," 8–11; Swinton, *Peasant Farming Practices*, 34; Pedro Sandoval, Affidavit, 8 August 1974, Folder 24, "Illegal Aliens, 1974–75," Box 30, UFW Administration Files Collection.

29 Kaiser and Dewey, "Migration, Cash Cropping," 1115–16.

30 Jenkins, *Politics of Insurgency*, 83–84, 208, 135–36.

31 Ibid., 135; Edid, *Farm Labor Organizing*, 40.

32 Jenkins, *Politics of Insurgency*, 208.

33 Pulido, *Environmentalism and Economic Justice*, 85–86, 105.

34 When the otherwise radical Ecology Action decided to organize an "ecology walk" against "agri-chemical powers," for example, the leadership attempted "to maintain a safe neutrality" regarding the farmworkers' strike "so they could reach all the people they wanted to reach." During the march, however, common participants, many of whom had worked on the grape boycott, decided to stay in the Delano area for Sunday Mass. A UFWOC organizer explained what the union thought about "neutrality" and argued that "the farm workers' struggle is a valid and important part of Ecology (not merely regarding the pesticides, but also in the important matter of preserving and respecting all our natural resources — including HUMAN)." This was

apparently convincing to many and they went back to educate the Ecology Action "officialdom." James Maguire to United Farm Workers Organization, 2 December 1969, Folder 15, "Ecology Walk, 1969–1970," Box 6, UFW Administration Files Collection; Jim Drake to César Chávez, 16 April 1970, internal memorandum, Folder 15, "Ecology Walk, 1969–1970," Box 6, UFW Administration Files Collection.

35 Pulido, *Environmentalism and Economic Justice*, 58–59; "Pesticides: The Poisons We Eat," Folder 20, "Pesticides, Leaflets, n.d.," Box 21, UFW Administration Files Collection.

36 "Statement of Jerome Cohen, 1 August 1969, Folder 1, "Pesticides 1964–1970," Box 24, UFW Information and Research Collection.

37 Pulido, *Environmentalism and Economic Justice*, 114–15.

38 Ibid., 116–17; Gordon, "Poisons in the Fields," 51, 62–3.

39 California Department of Public Health, Bureau of Occupational Health and Environmental Epidemiology, *Occupational Disease in California Attributed to Pesticides and Other Agricultural Chemicals, 1970* (Sacramento, 1971), 5.

40 Chris Meyer to Victoria A. Hays, 24 August 1973, Folder 21, "Environmental Action," Box 3, Work Department Collection, United Farm Workers, Archives of Labor and Urban Affairs, Wayne State University, Detroit, Mich. (hereafter cited as UFW Work Department Collection); Gordon, "Poisons in the Fields," 65; Edid, *Farm Labor Organizing*, 38–39.

41 "Coachella Valley Grape Crop Agreement," 16 April 1973, "Grape Contracts, 1970–1973," Box 15, UFW Information and Research Collection; Gordon, "Poisons in the Fields," 52.

42 California Department of Public Health, Bureau of Occupational Health and Environmental Epidemiology, *Occupational Disease in California Attributed to Pesticides and Other Agricultural Chemicals, 1971–1973* (Sacramento, 1974), 2.

43 Cathy Lerza to Ramon Romero, 30 April 1973, Folder 21, "Environmental Action," Box 3, UFW Work Department Collection.

44 César Chávez to Brock Evans, 9 May 1973, Folder 21, "Environmental Action," Box 3, UFW Work Department Collection; Brock Evans to César Chávez, 5 June 1973, Folder 21, "Environmental Action," Box 3, UFW Work Department Collection.

45 Pulido, *Environmentalism and Economic Justice*, 86; Chris Meyer to Victoria A. Hays, August 24, 1973, Folder 21, "Environmental Action," Box 3, UFW Work Department Collection.

46 Gordon, "Poisons in the Fields," 73–74; Edid, *Farm Labor Organizing*, 12, 42–43.

47 Robert Gottlieb, *Forcing the Spring: The Transformation of the American Environmental Movement* (Washington, D.C.: Island Press, 1993), 296–98.

CONCLUSION

1 Karl Marx and Frederick Engels, *The German Ideology* (New York: International Publishers, 2001), 42, 47.

2 Henry David Thoreau, *A Week on the Concord and Merrimack Rivers, Walden; or, Life in the Woods, The Maine Woods, Cape Cod* (New York: Library of America, 1985), 490.

3 Ibid., 454.

Bibliography

MANUSCRIPT COLLECTIONS

Concord, N.H.
  New Hampshire Historical Society
    Dame Family Papers, 1824–1951
    Deerfield Families Collection Papers, 1843–1915

Detroit, Mich.
  Archives of Labor and Urban Affairs, Wayne State University
    United Auto Workers
      Conservation and Recreation Departments Collection
      President's Office, Walter P. Reuther Collection
      Recreation Department Collection
    United Farm Workers
      Administration Files Collection
      Central Administration Files Collection
      Information and Research Department Collection
      Office of the President Collection
      Work Department Collection

Lansing, Mich.
  State Archives of Michigan
    Michigan Writers' Project, Department of Natural Resources, 89–55
    Occasional Issues of Out-of-Print Periodicals Devoted to Michigan Sports and
      Conservation, 1933–1965, 69-31-A
    Oscar Warbach Cartoons, Department of Natural Resources — Conservation Di-
      vision, 89–78
    Southern Michigan State Game Areas and Recreation Areas, 1949–1950, 68–6

Lowell, Mass.
  Center for Lowell History
    Lowell Horticultural Society, *Constitution and Premiums, 1854*

Morgantown, W.Va.

West Virginia and Regional History Collection, West Virginia University
New River Field Coal Co. Records, 1878–1956, A&M No. 2570
Cedar Grove Mining Company Ledger, 1883–1885, A&M No. 2936
Interviews, Appalachian Oral History Project

Topeka, Kans.

Kansas State Historical Society
Olive Capper Diary, 1895
Emma O. (Slygh) Clifton Diaries, 1910–1915
Gertrude Estelle (Stevens) Crane Diaries, 1885–1890
Susan (Bixby) Diamond Diaries, 1906 and 1914
Emma Drew Diaries, 1918–1924
Martha Farnsworth Diaries, 1882–1922
Lilla Day Monroe Collection of Pioneer Stories
Harriet Parkerson Diaries, 1891–1900

Washington, D.C.

National Archives
Records of the Assistant Commissioner for the State of Mississippi, Bureau of
Refugee, Freedmen, and Abandoned Lands, 1865–1869, RG 105

Worcester, Mass.

American Antiquarian Society
Anna Blackwood Howell Diaries, 1819–1839

MANUSCRIPT COLLECTIONS ON MICROFILM AND THE INTERNET

Born in Slavery: Slave Narratives from the Federal Writers' Project, 1936–1938, Library of Congress, Manuscript Division, <http:/memory.loc.government/am
mem/snhtml/snhome.html>
Interviews, Appalachian Oral History Project, Emory and Henry College, Emory, Va.
Uriah W. Oblinger Collection, Library of Congress/Nebraska State Historical Society,
<http://memory.loc.government/ammem/award98/nbhihtml/pshome .html>

NEWSPAPERS AND JOURNALS

Bay State Farmer and Mechanics Ledger (Worcester, Mass.)
Coal Age
Lowell (Mass.) Courier
Lowell (Mass.) Offering
New England Farmer (Boston, Mass.)
New England Offering (Lowell, Mass.)
Operatives' Magazine
United Mine Workers Journal
Voice of Industry

Boeger, E. A., and E. A. Goldenweiser. *Study of the Tenant Systems of Farming in the Yazoo-Mississippi Delta*. U.S. Department of Agriculture Bulletin No. 337. Washington: Government Printing Office, 1916.

California Assembly Committee on Agriculture. *The California Farm Labor Force: A Profile*. Sacramento, 1969.

California Department of Public Health, Bureau of Occupational Health and Environmental Epidemiology. *Occupational Disease in California Attributed to Pesticides and Other Agricultural Chemicals, 1970*. Sacramento, 1971.

California Department of Public Health, Bureau of Occupational Health and Environmental Epidemiology. *Occupational Disease in California Attributed to Pesticides and Other Agricultural Chemicals, 1971–1973*. Sacramento, 1974.

Commission on Agricultural Workers. *Report of the Commission on Agricultural Workers*. Washington: Government Printing Office, 1992.

Helsinki Commission. *Migrant Farmworkers in the United States*. Washington: Government Printing Office, 1993.

McGill, Nettie. *Welfare of Children in the Bituminous Coal Communities in West Virginia*. Children's Bureau, U.S. Department of Labor. Washington: Government Printing Office, 1923.

Mines, Richard, and Philip L. Martin. *A Profile of California Farmworkers*. University of California and the California Employment Development Department, 1986.

U.S. Coal Commission. *Report of the United States Coal Commission*. Senate Document No. 195. 68th Cong., 2nd sess., 1925. Washington: Government Printing Office, 1925.

U.S. Congress. Senate. Committee on Education and Labor. *Conditions in the Paint Creek District, West Virginia*. 63rd Cong., 1st sess., 1913. Washington: Government Printing Office, 1913.

———. Committee on Interstate Commerce. *Conditions in the Coal Fields of Pennsylvania, West Virginia, and Ohio*. 70th Cong., 1st sess., 1928. Washington: Government Printing Office, 1928.

———. Committee on Labor and Public Welfare, Subcommittee on Health. *Hearings on S. 2660, to Extend Provisions for Migrant Health Services . . . October 21st and 22d, 1969*. 91st Cong., 1st sess., 1969. Washington: Government Printing Office, 1969.

U.S. Department of Agriculture. *Economic and Social Problems and Conditions of the Southern Appalachians*. Miscellaneous Publication No. 205. Washington: Government Printing Office, 1935.

U.S. Women's Bureau. *Home Environment and Employment Opportunities of Women in Coal-Mine Workers' Families*. Women's Bureau Bulletin No. 45. Washington: Government Printing Office, 1925.

West Virginia State Board of Agriculture. *Fifth Biennial Report of the West Virginia State Board of Agriculture, 1899–1900*. Charleston, W.Va.: Butler Printing Company, 1900.

Armstead, Robert. *Black Days, Black Dust: The Memories of an African American Coal Miner*. Knoxville: University of Tennessee Press, 2002.

Ball, Charles. *Fifty Years in Chains: The Life of an American Slave*. Indianapolis: Dayton & Asher, 1858.

Barber, John Warner. *Historical Collections*. Worcester, Mass.: Dorr, Howland, 1839.

Beecher, Catherine. *A Treatise on Domestic Economy*. 1841. Reprint, New York: Schocken Books, 1977.

Berlin, Ira, Marc Favreau, and Steven F. Miller, eds. *Remembering Slavery: African Americans Talk about Their Personal Experience of Slavery*. New York: New Press, 1998.

Blassingame, John W., ed. *Slave Testimony: Two Centuries of Letters, Speeches, Interviews, and Autobiographies*. Baton Rouge: Louisiana State University Press, 1977.

Blewett, Mary H., ed. *Caught Between Two Worlds: The Diary of a Lowell Mill Girl, Susan Brown of Epsom, New Hampshire*. Lowell, Mass.: Lowell Museum, 1984.

Botkin, B. A., ed. *Lay My Burden Down: A Folk History of Slavery*. 1945. Reprint, Chicago: University of Chicago Press, 1969.

Bryant, Blanche Brown, and Gertrude Elaine Baker, eds. *The Diaries of Sally and Pamela Brown, 1832–38*. Springfield, Vt.: William S. Bryant Foundation, 1970.

Cather, Willa. *My Antonia*. 1918. Reprint, Boston: Houghton Mifflin, 1988.

——. *O Pioneers!* 1913. Reprint, New York: Quality Paperback Book Club, 1995.

Child, Lydia Maria. *The American Frugal Housewife*. Mineola, N.Y.: Dover Publications, 1999.

Dwight, Elizabeth Amelia. *Memorials of Mary Wilder White: A Century Ago in New England*. Boston: Everett Press Company, 1903.

Emerson, Ralph Waldo, and Henry David Thoreau. *Nature/Walking*. Boston: Beacon Press, 1991.

Emery, Sarah Anna. *Reminiscences of a Nonagenarian*. Newburyport, [Mass.]: William H. Huse, 1879.

Farley, Harriet. *Operatives' Reply to Hon. Jere. Clemens, Being a Sketch of Factory Life and Factory Enterprise and a Brief History of Manufacturing by Machinery*. Lowell, Mass.: S. J. Varney, 1850.

Feldman, Richard, and Michael Betzold, eds. *End of the Line: Autoworkers and the American Dream: An Oral History*. Urbana: University of Illinois Press, 1990.

Foner, Philip S., ed. *The Factory Girls: A Collection of Writings on Life and Struggles in the New England Factories of the 1840s*. Urbana: University of Illinois Press, 1977.

Ford, Henry. *My Life and Work*. 1922. Reprint, New York: Arno Press, 1973.

Hampsten, Elizabeth. *Read This Only to Yourself: The Private Writings of Midwestern Women, 1880–1910*. Bloomington: Indiana University Press, 1982.

The Housekeeper's Companion: A Practical Receipt Book and Household Physician, with Much Other Valuable Information. Chicago: Mercantile Pub. and Adv. Co., 1883.

Hughes, Langston, and Arna Bontemps, eds. *The Book of Negro Folklore*. New York: Dodd, Mead, 1958.

Hughes, Louis. *Thirty Years a Slave: From Bondage to Freedom*. Milwaukee: South Side Printing Company, 1897.

Kull, Nell, ed. "'I Can Never Be Happy There in Among So Many Mountains': The Letters of Sally Rice." *Vermont History* 38 (1970): 49–57.

Larcom, Lucy. *A New England Girlhood: Outline from Memory*. 1889. Reprint, Boston: Northeastern University Press, 1986.

———. *An Idyl of Work*. 1875. Reprint, Westport, Conn.: Greenwood Press, 1970.

Lowell Offering. Westport, Conn.: Greenwood Reprint Corporation, 1970.

Maguire, Jane. *On Shares: Ed Brown's Story*. New York: W. W. Norton, 1975.

Miles, Rev. Henry A. *Lowell, As It Was, and As It Is*. Lowell, Mass.: Nathaniel L. Dayton, 1846.

Mooney, Fred. *Struggle in the Coal Fields: The Autobiography of Fred Mooney*. Edited by J. W. Hess.Morgantown: West Virginia University Library, 1967.

Moore, Melissa Genett. *The Story of a Kansas Pioneer, Being the Autobiography of Melissa Genett Anderson*. Mt. Vernon, Ohio: Manufacturing Printers Co., 1924.

Obermiller, Phillip J., Thomas E. Wagner, and E. Bruce Tucker, eds. *Appalachian Odyssey: Historical Perspectives on the Great Migration*. Westport, Conn.: Praeger, 2000.

Olmsted, Frederick Law. *The Cotton Kingdom: A Traveller's Observation on Cotton and Slavery*. New York: Modern Library, 1984.

Olsson, Anna. *A Child of the Prairie*. Translated by Martha Winblad. Edited by Elizabeth Jaderborg. Lindsborg, Kans.: privately printed, 1978.

An Operative [Amelia Sargent]. *Factory Life as It Is*. 1845. Reprint, Lowell, Mass.: Lowell Publishing Company, 1982.

Orpen, Adela. *Memories of the Old Emigrant Days in Kansas, 1862–1865*. New York: Harper & Brothers, 1928.

Pioneer Stories of Custer County Nebraska. Broken Bow, Neb.: E. R. Purcell, 1936.

Rebecca Winters Genealogical Society. *Families of the Pioneer: Early Settlers of Scotts Bluff, Morrill, and Banner Counties of Western Nebraska*. Scottsbluff, Neb.: Rebecca Winters Genealogical Society, 1985.

Rebsch, Myrtle Brunkow. *Coming of Age in 1920's Kansas*. Universal Biorhythm Company, 1993.

Robinson, Harriet H. *Loom and Spindle, or Life Among the Early Mills Girls*. 1898. Reprint, Kailu, Hawaii: Press Pacifica, 1976.

Sandoz, Mari. *Sandhill Sundays and Other Recollections*. Lincoln: University of Nebraska Press, 1970.

Sigourney, Mrs. L. H. *Pleasant Memories of Pleasant Lands*. Boston: James Munroe, 1856.

Simpson, Harriet Arnow. *The Dollmaker*. 1954. Reprint, New York: Harper Collins, 1972.

Staadt, Olive Mitchell. *Gentle Memories: Kansas, 1900–1910*. n.p., n.d.

Stewart, Elinor Pruitt. *Letters of a Woman Homesteader*. 1914. Reprint, Lincoln: University of Nebraska Press, 1961.

Thoreau, Henry David. *A Week on the Concord and Merrimack Rivers, Walden; or, Life in the Woods, The Maine Woods, Cape Cod*. New York: Library of America, 1985.

Turner, J. A. *The Cotton Planter's Manual: Being a Compilation of Facts from the Best Authorities on the Culture of Cotton*. 1857. Reprint, New York: Negro University Press, 1969.

Turner, Janet Driskell. *Through the Back Door: Memoirs of a Sharecropper's Daughter*

Who Learned to Read as a Great-Grandmother. Boulder, Colo.: Creativa Press, 2000.

White, Tryphena Ely. *Tryphena Ely White's Journal*. New York: Grafton Press, 1904.

SECONDARY SOURCES

Aiken, Charles S. *The Cotton Plantation South Since the Civil War*. Baltimore: Johns Hopkins University Press, 1998.

Albanese, Catherine L. *Nature Religion in America: From the Algonkian Indians to the New Age*. Chicago: University of Chicago Press, 1990.

Anderson, Henry P. "The Bracero Program in California, with Particular Reference to Health Status, Attitudes, and Practices." University of California, Berkeley, 1961.

Andrews, Thomas G. " 'Made by Toile'? Tourism, Labor, and the Construction of the Colorado Landscape, 1858–1917." *Journal of American History* 92 (December 2005): 837–63.

——."The Road to Ludlow: Work, Environment, and Industrialization, 1870–1915." Ph.D. diss., University of Wisconsin–Madison, 2003.

Aron, Cindy. *Working at Play: A History of Vacations in the United States*. New York: Oxford University Press, 1999.

Bailey, Rebecca J. "Matewan Before the Massacre: Politics, Coal, and the Roots of Conflict in Mingo County, 1793–1920." Ph.D. diss., West Virginia University, 2001.

Blassingame, John W. *The Slave Community: Plantation Life in the Antebellum South*. New York: Oxford University Press, 1979.

Blum, Elizabeth. "Power, Danger, and Control: Slave Women's Perceptions of Wilderness in the Nineteenth Century." *Women's Studies* 31 (January/February 2002): 247–66.

Boyle, Kevin. "Little More than Ashes: The UAW and American Reform in the 1960s." In *Organized Labor and American Politics, 1894–1994*, edited by Kevin Boyle, 217–38. Albany: State University of New York Press, 1998.

——. *The UAW and the Heyday of American Liberalism, 1945–1968*. Ithaca: Cornell University Press, 1995.

Brandfon, Robert L. *Cotton Kingdom of the New South: A History of the Yazoo-Mississippi Delta from Reconstruction to the Twentieth Century*. Cambridge: Harvard University Press, 1967.

Braverman, Harry. *Labor and Monopoly Capital: The Degradation of Work in the Twentieth Century*. New York: Monthly Review Press, 1974.

Brighman, Loriman S. "An Independent Voice: A Mill Girl from Vermont Speaks Her Mind." *Vermont History* 41 (Summer 1973): 142–46.

Britton, Glenn Worth. " 'Improving' the Middle Landscape: Conservation and Social Change in Rural Southern Michigan, 1890 to 1940." Ph.D. diss., University of California, Los Angeles, 2005.

Camp, Stephanie M. H. *Closer to Freedom: Enslaved Women and Everyday Resistance in the Plantation South*. Chapel Hill: University of North Carolina Press, 2004.

Casper, Ellen. "A Social History of Farm Labor in California, with Special Emphasis on the United Farm Workers Union and California Rural Legal Assistance." Ph.D. diss., New School for Social Research, 1984.

Cecelski, David S. *The Waterman's Song: Slavery and Freedom in Maritime North Carolina*. Chapel Hill: University of North Carolina Press, 2001.

Chinoy, Eli. *Automobile Workers and the American Dream*. Boston: Beacon Press, 1955.

Cobb, James C. *The Most Southern Place on Earth: The Mississippi Delta and the Roots of Regional Identity*. New York: Oxford University Press, 1992.

Cohen, Deborah. "Caught in the Middle: The Mexican State's Relationship with the United States and Its Own Citizen-Workers, 1942–1954." *Journal of American Ethnic History* 20 (Spring 2001): 110–32.

Cohen, G. A. *Karl Marx's Theory of History: A Defence*. Princeton, N.J.: Princeton University Press, 2000.

Conley, Phil. *History of the Coal Industry of West Virginia*. Charleston, W.Va.: Education Foundation, 1960.

Corbin, David Alan. *Life, Work, and Rebellion in the Coal Fields: The Southern West Virginia Miners, 1880–1922*. Urbana: University of Illinois Press, 1981.

Cowan, Ruth Schwartz. *More Work for Mother: The Ironies of Household Technology from the Open Hearth to the Microwave*. New York: Basic Books, 1983.

Cutler, Jonathan. *Labor's Time: Shorter Hours, the UAW, and the Struggle for American Unionism*. Temple University Press, 2004.

Daniel, Pete. *Breaking the Land: The Transformation of Cotton, Tobacco, and Rice Cultures Since 1880*. Urbana: University of Illinois Press, 1985.

Davis, Donald Edward. *Where There Are Mountains: An Environmental History of the Southern Appalachians*. Athens: University of Georgia Press, 2000.

Davis, Kenneth S. *Kansas: A History*. New York: W. W. Norton, 1984.

Davis, Ronald F. *Good and Faithful Labor: From Slavery to Sharecropping in the Natchez District, 1860–1890*. Westport, Conn.: Greenwood Press, 1982.

Derickson, Alan. *Black Lung: Anatomy of a Public Health Disaster*. Ithaca, N.Y.: Cornell University Press, 1998.

Dewey, Scott. *Don't Breathe the Air: Air Pollution and U.S. Environmental Politics, 1945–1970*. College Station: Texas A&M University Press, 2000.

———. "Working for the Environment: Organized Labor and the Origins of Environmentalism in the United States, 1948–1970." *Environmental History* 3 (January 1998): 45–63.

Dix, Keith. *What's a Coal Miner to Do?: The Mechanization of Coal Mining*. Pittsburgh: University of Pittsburgh Press, 1988.

Dublin, Thomas, ed. *Farm to Factory: Women's Letters, 1830–1860*. New York: Columbia University Press, 1981.

———. "Rural-Urban Migrants in Industrial New England: The Case of Lynn, Massachusetts, in the Mid-Nineteenth Century." *Journal of American History* 73 (December 1986): 623–44.

———. *Women at Work: The Transformation of Work and Community in Lowell, Massachusetts, 1826–1860*. New York: Columbia University Press, 1979.

Du Bois, W. E. B. *Black Reconstruction in America*. 1935. Reprint, New York: Atheneum, 1992.

Earle, Alice Morse. *Home Life in Colonial Days*. 1898. Reprint, Stockbridge, Mass.: Berkshire Traveller Press, 1974.

Edid, Maralyn. *Farm Labor Organizing: Trends & Prospects*. Ithaca, N.Y.: ILR Press, 1994.

Eller, Ronald. *Miners, Millhands, and Mountaineers: Industrialization of the Appalachian South, 1880–1930*. Knoxville: University of Tennessee Press, 1982.

Emmet, Alan S. "Open Space in Lowell, 1826–1886." Research paper, Center for Lowell History, 1975.

Evanson, Howard N. *The First Century and a Quarter of American Coal Industry*. Pittsburgh: privately printed, 1942.

Fairbanks, Carol, and Sara Brooks Sundberg. *Farm Women on the Prairie Frontier: A Sourcebook for Canada and the United States*. Metuchen, N.J.: Scarecrow Press, 1983.

Feather, Carl E. *Mountain People in a Flat Land*. Athens: Ohio University Press, 1998.

Feurer, Rosemary. "River Dreams: St. Louis and the Fight for a Missouri Valley Authority." In *Common Fields: An Environmental History of St. Louis*, edited by Andrew Hurley, 221–41. Lawrence: University Press of Kansas, 1997.

Fine, Lisa. "Rights of Men, Rites of Passage: Hunting and Masculinity at Reo Motors of Lansing, Michigan, 1945–1975." *Journal of Social History* 33 (Summer 2000): 805–23.

Fitzgerald, Deborah. *Every Farm a Factory: The Industrial Ideal in American Agriculture*. New Haven: Yale University Press, 2003.

Genovese, Eugene. *Roll, Jordan, Roll: The World the Slaves Made*. New York: Vintage Books, 1976.

Gilbert, Charlene, and Quinn Eli. *Homecoming: The Story of African-American Farmers*. Boston: Beacon Press, 2000.

Gillenwater, Mack H. "Cultural and Historical Geography of Mining Settlements in the Pocahontas Coal Fields of Southern West Virginia, 1880 to 1930." Ph.D. diss., University of Tennessee, 1972.

Glave, Diana. "'A Garden So Brilliant with Colors, So Original in Its Design': Rural African American Women, Gardening, Progressive Reform, and the Foundation of an African American Environmental Perspective." *Environmental History* 8 (July 2003): 395–411.

Glave, Dianne D., and Mark Stoll, eds. *'To Love the Wind and the Rain': African Americans and Environmental History*. Pittsburgh: University of Pittsburgh Press, 2006.

Gonzalez, Gilbert G. *Labor and Community: Mexican Citrus Worker Villages in a Southern California County, 1900–1950*. Urbana: University of Illinois Press, 1994.

Gordon, Robert. "Environmental Blues: Working-Class Environmentalism and the Labor-Environmental Alliance." Ph.D. diss., Wayne State University, 2004.

———. "Poisons in the Fields: The United Farm Workers, Pesticides, and Environmental Politics." *Pacific Historical Review* 68 (February 1999): 51–77.

———. "'Shell No!': OCAW and the Labor-Environmental Alliance." *Environmental History* 3 (October 1998): 460–87.

Gottlieb, Robert. *Forcing the Spring: The Transformation of the American Environmental Movement*. Washington, D.C.: Island Press, 1993.

Graham, Abbie. *Working at Play in Summer Camps*. New York: Woman Press, 1941.

Greene, Janet. "Strategies for Survival: Women's Work in the Southern West Virginia Coalfields." *West Virginia History* 49 (1990): 37–54.

Gutierrez, David G. *Walls and Mirrors: Mexican Americans, Mexican Immigrants, and the Politics of Identity*. Berkeley: University of California Press, 1995.

Hahn, Steven. "Hunting, Fishing, and Foraging: Common Rights and Class Relations in the Postbellum South." *Radical History Review* 26 (October 1982): 37–64.

Harris, J. William. *Deep Souths: Delta, Piedmont, and Sea Island Society in the Age of Segregation*. Baltimore: Johns Hopkins University Press, 2001.

Henretta, James. *The Origins of American Capitalism: Collected Essays*. Boston: Northeastern University Press, 1991.

Herman, Daniel Justin. *Hunting and the American Imagination*. Washington, D.C.: Smithsonian Institution Press, 2001.

Herrera-Sobek, Maria. *Northward Bound: The Mexican Immigrant Experience in Ballad and Song*. Bloomington: Indiana University Press, 1992.

Hicks, Ruby Shepard. *The Song of the Delta*. Jackson, Miss.: Howick House, 1976.

Hogg, Charlotte. "'Private' Lives and 'Public' Writing: Rhetorical Practices of Western Nebraska Women." *Great Plains Quarterly* 22 (Summer 2002): 183–98.

Holt, Marilyn Irvin. *Linoleum, Better Babies, and the Modern Farm Woman, 1890–1930*. Albuquerque: University of New Mexico Press, 1995.

Holt, Sharon Ann. *Making Freedom Pay: North Carolina Freedpeople Working for Themselves, 1865–1900*. Athens: University of Georgia Press, 2000.

Hunt, Edward, F. G. Tyron, and Joseph Willits, eds. *What the Coal Commission Found*. Baltimore: Williams and Wilkins Company, 1925.

Hurley, Andrew. *Environmental Inequalities: Class, Race, and Industrial Pollution in Gary, Indiana, 1945–1980*. Chapel Hill: University of North Carolina Press, 1995.

Hurst, Mary. "Social History of Logan County, West Virginia, 1765–1928." M.A. thesis, Columbia University, 1924.

Jacoby, Karl. *Crimes Against Nature: Squatters, Poachers, Thieves, and the Hidden History of American Conservation*. Berkeley: University of California Press, 2001.

Jeffrey, Julie Roy. *Frontier Women: The Trans-Mississippi West, 1840–1880*. New York: Hill and Wang, 1979.

——. "'There is Some Splendid Scenery': Women's Responses to the Great Plains Landscape." *Great Plains Quarterly* 8 (Spring 1988): 69–78.

Jenkins, J. Craig. *The Politics of Insurgency: The Farm Worker Movement in the 1960s*. New York: Columbia University Press, 1985.

Johnson, Benjamin Heber. "Conservation, Subsistence, and Class at the Birth of Superior National Forest." *Environmental History* 4 (January 1999): 80–99.

Johnson, Susan. "West Virginia Rubber Workers in Akron." In *Transnational West Virginia: Ethnic Communities and Economic Change, 1840–1940*, edited by Ken Fones-Wolf and Ronald Lewis, 299–315. Morgantown: West Virginia University Press, 2002.

Jones, Jacqueline. *Labor of Love, Labor of Sorrow: Black Women, Work, and the Family from Slavery to the Present*. New York: Vintage Books, 1986.

Josephson, Hannah. *The Golden Threads: New England's Mill Girls and Magnates*. New York: Duell, Sloan and Pearce, 1949.

Judd, Richard. *Common Lands, Common People: The Origins of Conservation in Northern New England*. Cambridge: Harvard University Press, 1997.

Kaiser, Lucia L., and Kathryn G. Dewey. "Migration, Cash Cropping and Subsistence Agriculture: Relationships to Household Food Expenditures in Rural Mexico." *Social Science and Medicine* 33, no. 10 (1991): 1113–26.

Kantor, Shawn Everett. *Politics and Property Rights: The Closing of the Open Range in the Postbellum South*. Chicago: University of Chicago Press, 1998.

Kramer, Marie. *Homestead Fever*. York, Neb.: Service Press, 1993.

Kruse, Baldwin F. *Paradise on the Prairie: Nebraska Settlers Stories*. Lincoln, Neb.: Paradise Publishers, 1986.

Lahlum, Lori Ann. "'There Are No Trees Here': Norwegian Women Encounter the Northern Prairies and Plains." Ph.D. diss., University of Idaho, 2003.

Lewis, Ronald. *Transforming the Appalachian Countryside: Railroads, Deforestation, and Social Change in West Virginia, 1880–1920*. Chapel Hill: University of North Carolina Press, 1998.

Lichtenstein, Nelson. *Walter Reuther: The Most Dangerous Man in Detroit*. Urbana: University of Illinois Press, 1995.

Little, J. I. "A Canadian in Lowell: Labour, Manhood and Independence in the Early Industrial Era, 1840–1849." *Labour/Le Travail* 48 (Fall 2001): 197–264.

Maggard, Sally Ward. "From Farm to Coal Camp to Back Office and McDonald's: Living in the Midst of Appalachia's Latest Transformation." *Journal of Appalachian Studies* 6, no. 3 (1994): 14–38.

Maher, Neil. "A New Deal Body Politic: Landscape, Labor, and the Civilian Conservation Corps." *Environmental History* 7 (July 2002): 435–61.

Malone, Patrick, and Chuck Parrott. "Greenways in the Industrial City: Parks and Promenades along the Lowell Canals." *Journal of the Society for Industrial Archaeology* 24, no. 1 (1998): 19–40.

Mann, Susan Archer. *Social Change and Sexual Inequality: The Impact of the Transition from Slavery to Sharecropping on Black Women*. Memphis, Tenn.: Center for Research on Women, Memphis State University, 1986.

Marks, Stuart A. *Southern Hunting in Black and White: Nature, History, and Ritual in a Carolina Community*. Princeton, N.J.: Princeton University Press, 1991.

Marx, Karl. *Capital: A Critique of Political Economy*. Vol. 1. New York: International Publishers, 1967.

——. *A Contribution to the Critique of Political Economy*. New York: International Publishers, 1970.

——. *Pre-Capitalist Economic Formations*. New York: International Publishers, 2000.

Marx, Karl, and Frederick Engels. *The German Ideology*. New York: International Publishers, 2001.

McWilliams, Carey. *Factories in the Field: The Story of Migratory Farm Labor in California*. 1939. Reprint, Santa Barbara, Calif.: Peregrine Publishers, 1971.

Medellin, Rodrigo A. "Productivity and Employment in Subsistence Agriculture: An Experimental Case Study in Mexico." Thesis prospectus, Harvard University, 1974.

Meister, Dick, and Anne Loftis. *A Long Time Coming: The Struggle to Unionize America's Farm Workers*. New York: Macmillan Publishing Co., 1977.

Merchant, Carolyn. *Ecological Revolutions: Nature, Gender, and Science in New England*. Chapel Hill: University of North Carolina Press, 1989.

Mercier, Laurie. *Anaconda: Labor, Community, and Culture in Montana's Smelter City*. Urbana: University of Illinois Press, 2001.

Meyer, Stephen. *The Five Dollar Day: Labor Management and Social Control in the Ford Motor Company, 1908–1921*. Albany: State University of New York Press, 1981.

———. "Rough Manhood: The Aggressive and Confrontational Shop Culture of U.S. Auto Workers During World War II." *Journal of Social History* 36 (Fall 2002): 125–47.

Miles, Lisa. "A Land of Her Own: Independent Women Homesteaders in Lyon and Coffey Counties, Kansas (1860–1870)." M.A. thesis, Emporia State University, 1993.

Miller, Sondra Yvonne. "Free Grace in the Wilderness: An Aesthetic Analysis of Land and Space in African American Culture in the Narratives of Henry Bibb, Harriet Jacobs, and Josiah Henson." Ph.D. diss., Temple University, 1994.

Miller, Steven F. "Plantation Labor Organization and Slave Life on the Cotton Frontier: The Alabama-Mississippi Black Belt, 1815–1840." In *Cultivation and Culture: Labor and the Shaping of Slave Life in the Americas*, edited by Ira Berlin and Philip D. Morgan, 155–69. Charlottesville: University of Virginia Press, 1993.

Mitchell, Don. *The Lie of the Land: Migrant Workers and the California Landscape*. Minneapolis: University of Minnesota Press, 1996.

Montgomery, David. *The Fall of the House of Labor: The Workplace, the State, and American Labor Activism, 1865–1925*. Cambridge: Cambridge University Press, 1987.

Montrie, Chad. "Expedient Environmentalism: Opposition to Coal Surface Mining in Appalachia and the United Mine Workers of America, 1945–1977." *Environmental History* 5 (January 2000): 75–98.

———. *To Save the Land and People: A History of Opposition to Surface Coal Mining in Appalachia*. Chapel Hill: University of North Carolina Press, 2003.

Moore, John Hebron. *Agriculture in Ante-Bellum Mississippi*. New York: Octagon Books, 1971.

Mora, Gregorio. "New Directions in the Chicano History of California." *Mexican Studies/Estudios Mexicanos* 14 (Summer 1998): 451–70.

Morgan, Philip. "Work and Culture: The Task System and the World of Lowcountry Blacks, 1700 to 1880." *William and Mary Quarterly*. 39 (October 1982): 563–99.

Morse, Kathryn. *The Nature of Gold: An Environmental History of the Klondike Gold Rush*. Seattle: University of Washington Press, 2003.

Murray, Donald M., and Robert Rodney. "Sylvia Drake, 1784–1868: The Self Portrait of a Seamstress of Weybridge." *Vermont History* 34 (April 1966): 123–35.

Myres, Sandra. *Westering Women and the Frontier Experience, 1800–1915*. Albuquerque: University of New Mexico Press, 1982.

Nash, Linda. "The Fruits of Ill-Health: Pesticides and Workers' Bodies in Post–World War II California." *Osiris* 19 (2004): 203–19.

Nelson, Daniel. *American Rubber Workers & Organized Labor, 1900–1941*. Princeton, N.J.: Princeton University Press, 1988.

Norwood, Vera. *Made from This Earth: American Women and Nature*. Chapel Hill: University of North Carolina Press, 1993.

———. "Women's Place: Continuity and Change in Response to Western Landscapes." In *Western Women: Their Land, Their Lives*, edited by Lillian Schlissel, Vicki L. Ruiz, and Janice Monk, eds., 155–75. Albuquerque: University of New Mexico Press, 1988.

Ollman, Bertell. *Alienation: Marx's Conception of Man in Capitalist Society*. Cambridge: Cambridge University Press, 1976.

Peck, Gunther. "The Nature of Labor: Fault Lines and Common Ground in Environmental and Labor History." *Environmental History* 11 (April 2006): 212–38.

Penningroth, Dylan C. *The Claims of Kinfolk: African American Property and Community in the Nineteenth-Century South*. Chapel Hill: University of North Carolina Press, 2003.

Peters, J. T., and H. R. Carden. *History of Fayette County*. Fayetteville, W.Va.: Fayette County Historical Society, 1926.

Peterson, Joyce Shaw. *American Automobile Workers, 1900–1933*. Albany: State University of New York Press, 1987.

Powdermaker, Hortense. *After Freedom: A Cultural Study in the Deep South*. New York: Atheneum, 1968.

Proctor, Nicolas W. *Bathed in Blood: Hunting and Mastery in the Old South*. Charlottesville: University Press of Virginia, 2002.

Pruitt, Bettye Hobbs. "Self-Sufficiency and the Agricultural Economy of Eighteenth-Century Massachusetts." *William and Mary Quarterly* 41 (July 1984): 333–64.

Pulido, Laura. *Environmentalism and Economic Justice*. Tucson: University of Arizona Press, 1996.

Radke, Andrea G. "Refining Rural Spaces: Women and Vernacular Gentility in the Great Plains, 1880–1920." *Great Plains Quarterly* 24 (Fall 2004): 227–48.

Ransom, Roger, and Richard Sutch. *One Kind of Freedom: The Economic Consequences of Emancipation*. Cambridge: Cambridge University Press, 1977.

Ranta, Judith A. *The Life and Writings of Betsey Chamberlain: Native American Mill Worker*. Boston: Northeastern University Press, 2003.

Reiger, John. *American Sportsmen and the Origins of Conservation*. Norman: University of Oklahoma Press, 1975.

Rice, Otis. "Coal Mining in the Kanawha Valley to 1861." *Journal of Southern History* 31 (November 1965): 393–416.

Riley, Glenda. *The Female Frontier: A Comparative View of Women on the Prairie and Plains*. Lawrence: University Press of Kansas, 1988.

———. "Women's Responses to the Challenges of Plains Living." *Great Plains Quarterly* 9 (Summer 1989): 174–84.

Rodgers, Daniel T. *The Work Ethic in Industrial America, 1850–1920*. Chicago: University of Chicago Press, 1979.

Rome, Adam. "'Give Earth a Chance': The Environmental Movement and the Sixties." *Journal of American History* 90 (September 2003): 525–54.

Rosengarten, Theodore. *All God's Dangers: The Life of Nate Shaw*. New York: Alfred A. Knopf, 1973.

Rosenzweig, Roy. *Eight Hours for What We Will: Workers and Leisure in the Industrial City, 1870–1920*. Cambridge: Cambridge University Press, 1983.

Russell, Howard S. *A Long, Deep Furrow: Three Centuries of Farming in New England*. Hanover, N.H.: University Press of New England, 1976.

Sackman, Douglas Cazaux. *Orange Empire: California and the Fruits of Eden*. Berkeley: University of California Press, 2005.

Saville, Julie. *The Work of Reconstruction: From Slave to Wage Laborer in South Carolina, 1860–1870*. Cambridge: Cambridge University Press, 1994.

Schwab, Jim. *Deeper Shades of Green: The Rise of Blue-Collar and Minority Environmentalism in America*. San Francisco: Sierra Club Books, 1994.

Schwalm, Leslie. *A Hard Fight for We: Women's Transition from Slavery to Freedom in South Carolina* Urbana: University of Illinois Press, 1997.

Sellers, Charles. *The Market Revolution: Jacksonian America, 1815–1846.* New York: Oxford University Press, 1991.

Sellers, Christopher. *Hazards of the Job: From Industrial Disease to Environmental Science.* Chapel Hill: University of North Carolina Press, 1997.

Shifflet, Crandall A. *Coal Towns: Life, Work, and Culture in Company Towns of Southern Appalachia, 1880–1960.* Knoxville: University of Tennessee Press, 1994.

Smalley, Andrea. "'Our Lady Sportsmen': Gender, Class, and Conservation in Sport Hunting Magazines, 1873–1920." *Journal of the Gilded Age and Progressive Era* 4 (October 2005): 355–80.

Smith, Barbara. *Digging Our Own Graves: Coal Miners and the Struggle Over Black Lung Disease.* Philadelphia: Temple University Press, 1987.

Smith, Kimberly. "Black Agrarianism and the Foundations of Black Environmental Thought." *Environmental Ethics* 26 (Fall 2004): 267–86.

Smith, Michael. "'The Ego Idea of the Good Camper' and the Nature of Summer Camp." *Environmental History* 11 (January 2006): 70–101.

Smith, Norman W. "A Mature Frontier: The New Hampshire Economy, 1790–1850." *Historical New Hampshire* 24 (Fall 1969): 3–19.

Sobotka, Margie. *Nebraska, Kansas Czech Settlers, 1891–1895.* Evansville, Ind.: Unigraphic, 1980.

Stearns, Bertha M. "Early Factory Magazines in New England." *Journal of Economic and Business History* 2 (August 1930): 685–705.

Steinberg, Theodore. *Nature Incorporated: Industrialization and the Waters of New England.* Amherst: University of Massachusetts Press, 1991.

Steiner, Jesse Frederick. *Americans at Play: Recent Trends in Recreation and Leisure Time Activities.* New York: McGraw-Hill, 1933.

Stewart, Mart A. *"What Nature Suffers to Groe": Life, Labor, and Landscape on the Georgia Coast, 1680–1920.* Athens: University of Georgia Press, 2002.

Stoll, Mark. *Protestantism, Capitalism, and Nature in America.* Albuquerque: University of New Mexico Press, 1997.

Stoll, Steven. *The Fruits of Unnatural Advantage: Making the Industrial Countryside in California.* Berkeley: University of California Press, 1998.

Stratton, Joanna L. *Pioneer Women: Voices from the Kansas Frontier.* New York: Simon and Schuster, 1981.

Stricker, Frank. "Affluence for Whom? — Another Look at Prosperity and the Working Classes in the 1920s." *Labor History* 24 (Winter 1983): 5–33.

Strom, Albert, ed. *Swedish Pioneers in Saunders County, Nebraska: A Collection of Family Histories of Early Settlers in Nebraska.* Pittsburgh: n.p., 1972.

Sutter, Paul S. *Driven Wild: How the Fight Against Automobiles Launched the Modern Wilderness Movement.* Seattle: University of Washington Press, 2002.

Swinton, Scott. *Peasant Farming Practices and Off-Farm Employment in Puebla, Mexico.* Ithaca, N.Y.: Cornell University, 1983.

Sydnor, Charles S. *Slavery in Mississippi.* Baton Rouge: Louisiana State University Press, 1966.

Thomas, Jerry Bruce. "Coal Country: The Rise of the Southern Smokeless Coal Industry." Ph.D. diss., University of North Carolina, 1971.

Thorton, Tamara Plakins. *Cultivating Gentlemen: The Meaning of Country Life among the Boston Elite, 1785–1860*. New Haven: Yale University Press, 1989.

Thurow, Mildred. "A Study of Fifty Kansas Farm Women." B.S. thesis, Kansas State Agricultural College, 1927.

Trotter, Joe William. *Coal, Class, and Color: Blacks in Southern West Virginia, 1915–32*. Urbana: University of Illinois Press, 1990.

Tryon, Rolla Milton. *Household Manufactures in the United States, 1640–1860*. New York: August M. Kelley, 1966.

Turner, James Morton. "From Woodcraft to 'Leave No Trace': Wilderness, Consumerism, and Environmentalism in Twentieth-Century America." *Environmental History* 7 (July 2002): 463–84.

Ulrich, Laurel Thatcher. *The Age of Homespun: Objects and Stories in the Creation of an American Myth*. New York: Alfred A. Knopf, 2001.

Valencius, Conevery Bolton. *The Health of the Country: How American Settlers Understood Themselves and Their Land*. New York: Basic Books, 2002.

Wagner, Thomas E., and Phillip J. Obermiller. *African American Miners and Migrants: The Eastern Kentucky Social Club*. Chicago: University of Illinois Press, 2004.

Walker, Melissa. *All We Knew Was to Farm: Rural Women in the Upcountry South, 1919–1941*. Baltimore: Johns Hopkins University Press, 2002.

Warren, Louis. *The Hunter's Game: Poachers and Conservationists in Twentieth-Century America*. New Haven: Yale University Press, 1997.

Westmacott, Richard. *African-American Gardens and Yards in the Rural South*. Knoxville: University of Tennessee Press, 1992.

White, Richard. "'Are You an Environmentalist or Do You Work for a Living?': Work and Nature." In *Uncommon Ground: Rethinking the Human Place in Nature*, edited by William Cronon, 171–85. New York: W. W. Norton, 1996.

———. *The Organic Machine*. New York: Hill and Wang, 1995.

Williams, Barbara J. "Subsistence Agriculture and Wage Labor: A Mexican Case Study of Man-Land Relationships in a Changing Economy." Working paper, University of Wisconsin–Madison, 1968.

Williams, John Alexander. *West Virginia: A Bicentennial History*. Morgantown: West Virginia University Press, 1976.

Willis, John Charles. "On the New South Frontier: Life in the Yazoo-Mississippi Delta, 1865–1920." Ph.D. diss., University of Virginia, 1991.

Wilson, Harold Fisher. *The Hill Country of Northern New England: Its Social and Economic History*. New York: AMS Press, 1967.

Wood, Betty. *Women's Work, Men's Work: The Informal Slave Economies of Lowcountry Georgia*. Athens: University of Georgia Press, 1995.

Woofter, T. J., Jr. *Landlord and Tenant on the Cotton Plantation*. 1936. Reprint, New York: New American Library, 1969.

Worster, Donald. *Dust Bowl: The Southern Plains in the 1930s*. New York: Oxford University Press, 1979.

Index

Warbach, Oscar, 99, 100–101
Warren County, N.C., 113
Washing clothes. *See* Laundry
Water Pollution Control Act, 112
Wayne County Sportsmen's Club, 98, 104
Weaving: in mills, 9, 22; at home, 15, 17, 73
West, Melvyn, 103

West Virginia, 10, 72–90
Wildcats, 61
Wisconsin, 102
Wolves, 57
Woodcock, Leonard, 112
Wool, 15, 17, 73

Young, Bard, 109